TOUCHING THE ALTAR

The CALVIN INSTITUTE OF CHRISTIAN WORSHIP LITURGICAL STUDIES Series, edited by John D. Witvliet, is designed to promote reflection on the history, theology, and practice of Christian worship and to stimulate worship renewal in Christian congregations. Contributions include writings by pastoral worship leaders from a wide range of communities and scholars from a wide range of disciplines. The ultimate goal of these contributions is to nurture worship practices that are spiritually vital and theologically rooted.

Published

Touching the Altar

The Old Testament
for Christian Worship

Edited by

Carol M. Bechtel

WILLIAM B. EERDMANS PUBLISHING COMPANY
GRAND RAPIDS, MICHIGAN / CAMBRIDGE, U.K.

Published 2008 by
Wm. B. Eerdmans Publishing Co.
2140 Oak Industrial Drive N.E., Grand Rapids, Michigan 49505 /
P.O. Box 163, Cambridge CB3 9PU U.K.
www.eerdmans.com

Printed in the United States of America

12 11 10 09 08   7 6 5 4 3 2 1

Library of Congress Cataloging-in-Publication Data

Touching the altar: the Old Testament for Christian worship /
edited by Carol M. Bechtel.
p.   cm. — (Calvin Institute of Christian Worship
liturgical studies series)
Includes bibliographical references.
ISBN 978-0-8028-2848-4 (pbk.: alk. paper)
1. Worship — Biblical teaching. 2. Bible. O.T. — Criticism,
interpretation, etc.   I. Bechtel, Carol M., 1959-

BS1199.W76T68   2008

264 — dc22

2007043577

The sermons "Costly Vision" and "Lament over Jerusalem" in the essay "No Explanations in the Church: Two Sermons on the Prophets," by Ellen F. Davis, appeared previously in the *Virginia Seminary Journal* in July 2001 and January 2001, respectively, and are reprinted here with permission.

Unless otherwise noted, the Scripture quotations in this publication are from the New Revised Standard Version of the Bible, copyright © 1989 by the Division of Christian Education of the National Council of Churches of Christ in the U.S.A., and used by permission.

Contents

Contents

Contents

Contents

Series Preface

Making Connections

Christian corporate worship is an integrating practice at the center of the Christian life. It both reflects and shapes our view of God and the world. It grounds, sharpens, and humbles the work of the church in every sphere of ministry, including education, formation, pastoral care, evangelism, and justice. It gathers up every facet of our lives before God's face — our life at work and play; at home, school, and marketplace; in times of joy and sorrow — and then sends us out to live in obedience and joy.

Part of our mandate at the Calvin Institute of Christian Worship, and in this series of books, is to make the connections between worship and the various facets of Christian thought and life explicit and instructive, in ways that promote deeper and more vital worship practices.

This particular volume highlights the crucial connections between worship and Scripture. The past generation has witnessed an explosion of books about worship. The vast majority of these books, however, are about techniques of worship leadership, or prescriptions for stylistic changes that promise to make ministry more effective. Relatively few of these books focus on mining the riches of Scripture for wisdom to ground and sharpen our practices. Some ignore this task altogether. Many of the books that do discuss Scripture and worship practices limit their discussion to ancient practices, failing to probe what difference they might make for the life of faith today. And many of those books focus primarily on the New Testament and period of the early church.

The presence of these hymns also suggests that this book can be used in ways that bring study and worship together. Study groups and worship committees who discuss each essay over time can conclude their study in song. Pastors who don't use the revised common lectionary to guide their choice of preaching texts might consider a series of sermons based on the six themes of this book. The hymns included here will make preparing for worship for those weeks a bit easier. Students who are assigned to read these essays might find that the hymn texts published here serve to blur the distinction between theological study and prayer.

JOHN D. WITVLIET

Calvin Institute of Christian Worship
Calvin College and Calvin Theological Seminary
Grand Rapids, Michigan

Contributors

Carol M. Bechtel is Professor of Old Testament at Western Theological Seminary in Holland, Michigan. She is the author of *Esther* (*Interpretation* commentary series, Westminster John Knox, 2002) as well as several curricula, including *Job and the Life of Faith: Wisdom for Today's World* (Kerygma, 2005). She is an ordained Minister of Word and Sacrament and a General Synod Professor of Theology in the Reformed Church in America.

Thomas A. Boogaart is Professor of Old Testament at Western Theological Seminary in Holland, Michigan. He is the author of *Heaven Came Down* (Reformed Church Press, 1998), *Life on the Boundary* (World Vision, Inc., 1995), and numerous articles in *Reformed Review* and *Perspectives: A Journal of Reformed Thought*. He has helped Western Seminary launch a number of ministries to combat hunger, including The Bridge (a developing-world store) and the Community Kitchen (which serves a hot meal daily to the people in the seminary neighborhood). He is an ordained Minister of Word and Sacrament and a General Synod Professor of Theology in the Reformed Church in America.

Corrine L. Carvalho is an Associate Professor of Old Testament and Director of the Luann Dummer Center for Women at the University of St. Thomas in Saint Paul, Minnesota. She is the author of *Encountering Ancient Voices: A Guide to Reading the Old Testament* (Winona, Minn.: St. Mary's Press, 2006); co-editor (with Stephen L. Cook) and contributor to

Ezekiel's Hierarchical World: Wrestling with a Tiered Reality, SBL Sym. 31 (Atlanta: Society of Biblical Literature, 2004); and co-editor (with Stephen L. Cook and James W. Watts) of *The Whirlwind: Essays on Job, Hermeneutics, and Theology in Memory of Jane Morse,* JSOT Supp. 336 (Sheffield: Sheffield Academic, 2001). She has also authored numerous articles and essays for both scholarly and popular audiences.

Ellen F. Davis is Professor of Bible and Practical Theology at Duke Divinity School in Durham, North Carolina. Two of her most recent books are *Wondrous Depth: Preaching the Old Testament* (Westminster John Knox, 2005) and *Who Are You, My Daughter? Reading Ruth through Image and Text,* with woodcuts by Margaret Adams Parker (Westminster John Knox, 2003). She is currently writing a book on reading the Bible through agrarian eyes. Davis is a lay Episcopalian.

J. Clinton McCann Jr. is Evangelical Professor of Biblical Interpretation at Eden Theological Seminary in Webster Groves, Missouri. A Minister of Word and Sacrament in the Presbyterian Church (USA), he is the author of the Psalms commentary in *The New Interpreter's Bible,* volume 4 (Abingdon, 1996), and *Judges* (*Interpretation* commentary series, Westminster John Knox, 2002). His introduction to and annotations on the Psalms will appear soon in *The Westminster Discipleship Study Bible,* a work oriented to persons especially interested in themes of justice, righteousness, and peace in Scripture.

Dennis T. Olson is Charles T. Haley Professor of Old Testament Theology at Princeton Theological Seminary in Princeton, New Jersey. He is an ordained Minister of Word and Sacrament in the Evangelical Lutheran Church in America. His publications include *Numbers* (*Interpretation* commentary series, Westminster John Knox, 1996); "Book of Judges," in *The New Interpreter's Bible,* volume 2 (Abingdon, 1998); and *Deuteronomy and the Death of Moses: A Theological Reading* (Wipf & Stock, 2005).

Margaret Adams Parker works as a printmaker and sculptor. She has served on the adjunct faculty at Virginia Theological Seminary since 1992. The Library of Congress has purchased her *WOMEN — 15 Woodcuts.* The High Commissioner for Refugees of the United Nations published her woodcut entitled *African Exodus* as the frontispiece to *Refugee Children,* volume 23 of *Refugee Survey Quarterly* (Oxford University Press). Twenty of her woodcuts appear in a book she produced with Ellen Davis entitled *Who Are You, My Daughter? Reading Ruth through Image and Text* (Westminster John Knox, 2003). She recently completed a set of woodcuts called *Stations of the Cross.* Parker's sculpture entitled *Reconciliation,* based on the parable of the prodigal son and commissioned by Duke Divinity School, was installed there in 2005. Her *Mary* is installed at the College of Preachers at Washington's National Cathedral; at St. Mary's Episcopal Church and at Iglesia Santa Maria in Arlington, Virginia; at St. John's Church, West Hartford, Connecticut; and at The Episcopal Church of St. Mary the Virgin, San Francisco.

John D. Witvliet is Director of the Calvin Institute of Christian Worship and serves as Associate Professor of Worship, Theology, and Music at Calvin College and Calvin Theological Seminary. An ordained minister in the Christian Reformed Church, he is the author of *Worship Seeking Understanding* (Baker Academic, 2003) and co-editor of *Worship in Medieval and Early Modern Europe* (University of Notre Dame Press, 2004). He also serves as the editor of book series for both Eerdmans and the Alban Institute.

Introduction

What does it mean to be "sucked up into the vortex of sacred reality and tumbled head over heels before God's presence"? This is the question that Corrine Carvalho asks in her essay in this volume (see p. 149).

This is not the kind of question Christians typically ask themselves. And yet, perhaps we should. God's electrifying holiness is not to be trifled with. Whether we actively seek it or tumble into it unawares, we should know, as Carvalho points out, that "God's presence makes demands on us, requires from us a new way of living, [and that] the ripples of holiness extending out from God's presence change all of reality" (p. 132).

There is a sense in which this entire volume seeks to explore this question, which is, whether we realize it or not, at the heart of Jewish and Christian worship. All of the contributing authors are Christians. Though we represent a range of Christian traditions (Christian Reformed, Episcopalian, Lutheran, Presbyterian, Reformed Church in America, and Roman Catholic), we all agree on one thing: that what Christians call the Old Testament is essential for knowing what we're about when we come into God's presence to sing "Alleluia!"

The other thing that six out of the seven contributing authors have in common is that we are Old Testament professors. That means we are all too familiar with the challenges of teaching this part of the Bible. Fewer and fewer students come to us with even a passing familiarity with the text, and many arrive with attitudes and assumptions that can make the process of teaching and learning more difficult. Some students are simply indifferent to the material; others are openly hostile; still others profess enthusiasm, but seem more interested in contrasting the Old Testament with the New than in seeing the essential connection between them. This volume is intended to challenge such attitudes and present a compelling alternative.

Because most of the authors teach Old Testament, either at the undergraduate or graduate/seminary level, we have designed this book in such a way as to make it useful as a supplementary text for introductory or elective courses. In light of the intensifying interest in worship worldwide, especially among those who seek a deeper understanding of worship's Old Testament roots, one might well expect that this volume would provide a rich resource for Christians generally. Notice that the essays move with the flow of the Hebrew canon, beginning with the Pentateuch and reaching to the Psalms and the Wisdom Literature.

Dennis Olson's essay is focused on the Sabbath commandment in Exodus 20 and Deuteronomy 5, but draws on Genesis as well. Its placement at the beginning of the book reflects not only the canonical sequence but also our culture's desperate need to make Sabbath a priority.

Tom Boogaart's provocative piece focuses primarily on the book of Kings but has profound implications for the way we read and interact with all Old Testament narratives. Boogaart ably demonstrates that the contemporary trend toward utilizing drama in worship is not new, but rather the resurrection of an ancient and inspired practice.

John Witvliet's essay, "Isaiah in Christian Liturgy," ushers us into the Major Prophets, and also functions as an extended meditation on idolatry. Witvliet makes the case that idolatry is a very contemporary problem, and is in fact "the most obvious form of false worship" (p. 75).

Ellen Davis helps us to see the way in which Jeremiah, the Minor Prophets, and Jesus himself used imaginative vision to reveal reality from God's perspective. The images Davis sets before us in her two illustrative sermons are not ones we'll soon forget — and we may find them impossible to ignore.

Corrine Carvalho takes on the topic of sacred space in an essay that draws on Temple texts in both Ezekiel and 1 Kings. From lesser questions ("Why do we call worship spaces 'sanctuaries'?") to larger ones ("What does the Incarnation have to do with the Temple?"), Carvalho helps us to understand why the Temple texts are much more than bits of historical trivia.

J. Clinton McCann Jr. mines the psalms for justice and helps us to appreciate the Old Testament's insistence that "worship without justice is empty" (p. 156). McCann believes that the psalms not only inspire us to search for justice, but also give us the language to begin speaking it into being.

Carol Bechtel's essay rereads the book of Job through the lens of our human limitations (as opposed to the usual theme of "theodicy") and makes applications for both life and worship.

Following the flow of the whole canon is the artwork of Margaret Adams Parker, which graces both the cover and each essay in this book. Alert readers will recognize in these woodcuts an opportunity to experience exegesis in another medium. Like good postludes, they not only complement our "sermons" — they complete them.

One of the things the above survey also underscores is the way these essays address what is probably the most ubiquitous question in classrooms of all kinds, namely: "So what?" Readers of this book will not have to wait long to find that question engaged. While the essays touch on many aspects of contemporary concern (e.g., ecology and politics), our primary arena of application is Christian worship. The recent resurgence of interest in worship should make hermeneutical bridge-building much easier.

Perhaps it would be well to say a few words about how a group of Old Testament professors came to write a book about worship.

This collaborative effort would not have been possible without the support of the Calvin Institute of Christian Worship and the generosity of the Lilly Endowment Inc. John Witvliet, the director of the Institute and the one worship professor among us, convened the group and kept us honest as we sought to discern applications for worship. He also made sure that we came up with a book that would be useful and interesting to readers who come to the book with worship as a primary interest. Preachers particularly will enjoy Witvliet's essay on Isaiah, as well as Davis's essay, which includes two actual sermons.

One of the real strengths of our creative process was that it was allowed to develop over a period of time. This book is the result of a series of meetings and continued conversations in which all of the participants influenced each other's thought. We were enriched by the mutuality of the process, and the book is stronger for it as well. It is our sincere hope that this volume will also enrich the current discussion of worship generally by helping to anchor the study of worship in Scripture — particularly that part of Scripture that is sometimes neglected and/or misunderstood. As a group we often lamented the fact that many Christians do not realize the enormous importance of the Old Testament for worship. We hope that the specificity of these essays will make its importance more obvious.

The title we have chosen for this volume is itself an instance of such specificity. It is based on the last phrase of Exodus 29:37: ". . . whatever touches the altar shall become holy." This text is apt to spark controversy among Christians who may balk at the idea of holiness being somehow "contagious." In truth, it has engendered significant discussion among

Jews as well. Jacob Milgrom devotes a full eleven pages to it in his massive commentary on Leviticus.[1] We chose it not to provoke controversy, however, but simply because it speaks — both eloquently and mysteriously — to the power of God's holy presence. Of course, we recognize that we could not presume to come into God's presence at all if we did not come at God's own invitation. This gracious dynamic is evident in all of the ways God seeks us out — in history, Scripture, sacrament, and prayer. We cannot pretend to understand this gracious habit of God's heart, but we can certainly celebrate it.

Finally, we would like to dedicate this book to our students. Thank you for asking us hard questions and for joining us in the search for faithful and compelling answers.

CAROL M. BECHTEL

1. Jacob Milgrom, *Leviticus,* Anchor Bible (New York: Doubleday, 1991), vol. 1, p. 443.

Sacred Time: The Sabbath and Christian Worship

Dennis T. Olson

EXODUS 20

Remember the sabbath day, and keep it holy.

Exodus 20:8

Some Salient Questions on Sabbath

Does the Old Testament commandment for sabbath rest on the seventh day of the week (Saturday) apply to Christians who typically gather for worship on Sundays? Or does the sabbath command apply only to Jews? Is the Christian Sunday properly called a sabbath, or is it something entirely different from the Jewish day of rest? If Sunday is a sabbath day, does that mean that we are not supposed to do any work on Sunday at all? What constitutes work? Should people in school do homework on the sabbath? Should doctors and nurses work on the sabbath? Can you cook food, clean the house, or go to the movies? Should stores be open on Sundays?

Christians today don't seem to take the sabbath as seriously as the Old Testament itself, which prescribes that "whoever does any work on the sabbath day shall be put to death" (Exod. 31:15). The question is, Why don't we? Is the command to rest every seven days meant only for religious people, or is it built into us as a basic need for all human beings? Why are there two different versions of the same sabbath commandment — Exodus 20 and Deuteronomy 5? What indeed is the meaning of this commandment for us today?

As we begin to explore these questions, we will discover many and varied biblical traditions associated with the sabbath commandment in the Old Testament. The biblical theme of the sabbath offers rich resources for fundamentally reshaping our view of time as it integrates and balances the ways we relate to all our primary connections in life — our relationship with God, with other humans, with nonhuman creation, and even with ourselves. The sabbath provides a window into the biblical view of time and all the meanings and values associated with it.

In his book entitled *A Geography of Time*, Robert Levine notes that modern Western industrialized societies tend to be ruled by the clock — fast-paced, punctual, and highly efficient. Instant messages, fast food, being on call "24/7," impatience with delay, and insistence on "being on time" characterize our society's time values. We are defined and valued by how efficiently we use our time. After all, we are told, time is money. Overfilled schedules and a fast-paced lifestyle somehow signify status, importance, and value. But not all human societies are like that. For some cultures, life is slower, interruptions are welcomed, and a balance of rest and work is the norm. Some societies don't even use clocks with minutes and hours, but instead mark time through the slow movement of the stars, the seasons of nature, the rhythms of the human body, or simply events as they occur.[1] In a study entitled *Time Wars,* Jeremy Rifkin writes, "Every culture has its own unique set of temporal fingerprints. To know a people is to know the time values they live by."[2] In many ways, the biblical sabbath represents a set of time values at odds with contemporary culture.

Modern culture's time values often seem enslaving and oppressive. Bookstore shelves are lined with titles like *The Time Trap* and *Timelock* and *The Time Bind.* Work time seems increasingly to expand and rob us of time with family and friends. Computers and the Internet bombard us with a constant flow of data, messages, and information. Hectic schedules and crowded calendars often restrict our options, sap our energies, and rob us of time for thoughtful reflection. Like circus performers desperately trying to keep multiple plates spinning on the ends of wobbly sticks, we rush back and forth from one function or activity to another. We sometimes feel harried and hurried, out of balance, out of sync, not in rhythm. Sociologists tell us that the average American workday has gradually gotten longer, while the time we devote to sleep has grown shorter. We spend less time with family and friends and in voluntary organizations and service. For others in our society, time is out of balance and oppressive in other ways. Some people's lives are marked by having too much time on their hands, feeling bored and isolated, watching the hours pass by without a genuine sense of meaning and purpose. They are the lonely, the unemployed, the depressed, the imprisoned, the bored workers, the elderly in a nursing home, the children with no friends, the poor with few options for play or work.

The biblical vision of time is something quite different from all of this. Time is a gift intended to give human life a sense of balance, meaning, and purpose. God's eternity puts human time in perspective. At the beginning of the Bible in Genesis 1, we read, "In the beginning, God created." Creation happens within a God-given framework of time defined

---

1. Robert Levine, *A Geography of Time* (New York: Basic Books/Perseus, 1997), p. xi.

2. Jeremy Rifkin, *Time Wars: The Primary Conflict in Human History* (New York: Henry Holt, 1987); quoted in Levine, *A Geography of Time,* p. xi.

as the days of the week — six days of work and a sabbath day of rest. At the end of the Bible in John's grand apocalyptic vision, God reaffirms the absorbing of all human time within the all-encompassing eternity of God: "I am the Alpha and the Omega, the beginning and the end" (Rev. 21:6). One of the most important features of this biblical vision of time is the Old Testament sabbath. The Hebrew noun "sabbath" is related to the verb *shabat,* meaning "to cease, stop, interrupt." The sabbath involves breaking into the routine, interrupting what is presumed normal, periodically stopping us in our tracks in order to return us to a healthy rhythm of worship and work, a balance between focusing on God and focusing on others, an equilibrium between caring for our own basic needs and caring for God's whole creation. Such interruptions open up space in time for us to remember, to redirect our lives to what is true and good, to regain perspective, to be broken and then freed, to be stopped and made new again.

Biblical scholars have sought to find parallels to the Old Testament sabbath and the seven-day week in texts from other ancient Near Eastern cultures who were neighbors to ancient Israel, but no clear or direct parallels have emerged.[3] Regular sabbath rest appears to be a fairly distinctive element of ancient Israel's own practice and reflection. The sabbath and the seven-day week were subsequently adapted and reshaped by the early Christians (the earliest of whom were Jewish in background) and then eventually implemented and enforced by Christian rulers and other political authorities as an agreed-upon and common way of reckoning time, weeks, and months in a now widely shared system of marking time across the globe. Although we may work within the seven-day framework of the sabbath, many of us have lost a basic understanding of the full and integrating meanings of the sabbath in relationship to the worship of God, human justice, the rejuvenation of the self, and concern for God's whole creation.

---

3. Some proposals for parallels to the Israelite sabbath have been made. For example, scholars have pointed to one ancient Babylonian text that seems to mark time in seven-day increments according to cycles of the moon. Other texts indicate that the Babylonians may have offered sacrifices to their gods on the day of each full moon, called a *sabbattu* (a word similar to the Hebrew word *shabbat,* "sabbath"). However, the general consensus is that these alleged parallels do not stand up under scrutiny. The Babylonian texts in question seem to apply quite narrowly to certain religious rites and do not signify a society-wide way of marking time.

We will begin our exploration of the Old Testament sabbath by looking at the two versions of the sabbath commandment as they appear in Exodus 20 and Deuteronomy 5.

The Sabbath Commandment in Exodus 20 and the Book of Exodus

Remember the sabbath day, and keep it holy. Six days you shall labor and do all your work. But the seventh day is a sabbath to the LORD *your God; you shall not do any work — you, your son or your daughter, your male or female slave, your livestock, or the alien resident in your towns. For in six days the* LORD *made heaven and earth, the sea, and all that is in them, but rested the seventh day; therefore the* LORD *blessed the sabbath day and consecrated it.*

Exodus 20:8-11

The book of Exodus tells the story of God's rescue of the enslaved people of Israel, who are forced against their will to work for Pharaoh in ancient Egypt. God's servant, Moses, leads Israel across the Red Sea and into the wilderness on a journey toward the promised land of Canaan. Along the way, Israel stops at the mountain of God called Mount Sinai, where God makes a covenant with Israel as God's special people. At the heart of this covenant are the Ten Commandments. Among the most important of these ten imperatives is the command to "remember the sabbath day, and keep it holy" (Exod. 20:8). The sabbath commandment is the lengthiest of all the commandments, making up about a third of the text of the Decalogue. Moreover, the sabbath commandment stands structurally at a central and integrative transition point between the first group of commandments, which articulate obligations to God (no other gods, no worship of images, careful use of the divine name), and the second group of commandments, which articulate obligations to other humans (honoring parents, not killing, not stealing, not committing adultery, not bearing false witness, not coveting). Between these two groups stands the sabbath commandment, which ties together our obligations to God, to other humans, to our own well-being, and to nature (animals are also included in the sabbath rest). All of these relationships come together in this one commandment.

The Sabbath and the Holy

The commandment in Exodus 20 begins, "Remember the sabbath day, and keep it holy" (v. 8). To keep something holy means to set it apart from what is ordinary. The day is special and devoted to God, who is holy. Israelites periodically stop the normal routine of ordinary weekday work and set aside a day as an offering of time to God. What is holy is typically associated with worshiping God and coming together as a community around God's revealed and holy presence. Thus the sabbath is holy "to the Lord" (Exod. 16:23; 20:10; 31:15; 35:2; Lev. 19:3; 23:3). But the sabbath is also holy "to you," the people of God (Exod. 16:29; 31:14; Lev. 16:31). The holiness of the sabbath binds together *God's* holiness with *Israel's* holiness as the beloved and chosen people of God. "You shall keep my sabbaths, for this is a sign between me and you throughout your generations, given in order that you may know that I, the Lord, sanctify you. You shall keep the sabbath, because it is holy for you" (Exod. 31:13-14). Israel rests on the sabbath so that they might have the time to remember and know that it is the Lord who sanctifies or makes them holy. It is not their human work, not their frantic activity, not their human power or efforts that make them holy, special, and set apart from others. Rather, it is God who makes them whole and holy. The friendly commandment of weekly rest reminds the people of Israel of their reliance on God's gracious presence and activity to sustain their life, their freedom, their identity, and their hope.

The Sabbath and Work

Every seventh day is to be a day on which "you shall not do any work." Specific types of work are prohibited in the Old Testament. On the sabbath, there is to be no kindling of fire or cooking (Exod. 35:3), no gathering of wood with the intention of starting a fire (Num. 15:32-36), no carrying of burdens (Jer. 17:21-22; 24:27), no trade or commerce (Neh. 10:32; see Amos 8:5), no treading of winepresses or loading of beasts (Neh. 13:15-22), and no traveling away from your home territory ("each of you stay where you are; do not leave your place on the seventh day" — Exod. 16:29). The literal Hebrew of Isaiah 58:13 even prohibits "speaking words" on the sabbath. Some interpret this injunction as a requirement to main-

tain total silence during the sabbath, and others suggest it is a requirement simply not to speak about work matters on the sabbath. Given the
imprecision and ambiguities in the biblical sabbath instructions, the Jewish rabbinic tradition developed a large number of clarifying interpretations about what one was and was not allowed to do on the sabbath. But
strict observance of sabbath rest from all work was assumed, even in the
busiest times of the year: "even in plowing time and in harvest time you
shall rest" (Exod. 34:21).

Within the larger literary context of the book of Exodus, the sabbath
commandment provides a thoughtful commentary on the nature of human work and vocation. The book of Exodus contrasts two major work
projects. The one described in Exodus 1–13 is oppressive, enslaving, and de-
humanizing. It is the Egyptian empire's enslavement of the Israelites, who
are forced to do menial and hard labor against their will and without just
compensation. The other work project in Exodus 25–31 and 35–40 is Israel's eager and willing building of the Tabernacle, the seat of God's presence in their midst, a portable shrine and sanctuary that is the visible sign
of God's presence in their midst. It is only this — the divine presence,
"God with us" — that makes Israel holy and set apart from every other
people (Exod. 33:16). And so Israel willingly offers its resources, time, and
energy to construct the Tabernacle. Concerning these two large work projects in Exodus, Ellen Davis makes this observation:

> Exodus is setting before us two lengthy, vivid pictures. In the first thir-
> teen chapters, we see Israel enslaved in Egypt, trapped in "that iron fur-
> nace" (Dt 4:20), the great industrial killing machine of Pharaonic Egypt.
> There Israel builds store cities for a king so deluded he thinks he is a
> god. Then at the other end of the book, thirteen chapters portray Israel's
> first concerted activity in freedom. Israel's first "public work" is to build
> a sanctuary for her God, who is of course the real God. These two long
> narratives at beginning and end are a sort of unmatched pair, designed
> to contrast absolutely. They are, respectively, perverted work, designed
> by Pharaoh to destroy God's people, and divinely mandated work, de-
> signed to bring together God and God's people, in the closest proximity
> possible in this life. That is what worship is for.[4]

4. Ellen F. Davis, "Slaves or Sabbath-Keepers? A Biblical Perspective on Human Work,"
Anglican Theological Review 83 (2001): 30-31.

How Do Pastors Observe the Sabbath?

This requirement of Isaiah 58 to maintain silence about one's work on the sabbath raises the issue of how the clergy and other religious professionals are to observe the sabbath. For priests and ministers, Sunday is a day not of silence but of much talking and preaching. Sunday is typically their busiest day of the week. How do ministers properly keep the sabbath and reap its blessings of rest? Clergy self-care has become an increasingly crucial concern as the demands and expectations placed on many pastors continue to mushroom. In his book *Rest in the Storm: Self-Care Strategies for Clergy and Other Caregivers* (Valley Forge, Pa.: Judson Press, 2001), Kirk Byron Jones shares the lament of one pastor stretched to the breaking point. After enumerating a long list of all the responsibilities and roles that congregations place on their pastors, from preaching to administering to counseling to conflict management and the like, the pastor concludes, "Right now, I am not filling any of those expectations very well . . . and I am tired" (p. 4).

Clearly, some measure of regular sabbath-keeping is imperative for clergy. Sabbath-keeping may include carefully guarded days off each week, boundaries to protect time for weekly study and reading, a sustained devotional life, a study sabbatical for long-term pastorates, regular and full vacations, continuing education, hobbies and interests outside of church work, confidential friendships, a network of mutual support among colleagues in ministry or a trusted counselor, and an overall healthy lifestyle. These and

The instructions for the "divinely mandated work" of building the Tabernacle in Exodus 25–31 divide into six sections or speeches that correspond to the six days of creation in Genesis 1. And just as the sabbath day comes at the end of six days of God's work in the creation story (Gen. 2:1-3), so the six sections of the Tabernacle instructions conclude with a seventh speech that repeats the sabbath commandment (Exod. 31:12-17).[5]

5. Peter Kearney, "Creation and Liturgy: The P Redaction of Ex 25–40," *Zeitschrift für die alttestamentliche Wissenschaft* 89 (1977): 374-87; Peter Weimar, "Sinai und Schöpfung, Komposition und Theologie der priesterschriftlichen Sinaigeschichte," *Revue Biblique* 95 (1988): 337-85; and Bernd Janowski, "Tempel und Schöpfung, Schöpfungstheologische Aspekte der priesterschriftlichen Heiligstumskonzeption," in *Schöpfung und Neuschöpfung,*

many other "sabbath habits" can interrupt the routine pressures of ministry and help to restore the balance of work, rest, and worship. Pastor and scholar Barbara Brown Taylor recounts her decision to move from a seven-day workweek as a pastor to a six-day workweek as part of her Lenten discipline:

> I continued to work seven days a week, until this past Lent, when I decided to obey the fourth commandment. One day a week, I would lie back in God's arms. One day a week, whether or not my work was done, I would live as if I were free. . . . Once when I attended a funeral at a black Baptist church, the preacher consoled us by telling us that the person we loved had gone on to that place where every day is Sunday. . . . Now I know what he meant. We do not have to wait until we die to experience resurrection. God is ready whenever we are, with a weekly rehearsal for those who are willing to lie back in God's arms. ("Remember the Sabbath," *Christian Century* 116 [1999]: 510)

One active local church reviewed its crammed calendar of meetings, programs, and events and decided that it needed to model the sabbath principle in the way it put together its schedule. Thus, one month every year is designated as a sabbath, a month when no meetings, events, or activities apart from Sunday worship are held. Clergy and congregations have a responsibility to be examples of sabbath-keeping and to hold each other mutually accountable for finding a balance between rest and work.

What is the significance of this correspondence between God's creating work in Genesis 1 and Israel's Tabernacle building in Exodus 25–31? It is important to note that God's creating in Genesis 1 works with the resources at hand and empowers intermediaries to participate with God in the creation and stewardship of the world. "Let the waters bring forth swarms of living creatures" (Gen. 1:20). "Let the earth bring forth living creatures" (Gen. 1:24). "God set [the sun and the moon] in the dome of the sky . . . to rule over the day and over the night" (Gen. 1:17-18). "God said to

Jahrbuch für Biblische Theologie, vol. 5, ed. Luis M. Alonso Schöckel et al. (Neukirchen-Vluyn: Neukirchener Verlag, 1990), pp. 37-70.

[the humans], '. . . have dominion . . . over every living thing that moves upon the earth" (Gen. 1:28).[6] Earth, water, sun, moon, and humans participate with God in co-creating the world in the midst of the watery primeval chaos with which Genesis 1 begins. God is the master architect and builder, but creation is less a one-God show and more an orchestrated community effort in which the created order participates under God's direction.

Similarly, God's instructions to build the Tabernacle (the center of God's presence and Israel's worship) are ultimately God's work that at the same time invites human intermediaries to participate and cooperate in this new creation in the midst of the chaos of the wilderness. Both the creation of the world and the creation of the Tabernacle have as their culmination and goal the sabbath day and its rest. Sabbath rest interrupts work time with time to enjoy, reflect, remember, and worship the God who rules over all creation and yet comes near and is present in the midst of God's people as they gather as a community in worship. Regular sabbath rest and worship remind us that the work we do on the other days of the week should align itself in a cooperative way with God's continuing presence and creative activity in loving service to the world and its inhabitants, human and nonhuman alike.

The Sabbath and Worship

In its earliest stages of development in ancient Israel, the sabbath, scholars believe, was simply a day of rest from work without any association with worship. The motivation for the earliest version of the sabbath law in the Book of the Covenant in Exodus 23:12-13 is simply "so that your ox and your donkey may have relief, and your homeborn slave and the resident alien may be refreshed." But gradually the sabbath became associated more and more with a time for the community of God's people to be gathered for worship. Some texts already before Judah's exile into Babylon (587 B.C.E.) associate the sabbath and worship (Hos. 2:11; Isa. 1:13). However, it is in later exilic or post-exilic texts (after 587 B.C.E.) that we find a more

---

6. Eric Elnes, "Creation and Tabernacle: The Priestly Writer's 'Environmentalism,'" *Horizons in Biblical Theology* 16 (1994): 144-55; Terence Fretheim, "Creation and Co-Creation," in *Making All Things New: Essays in Honor of Roy Harrisville*, Word & World Supplement, Series 1 (St. Paul: Luther Seminary, 1992).

frequent connection between the sabbath day and acts of community worship (Leviticus; 2 Chronicles). Leviticus 23 defines the sabbath as a day of convocation, festival, and the giving of offerings to God (vv. 2-3, 37-38; see also Lev. 24:8). The sabbath is a day to "reverence the sanctuary" as the community gathers around the Tabernacle in its tent or in the temple as the seat of God's holy presence in the community (Lev. 26:2). The prophets condemn sabbath worship and the bringing of offerings to God if justice for the poor and righteousness in everyday life are not maintained (Isa. 1:13-17; see also Amos 5:21-24). The post-exilic book of 2 Chronicles retells the earlier stories of 2 Kings and adds a reference to sabbath worship and the giving of offerings at the temple when King Solomon builds the first temple in Jerusalem (2 Chron. 2:4; 8:12-13). These texts mention three categories of regular worship and assembly by post-exilic Jews: three "annual festivals"; twelve assemblies, one every month at the "new moon"; and weekly "sabbaths." The role of priests in sabbath worship is also noted in 2 Chronicles 23:4, 8. The association of sabbath worship with music, prayer, and the singing of the psalms is suggested by Psalm 92, which is entitled "A Song for the Sabbath Day." The psalm is a hymn of praise and begins with these words:

> It is good to give thanks to the LORD,
> to sing praises to your name, O Most High;
> to declare your steadfast love in the morning,
> and your faithfulness by night,
> to the music of the lute and the harp,
> to the melody of the lyre.
> For you, O LORD, have made me glad by your work;
> at the works of your hands I sing for joy.

Sabbath worship likely involved the use of the full range of psalms from lament to praise, from prayers of confession to songs of thanksgiving. One important biblical text brings together the sabbath and worship as it offers an ideal and distant future vision of all humanity gathered together before God: "from sabbath to sabbath, all flesh shall come to worship before me, says the LORD" (Isa. 66:23).

The Sabbath and Food: Greed versus Trust

Another important story related to the sabbath is Exodus 16 and the divine gift of manna. The manna is a special food that appears every morning to the Israelites during their wilderness journey. Remarkably, although on a given day some Israelites would gather more of the manna and some less, "those who gathered much had nothing over, and those who gathered little had no shortage; they gathered as much as each of them needed" (Exod. 16:18). Two important themes associated with the sabbath and worship appear here for the first time: the theme of feasting and food as gifts of God, and the theme of the basic equality of God's provision to all, regardless of effort, ability, or status. What is given is what is sufficient to meet one's basic needs — that is all that is required. When in the Lord's Prayer we pray "Give us this day our daily bread," we are praying out of the tradition of the manna story for only what we need for this particular day, no more and no less.

The sabbath enters the story explicitly in God's instruction to Moses that the people are to gather twice as much as usual on the sixth day in order that they may rest on the sabbath or seventh day from the work of gathering food. The people must learn to trust that God will provide what they need, even though they do not work on the sabbath. There are those who went out on the sabbath day looking to gather more manna, "but they found none" (Exod. 16:27). The greedy desire to hoard, to wring something more out of the gift of time given to us, to refuse to trust God and trust only one's own hard work and "efficient" use of time and energy — and all of these are put under critique and judgment in the story of the manna. As a constant reminder of the lessons of the manna, God commands Moses to take some of it, put it into a jar, and place the jar with the manna "before the LORD, to be kept throughout your generations" (Exod. 16:33). The jar of manna is a visible sign in worship "before the LORD" of God's gracious gift of food, the equality of all before God, the character of the sabbath as a special day to lean back in trust into the comforting arms of God, and the trustworthiness of God to "give us this day our daily bread."

Sabbath Rest and Creation

One of the most central features of the sabbath commandment in Exodus 20 is that the primary motivation and reason for resting on the sabbath day is rooted in the model or example provided by God as Creator in Genesis 1–2: "For in six days the LORD made heaven and earth, the sea, and all that is in them, but rested the seventh day; therefore the LORD blessed the sabbath day and consecrated it" (Exod. 20:11). This grounding in God's activity as Creator is the most distinctive element of the Exodus version of the sabbath commandment in comparison with its alternate version in Deuteronomy 5. The commandment in Deuteronomy 5 grounds the sabbath not in creation but in God's rescue of Israel from Egyptian slavery. The focus of Exodus 20 on God as a kind of teaching model, One who labors in creation for six days and then takes a rest (Gen. 2:1-3), raises some theological issues. Another version of the sabbath commandment in Exodus 31:17 suggests that the LORD "rested" and indeed "was refreshed" on the seventh day of creation. But does God, the LORD of eternity and Creator of the world, really need to take a rest? Does the almighty God actually become tired and exhausted? Do not the Psalms confess that the God "who keeps Israel will neither slumber nor sleep" (Ps. 121:4)? Is not God always at work, always active, always awake?[7]

Precisely here is an important insight into the meaning of the sabbath. In Genesis 1:1–2:3 God creates time. The modern reader need not take the creation account as a literal scientific description of the origins of the universe in order to appreciate the profound truth expressed in the creation story. God fashions the framework of the six days of creation and the seventh day of rest in Genesis 1:1–2:3 with the alternation of light and darkness along with the sun, moon, and stars as markers of the passage of time. God is Alpha and Omega, beginning and end, sovereign over all human time. But by resting on the sabbath, God willingly enters into and becomes subject to the created framework of human time that God had just created. This act of divine resting on the sabbath day of creation is the first instance of God's gracious accommodation, God's self-limiting, the first step toward the eventual coming of God in human flesh in the person of Jesus. In the Gospel story of Jesus calming the storm on the sea, Jesus combines the power of the Creator God to still the raging waters of primeval chaos (see Gen. 1:2) with the human need for sleep:

---

7. On the interesting theme of God and sleep in the Old Testament and its ancient Near Eastern environment, see Thomas McAlpine, "Sleep, Human and Divine, in the Old Testament," *Journal for the Study of the Old Testament*, Supp. 38 (Sheffield: JSOT, 1987).

And when [Jesus] got into the boat, his disciples followed him. A wind-
storm arose on the sea, so great that the boat was being swamped by the
waves; but he was asleep. And they went and woke him up, saying,
"Lord, save us! We are perishing!" And he said to them, "Why are you
afraid, you of little faith?" Then he got up and rebuked the winds and
the sea; and there was a dead calm. They were amazed, saying, "What
sort of man is this, that even the winds and the sea obey him?" (Matt.
8:23-27; cf. also Mark 4:35-41; Luke 8:22-25)

The community of Jesus' disciples gathered in a boat was for the early
church a common symbol of Christians gathered in community for worship. Even today the inside architecture of many church buildings represents an inverted boat or ship. The image also recalls the story of Noah and
the ark, with Noah's family being saved from the raging floods of Genesis
6–9. The Noah narrative is the story of another new creation. This same
divine power to create, tame chaos, and bring sabbath rest is evident here
in Jesus, who both rests and acts in power to save. Rest, peace, calm — creation's seventh day offers to worshipers a sabbath refuge from the winds,
storms, and waves that buffet our workdays and threaten to throw us off
balance or even drown us in the waters of chaos. The sabbath and sabbath
worship are first of all about God's coming down into our lives and communities to act, to create, to calm, and to give rest. Sabbath worship is an
interruption in human time whereby God becomes revealed and present
in power among a gathered community of faith.

This is why the sabbath day is described as "blessed" by God (Exod.
20:11; Gen. 2:3). Sabbath time becomes an arena or sphere of God's blessing, a temporal space set aside to give life, well-being, and wholeness. In
this way, the sabbath holds together in some tension a more somber sense
of holiness, obligation, and "solemn rest" (Exod. 16:23; 31:15; 35:2) and a
more joyful sense of the sabbath as a gracious gift that is received, embraced, and celebrated in an atmosphere of freedom and feasting. Thus the
prophet in Isaiah 58 promises that "if you call the sabbath a delight . . . then
you shall take delight in the LORD, and I will make you ride upon the
heights of the earth" (Isa. 58:13-14). There are echoes of this promise elsewhere in Isaiah. "Happy is the mortal . . . who keeps the sabbath" (Isa.
56:2). "All who keep the sabbath, and do not profane it . . . these I will bring
to my holy mountain, and make them joyful in my house of prayer" (Isa.
56:6). The sabbath is associated with festivals and feasts involving the shar-

ing of food and celebration (Lev. 23:37-38; 2 Chron. 8:12-13). As with many of its facets, the sabbath holds together a dialogical tension between holy, solemn obligation and joyful, gracious freedom.

The Sabbath and Caring for Others

We have seen that the sabbath in Exodus 20 carries with it several important themes: the holiness of the seventh day, the primacy of God's gracious action, a balanced understanding of work and vocation, the experience of God's re-creating power and presence in worship, and the joyful receiving of the sabbath as a blessing and a gift for oneself. The Exodus 20 version of the sabbath imperative adds one more theme to this list: Sabbath rest is not just for us but, just as important, it is for others — for family members, for workers, and even for animals. Grounded in God's creating of the whole universe in Genesis 1–2, the need for periodic and regular sabbath rest is built into every creature created by God, whether human or nonhuman. Humans are created in the image of God (Gen. 1:26) and thus have built into them a resonance to God's exemplary rhythm of working six days and resting on the seventh. The gift of the sabbath is for all humans, even the non-Israelite "alien resident in your towns" (Exod. 20:10). Foreigners and strangers are welcomed into receiving the blessing of sabbath rest.

In the creation story in Genesis 1, humans are given dominion over the animals (Gen. 1:26). But that dominion is to be exercised graciously "in the image of God," who limited and accommodated God's self in order to provide the blessing of the sabbath to humans. Similarly, humans are to give rest not only to their human workers but also to their animals in benevolent oversight and stewardship of all of God's creatures. The sabbath as rooted in God's creating activity readily enables connections among practices of rest, worship, justice, and the care of the earth. The sabbath is about interrupting the routine of our daily work and lives not only so that *we* might be refreshed and restored but also so that others, human and nonhuman alike, may rest and be reinvigorated and renewed. Indeed, what may be the oldest version of the sabbath commandment in Exodus 23:12 offers a singularly practical and humane justification for the commandment: the sabbath is to be a day of rest "so that your ox and your donkey may have relief, and your homeborn slave and the resident alien may be refreshed." Isaiah 56:1-2 affirms this dimension of "keeping the sabbath" as not just passive rest and not just worship of God but also the active concern to "maintain justice, and do what is right" for the sake of others. Doing justice for the sake of others properly flows out of gratitude for the gift of sabbath rest and blessing that we receive along with God's transforming activity within us in sabbath worship. This concern for active justice for the sake of the other is present in the Exodus 20 version of the sabbath commandment, but it is highlighted even more in the version we find in Deuteronomy 5, to which we now turn.

The Sabbath Commandment in Deuteronomy 5
and the Book of Deuteronomy

Observe the sabbath day and keep it holy, as the LORD your God commanded you. Six days you shall labor and do all your work. But the seventh day is a sabbath to the LORD your God; you shall not do any work — you, or your son or your daughter, or your male or female slave, or your ox or your donkey, or any of your livestock, or the resident alien in your towns, so that your male and female slave may rest as well as you. Remember that you were a slave in the land of Egypt, and the LORD your God brought you out from there with a mighty hand and an outstretched arm; therefore the LORD your God commanded you to keep the sabbath day.

Deuteronomy 5:12-15

The alternate version of the sabbath commandment appears in Deuteronomy 5 in the context of an elderly Moses who is at the end of his life and wishes to leave a legacy for future generations. Moses has led a new generation of young Israelites through the wilderness to the edge of the promised land of Canaan. Moses is about to die and will not enter Canaan with them. But in the words of Deuteronomy, Moses leaves a final catechetical book that will teach and shape the faith and lives of new generations of God's people. In Deuteronomy 5, Moses repeats the Ten Commandments (found first in Exodus 20) with some variation, especially in the sabbath commandment. It is important to observe that the Ten Commandments are central to the structure of the whole book of Deuteronomy. All the laws that follow in Deuteronomy 6–28 are laid out roughly according to the sequence of the Ten Commandments in Deuteronomy 5. Thus, the many particular laws in chapters 6–28 function as commentary on the Ten Commandments. In this way, the sabbath commandment in Deuteronomy 5:12-15 is expanded and interpreted by a group of laws related to the sabbath in Deuteronomy 14:22–16:17.[8] We will consider first the variations of the sabbath commandment itself in Deuteronomy 5:12-15 (relative to the earlier version in Exodus 20:8-11), and then some implications of the ways in which the sabbath commandment is expanded in the group of laws found in Deuteronomy 14:22–16:17.

The Sabbath: A Practice That Generates Memory

One interesting change in the sabbath commandment in its Deuteronomic version is a shift in the verbs. Exodus 20:8 begins, "*Remember* the sabbath day, and keep it holy." Deuteronomy 5:12 begins, "*Observe* [Hebrew *shamar* — "to keep, watch, observe, guard"] the sabbath day and keep it holy." In the Deuteronomic version, the emphasis is on being careful to preserve the doing of the sabbath. Watch that you do the sabbath regularly and maintain its practice. However, the notion of "remembering" that begins the commandment in Exodus 20 is not lost in Deuteronomy's version. But a different dynamic is set up that is instructive for understanding the practice of the sabbath. The verb "remember" comes later in the Deuteronomic sabbath commandment so that the logic is now this: "*Observe* the sabbath day" (v. 12) in order that you may do the following: "*Remember* that you were a slave in the land of Egypt, and the LORD your God brought you out from there with a mighty hand and an outstretched arm; therefore the LORD your God commanded you to keep the sabbath day" (v. 15). In other words, "observing" the sabbath, actually doing the practice of resting from work every seventh day and gathering in worship, serves to generate memory. We remember who we were and who we are: we were slaves, and now we are free. We remember what God did for us: the LORD brought us out of slavery. We remember our core identity: we are God's own people.

But the Deuteronomic version knows that the people of God often suffer from a kind of spiritual amnesia. We are prone to forget who we truly are and whose we truly are. Thus, the practice of the sabbath serves

---

8. Dennis T. Olson, *Deuteronomy and the Death of Moses*, Overtures to Biblical Theology (Minneapolis: Fortress, 1994), pp. 14-17, 73-78.

regularly to jog our memories back to the truth of our authentic identity and purpose as the people of God. This has implications for understanding the role of liturgy and practice within worship. Liturgy creates and shapes memory, which in turn shapes our core commitments, actions, and beliefs.

The Sabbath: A Memory That Generates Compassion

Exodus 20 grounded the sabbath in a focus on God as Creator. Deuteronomy 5 grounds the sabbath in God as Liberator of those enslaved to work. The Deuteronomic version adds as a motivation for observing the sabbath, "so that your male and female slave may rest as well as you" (v. 14). The command seeks to protect the well-being of those who have relatively less power in the community and who may more easily be exploited, abused, and overworked. The commandment appeals to a memory of Israel's foundational story of its own slavery, abuse, and exploitation at the hand of Pharaoh in Egypt. "Remember that you were once a slave in Egypt." Being a slave in Egypt was an identity that was not literally true for many later generations who read the Bible as their book. Nevertheless, the Exodus story was a primal narrative that each new generation adopted as their own life story and core identity. In the annual celebration of Passover, each new generation was to confess, "By strength of hand the LORD brought us out of Egypt" (Exod. 13:14). When each new generation of Israelites would bring its offering to the LORD's sanctuary, they were to reclaim the ancient story as their own: "When the Egyptians treated us harshly and afflicted us . . . the LORD brought us out of Egypt with a mighty hand and an outstretched arm" (Deut. 26:6-8). These sabbath memories that interrupt our normal routine of business and work serve to generate empathy, compassion, acts of justice, and humane concern for workers, children, animals, and other vulnerable members of the community. These concerns are present as well in the laws that expand upon the sabbath commandment in Deuteronomy 14–16.

Sabbath Interruptions and the Integration of Justice and Worship

The statutes and ordinances in Deuteronomy 14:22–16:17 all specify in some way regular interruptions in time, work, and ambition. In the cycle

A Broader Understanding of Sabbath Worship: A Matter of Days, Weeks, and Years

Deuteronomy's laws on the sabbath suggest that the blessing of regular sabbath interruption is not confined just to the time frame of a week. The sabbath principle extends as well to yearly festivals or cycles of seven years. The book of Leviticus calls the annual observance of the Day of Atonement (Yom Kippur) "a sabbath of complete rest" (Lev. 23:32). The yearly harvest celebration, the Festival of Booths (Succoth), and the Festival of Unleavened Bread and Passover include within them designated days of "sabbath" that involve "a holy convocation" and a command that "you shall not work at your occupations" (Lev. 23:7-8, 39). Moreover, the Psalms testify to the practice of daily morning prayer ("O LORD, in the morning you hear my voice" — Ps. 5:3) and prayer in the evening ("Let my prayer be counted as incense before you, and the lifting up of my hands as an evening sacrifice" — Ps. 141:2). Indeed, the sabbath blessing may be understood to underlie any regular worshipful, restful, or caring interruption of our routine, whether the practice or ritual occurs within the framework of a day, a week, a month, a year, or a series of years.

Thus, daily prayer, family devotions, grace at meals, the seasonal disciplines of Advent and Lent, annual festivals like Christmas, Easter, and Pentecost, and the whole pattern of the church year — all of these are sabbath interruptions of our routines in the various time frames in which we live. And they all share the same basic sabbatical significance that we attach to the weekly rest and worship on every seventh day of the week: worship, rest, and activity that reorient our lives and priorities to their true compass points in loving God and loving neighbor.

of years and annual harvests, the laws' interruptions include structured time to remember the gifts that God has given, time to give offerings back to God, time for worship, time for celebration, time for sharing with those in need, and time for periodically canceling debts and releasing slaves to ease the burdens of others. The many laws in this section speak of regular cycles of days, weeks, and years in which offerings, festivals, and releases are to occur: "yearly" (14:22), "every third year" (14:28), "every seventh year" (15:1), "in the seventh year" (15:12), "year by year" (15:20), "the month of Abib" (16:1), "for seven days" (16:3), "on the seventh day" (16:8), "seven weeks" (16:9), "seven days" (16:13, 15), and "three times a year" (16:16). Time is punctuated by interruptions that call the members of the community back to remember their vocation as the people of God. These interruptions are structured, routinized, and institutionalized rather than left merely to the voluntary charity, decisions, and whims of the individual. The sabbath day is to be observed every seven days. The tithe is to be given yearly. The canceling of all debts and the freeing of slaves is to occur every seventh year. The Passover, the Festival of Weeks, and the Feast of Booths are to be celebrated annually. Such discipline and planned interruption are a form of teaching and shaping human minds and hearts to remember who they were, who they are, and who their true God is.

The sabbath laws in Deuteronomy 14:22–16:17 break down into three groups of laws:

1. The laws in 14:22-29 treat the offering of tithes of crops and the first-born of animals to God. The purpose of such offerings is educational: "so that you may learn to fear the LORD your God always" (14:23). Giving a portion back to God reminds us that all we have is a gift from God that rightly belongs to God, a truth which should lead to fear, love, and trust in God alone above all other allegiances. When the offering is given to God, it does not just disappear into the temple. Rather, the offering is immediately shared with others in the community who are in need: the landless Levites, the resident aliens, the widows, the orphans, and the poor so that they "may come and eat their fill" (Deut. 14:29). Gathering for worship and offerings to God is intimately tied to compassionate acts of justice and sharing with those in need.

2. The laws in Deuteronomy 15:1-10 reach into areas of social and economic life within the community or society. They keep an important connection with the themes of the sabbath centered on the so-called sabbatical year or year of release that is to be observed every seventh year. In 15:1-6, all debts are to be forgiven and canceled every seventh year. The goal is that there will "be no one in need among you" (15:4). In 15:7-11, the laws encourage generous sharing with the poor in case the ideal set out in verse 4 is not realized. In 15:12-18, the laws mandate the release of slaves every seventh year (see Jer. 34:8-22). In all of these

laws, the periodic interruption in the holding of debts or slaves serves to prevent those who are rich or in power from abusing the poor or other vulnerable members of the community. The sabbath puts limits on human greed and power.

3. The laws in 15:19-23 return to the theme of making offerings to God. The firstborn animal that is given as an offering to God at the sanctuary or place of worship is immediately slaughtered. The meat is eaten by the worshiper but also shared with others in need in a joyous feast.

What is striking about all of these sabbath laws is the way in which worship and the giving of offerings are intimately connected with acts of justice, compassion, and concern. Such acts of justice and sharing are grounded again and again in the memory of who the Israelites were and what God had done for them: "Remember that you were a slave in Egypt" (15:15; 16:12).

The Sabbath, the Jubilee Year, and an Ethic for Land Use

The sabbath theme that links worship and justice encompasses one other important dimension — namely, the care and distribution of land among the various families and communities of Israel. In Leviticus 25:23, God reminds Israel of the fundamental divine ownership of all land: "the land is mine; with me you are but aliens and tenants." The land is to be worked for six years and then allowed to lie fallow and rest so that it may regenerate itself in the seventh year. The sabbath commandment's concern for the humane treatment of animals embodies a larger ecological concern that extends beyond animals to the land itself. The so-called Year of Jubilee occurs after seven cycles of seven years (thus every fiftieth year). In every Jubilee or fiftieth year, any land sold during the previous cycle of forty-nine years was to be returned to the family who originally owned the land at the beginning of the cycle. Thus, land could be freely bought and sold over the years. But this cycle of buying and selling was to be interrupted every fifty years with a land redistribution program so that all families would start over with what they originally had as their family's land inheritance. No one family or group could permanently amass unduly large tracts of land for itself, on the one hand, or be forced into permanent poverty on the other. Every family was periodically to gain access again to their fair portion of the economic pie.

The Babylonian Exile of Judah
as an Enforced Sabbath for the Land

One Old Testament tradition interprets the exile of 587 B.C.E., when many in Judah were forcibly removed from their native land and relocated to Babylon, as an enforced sabbath of rest for the land of Judah. Leviticus 26:34-35 understands the exile as a consequence of Israel's failure to obey God's law which commanded that the land be allowed to rest every seven years:

> Then the land shall make up for its sabbath years as long as it lies desolate, while you are in the land of your enemies; then the land shall rest, and make up for its sabbath years. As long as it lies desolate, it shall have the rest it did not have on your sabbaths when you were living on it.

There can be grave consequences when we abuse or neglect the natural resources that God has entrusted to us. That is true of the land and of other basic resources of life: water, air, forests, and wildlife. It is also true of our own human bodies. If we neglect or abuse our bodies through overwork, lack of sleep, bad eating habits, lack of exercise, and the like, our bodies will sometimes impose on us an enforced sabbath. It is true that an illness, a heart attack, an accident, or some other traumatic event may occur, as it did in Job's case, without any apparent reason and in spite of our best efforts to follow the guidelines of healthy and faithful living. However, such an event may be a time when some people realize that their bodies or circumstances are telling them to slow down, to take stock, to regain balance and perspective in their lives. Like the people of Judah in exile, they may see the enforced rest as a time when "they shall make amends for their iniquity" (Lev. 26:43).

We have no evidence that the Year of Jubilee was ever actually implemented in ancient Israel. But it remained a vision and an ideal that eventually came to define a future hope of what God would one day bring. Thus the prophets pick up the theme of the Jubilee year or "the year of the LORD's favor" as an eschatological vision of what God's chosen servant will bring:

The spirit of the Lord GOD is upon me,
because the LORD has anointed me;

he has sent me to bring good news to the oppressed,
to bind up the brokenhearted,
to proclaim liberty to the captives,
and release to the prisoners;
to proclaim the year of the LORD's favor.

(Isa. 61:1-2)

It was this text from Isaiah 61 with its promise of the sabbatical release of slaves and debts and the Jubilee year of land redistribution that Jesus used in his first inaugural sermon at his home synagogue in Nazareth (Luke 4:16-19). The sabbath and its integration of worship and justice evident in the laws in Deuteronomy 14–16 continued as a powerful theme in the Old Testament prophets and on into the New Testament.

From Saturday to Sunday:
The Sabbath Day and the Lord's Day

In what ways were the practice and the themes of the sabbath in the Old Testament continued or changed in the New Testament and the early church? The Gospels portray Jesus and his disciples as devout Jews who regularly attend synagogue worship on the sabbath (Mark 1:21; Luke 13:10; John 6:59). However, the Gospels do portray Jesus and his disciples in some conflict with the Jewish Pharisees and scribes concerning the proper observance of the sabbath. On one sabbath, Jesus' disciples pluck some grain from the fields, something that might be construed as work (Mark 2:23-28). When the Pharisees object that the disciples are thus disobeying the sabbath, Jesus replies with a principle that was also well known in other Jewish rabbinic traditions: "The sabbath was made for humankind, and not humankind for the sabbath" (Mark 2:27). Exceptions could be made for doing work on the sabbath when it served human life or when emergency conditions demanded it. (See also Jesus healing the sick on the sabbath — Mark 3:1-6; Matt. 12:9-14; John 5:1-24; 9:1-41.) But then Jesus adds a second and more radical claim that goes beyond any previous discussions of the sabbath: "so the Son of Man is lord even of the sabbath" (Mark 2:28). Jesus here claims for himself the role of arbiter and ruler over the practice of the sabbath law instituted by God at creation (Gen. 2:1-3). Jesus as the Son of God has the power to release his followers from the obligations of the sabbath.

According to the book of Acts, the earliest Jewish Christians after the death and resurrection of Jesus faithfully observed the sabbath (Saturday) and attended synagogue worship services where they proclaimed the Gospel message of Jesus the Christ (Acts 13:14-16; 17:1-3). But the early followers of Jesus also felt a need to gather together on Sunday, "the first day of the week" (Acts 20:7), to worship, break bread together, and collect offerings to help the poor of the community (1 Cor. 16:2). All the Gospels agree that Sunday was the day on which Jesus was resurrected from the dead (Mark 16:2; Matt. 28:1; Luke 24:1; John 20:1, 19). Accordingly, Sunday came to be called "the Lord's Day" by the earliest Christians (Rev. 1:10). While the early Jewish Christians continued to observe the sabbath, the letters of Paul suggest that Gentile or non-Jewish converts to Christianity were not subject to the Jewish law of the sabbath. In fact, Paul urged Gentile believers of Jesus not to impose upon themselves the yoke of the Jewish law, including the observing of festivals and other special days like the sabbath (Gal. 4:8-11). Colossians 2:16-19 admonishes Gentile Christians, "Therefore do not let anyone condemn you in matters of food and drink [the Jewish dietary laws] or of observing festivals, new moons, or sabbaths." The general principle for Gentile Christians is stated in Galatians 5:1: "For freedom Christ has set us free. Stand firm, therefore, and do not submit again to a yoke of slavery." Clearly, Gentile Christians were free to disregard the obligation of the sabbath.

As the Gentile Christian community grew and the Jewish Christian community diminished in size and influence, the early church more and more established Sunday, the first day of the week, as the primary day to gather for worship. For Christians, each Sunday commemorated the resurrection of Jesus on the first day of the week and could be celebrated as "a little Easter." The beginning day of the new week came to represent "the eighth day of creation" and the dawn of a new creation in light of Jesus rising from the dead. Some early Christian writers rejected the Jewish sabbath as in any way binding on Christians (*Letter of Barnabas* 15). The Church Father Athanasius (296-373 c.e.) in his treatise *On the Sabbath and Circumcision* argued that Sunday was superior to the sabbath — Saturday — because the sabbath represented the end of the old creation, while Sunday represented the beginning of the new creation in Christ. On the other hand, the so-called *Constitutions of the Holy Apostles* (380 c.e.) recommended that Christians observe both the sabbath and the Lord's Day (Saturday and Sunday), since they both commemorated worthy fundamentals of the faith: creation (sabbath) and resurrection (Sunday). Augustine (354-430 C.E.) reinterpreted the ongoing significance of the Old Testament sabbath in two ways: eternal sabbath rest in God as the goal of the history of the world (*City of God* 22.30), and eternal sabbath rest in God as the goal of the individual soul of the believer (*Confessions* 13.35-36).

However, a significant development occurred in 321 C.E. when the Christian emperor Constantine decreed legislation that took the requirement of rest from work, a requirement applied only to the sabbath or Saturday in the Bible, and applied it to Sunday. Whereas before the sabbath and Sunday had been separate and distinct, the Sunday law of 321 merged them together as one concept. For Constantinian Christendom, Sunday took over as the sabbath. The sabbath commandment in the Old Testament became reinterpreted as requiring rest not on the seventh or last day of the week (Saturday) but on one day in every seven, whatever that day might be. Christians could then freely assign the sabbath with all of its requirements to the first day of the week, Sunday.

This begins an ongoing debate and tension within the Christian tradition about the sabbath. Was the Old Testament law, including the requirements of the sabbath rest, applicable to Christians or not? The medieval theologian Thomas Aquinas interpreted sabbath rest as a spiritual rest in God but rejected the need to observe a literal sabbath day of no work. The sixteenth-century Reformer Martin Luther was suspicious about any imposition of the Old Testament law of the sabbath as a legalistic requirement. Luther feared that making the sabbath obligatory would rob the gospel of its freedom. Consequently, Luther reinterpreted the sabbath commandment as a general admonition to stop work regularly and make time to hear and study God's Word. Following John Calvin, the Reformed tradition (Puritans, Presbyterians, Congregationalists, Methodists, and Baptists) tended to see the sabbath as a continuing universal and binding law of creation for all humans but Christianized in part so that the sabbath obligation was transferred to Sunday with more discipline and strictness than in the Lutheran tradition.[9] The debate and tension concerning the meaning of the sabbath for Christians continue unresolved even to the present day. How then do we best understand the significance of the Old Testament sabbath for Christian worship, life, and practice?

---

9. Samuele Bacchiocchi, "Remembering the Sabbath: The Creation-Sabbath in Jewish and Christian History," in *The Sabbath in Jewish and Christian Traditions*, ed. Tamara Eskenazi et al. (New York: Crossroad, 1991), pp. 78-86.

Breaking Open the Category of "Sabbath Hymns"

Worship leaders and planners may be familiar with a category of hymns sometimes called "sabbath hymns," which traditionally celebrate Sunday as the weekly day of rest and worship. One example is Christopher Wordsworth's hymn "O Day of Rest and Gladness," retitled in the *Presbyterian Hymnal* as "O Day of Radiant Gladness":

O day of radiant gladness, O day of joy and light,
O balm of care and sadness, most beautiful, most bright;
this day the high and lowly, through ages joined in tune,
sing "Holy, holy, holy" to the great God triune.

[Hymn 470, *The Presbyterian Hymnal*
(Louisville: Westminster John Knox, 1990)]

But the sabbath is a much more expansive theme that touches on a large number of entries in the topic index of a typical hymnal: comfort and rest, stewardship and possessions, social concern and justice, vocation and work, heaven and hope, nature and creation, worship and trust, to name but a few. Charles Wesley's Advent hymn, "Come, Thou Long-Expected Jesus," petitions God for sabbath release and rest: "From our fears and sins release us; let us find our rest in thee." In her Holy Week hymn, Elizabeth Cecilia Clephane stands "beneath the cross of Jesus" and finds there "a home within the wilderness, a rest upon the way."

The black Baptist tradition affirms that "in heaven every day is Sunday."

The Old Testament Sabbath and Christian Life and Worship

We conclude with a series of brief reflections on how the sabbath commandment in its two versions in Exodus 20 and Deuteronomy 5 and their larger Old Testament contexts might inform and shape Christian faith and practice. In keeping with the number seven and its association with the sabbath, let us consider seven concluding observations.

The medieval theologian Peter Abelard echoes that sentiment as he contemplates the fate of those who have died in Christ in his hymn "O What Their Joy": "O what their joy and their glory must be, those endless Sabbaths the blessed ones see!" The habit of sabbath offerings given to God and shared with others in need embodies a core sabbatical premise, expressed in the hymn by William How entitled "We Give Thee But Thine Own": "All that we have is thine alone, a trust, O Lord, from thee." A line from Matthew Bridges' "Crown Him with Many Crowns" summarizes well the sabbath's affirmation of the rule of God as the Alpha and the Omega, the beginning and the end of all temporality: "Crown him the Lord of years, the Potentate of time." Finally, John Greenleaf Whittier's nineteenth-century hymn "Dear Lord and Father of Mankind" expresses well in its verses the yearning for sabbath rest in the midst of harried lives:

O sabbath rest by Galilee,
    O calm of hills above,
where Jesus knelt to share with thee
    the silence of eternity, interpreted by love!
Drop thy still dews of quietness,
    till all our strivings cease;
take from our souls the strain and stress,
    and let our ordered lives confess
the beauty of thy peace.

[Hymn 358, *The United Methodist Hymnal*
(Nashville: United Methodist Publishing House, 1989)]

1. Creation and Exodus

The two different versions of the sabbath commandment in Exodus and Deuteronomy (one rooted in the creation story and the other in the Exodus) imply an inner tension or dialogue in the understanding of the sabbath, a fruitful tension that invites ongoing interpretation and resists legalistic precision. If we then add the larger context of other biblical laws and the sayings of the prophets, we soon see that the theme of the sabbath is an exceedingly rich but complex concept within the Old Testament. The sabbath theme touches on numerous fundamental aspects of life: time, worship, work, creation, justice, compassion, ecology, economics, land use, future hope, memory, identity, and purpose. The biblical sabbath is much more than simply not doing any work or worshiping on Saturday or Sunday. This rich meaning of the sabbath may be expressed in a number of dialogical polarities or tensions that emerge from the full biblical witness to the theme of the sabbath. Some of those polarities are noted below.

2. Holy to God, Holy to Humans

The sabbath maintains a polarity of holiness to the Lord and to humans. The sabbath is "holy to the Lord," but it is also "holy to the people of God." The sabbath represents an obligation of time and attention set apart for God. But the sabbath is also time and rest set apart for the benefit of human beings ("the sabbath is made for humankind, and not humankind for the sabbath").

3. Rest and Work

The sabbath reflects a polarity between rest and labor. God has created humans for meaningful work. Even in the Garden of Eden, the human from the very beginning was called "to till it and keep it" (Gen. 2:15). But such work is to be balanced by regular periods of rest. We need time and activities that restore our energies, quiet our anxious minds, and regenerate our troubled spirits. Regular sabbath rest enables our work and service to God and neighbor to continue in healthy and productive ways. Without the sabbath, work can become an idol or an oppressor.

4. Anxiety and Trust

The sabbath introduces a "test" in the struggle between worrisome fretting and confident trusting. God provided the miraculous food of manna to the Israelites during their wilderness journey from Egypt to Canaan. But they could gather only what they could use in one day, and they could not gather manna on the sabbath. In this context, God says, "I will test them, whether they will follow my instruction or not" (Exod. 16:4). The sabbath may be seen as an ongoing test of our willingness to trust God to provide or not. Do we know that not everything depends on what we accomplish? Have we learned the art of letting go and saying no? Have we focused our energies on gathering huge surpluses for a rainy day, or do we live simpler, leaner, and more trusting lives, confident that God will provide what we need for the day?

5. Somber Holiness and Joyful Delight

Several polarities revolve around the theme of the sabbath and creation (Gen. 2:1-3). Sabbath rest is built into creation and so applies to all humans and all nonhuman creatures. And yet the sabbath is also distinctive and unique, a "sign" of God's special covenant with Israel (Ezek. 20:12, 20). God's resting on the sabbath after six days of creation invites reflection on the mystery of the eternal God who is beyond time and yet enters into time out of love for the world. Within human time, God models the practice of rest and refreshment for the sake and benefit of God's creatures. In the creation story, God both "hallows" or makes holy the sabbath day and "blesses" the holy day. As both a holy day and a blessing, the sabbath holds together the more somber traits of holiness, obligation, and "solemn rest" (Exod. 16:23) alongside the more positive characteristics of a gracious gift, a liberating freedom, and a generous blessing. If we emphasize too much the sabbath as somber obligation, we lose its freeing delight and joy (Isa. 58:13-14). On the other hand, if we lose the discipline, respect, and importance implied in its holiness, we tend to neglect and drift away from the gifts and joy of regular sabbath-keeping.

6. For Us and for Others

The sabbath carries within it a basic polarity between its benefits for us ourselves and its benefits for others: family members, workers, animals, and even the land that provides our food. Indeed, the sabbath commandment integrates all our relationships as none of the other Ten Commandments does: (a) our relationship to God, who is worshiped on the sabbath as both Creator and Deliverer from bondage; (b) our relationship to other human beings as we give workers time off for sabbath rest; (c) our relationship to nonhuman creation as we rest both animals and the land in order that they may be refreshed; and finally, (d) even our relationship to ourselves as we benefit from the balance of work and sabbath rest and regain our identity as we remember who we were (slaves in Egypt) and who at the core of our being we are (people saved and loved by God).

7. Worship and Justice

One final and crucial polarity that the sabbath holds together in the Old Testament is an essential integration of and commitment to the worship of God *and* the doing of justice for the neighbor in need. The biblical sabbath is the bridge which insists that both of these aspects of the life of faith must be held together. We began the essay by talking about cultures and the time values they display in their beliefs and practices. The Old Testament sabbath may be one of the most strongly countercultural concepts in the Bible in relation to our modern society and its values. Our secular world tends to worship money, power, success, and fame. Our self-indulgent and individualistic culture asks "What's in it for me?" not "What would be just and good for my neighbor or for the community as a whole?"

Christians will likely continue to debate and disagree about how to implement and be faithful to these many polarities and tensions associated with the sabbath. Many of the questions with which we opened this essay defy easy answers. Much will depend on the particular contexts and specific issues for which we may be seeking guidance. Nevertheless, the biblical sabbath has the capacity to speak a helpful and powerful word to us today. We live in the midst of worship wars, terrorist wars, battles of denominational unrest, the disestablishment of the church, increasing blindness toward the needs of the poor, human ravaging of the world's environment, and all manner of personal and community unrest and turmoil. The recovery of a full biblical understanding of the sabbath will be an essential resource as the people of God navigate their way through the stormy and chaotic waters of our day, straining to hear the voice of the One who is Lord even of the sabbath saying, "Peace, be still!" In order to hear that voice, time must be broken, routines must be interrupted, business as usual must be stopped. Only then can the God of the sabbath infiltrate our minds, integrate our spirits, and make us whole.

O Day of Radiant Gladness

O day of radiant gladness,
O day of joy and light,
O balm of care and sadness,
most beautiful, most bright;
this day the high and lowly,
through ages joined in tune,
sing "Holy, holy, holy"
to the great God Triune.

This day at the creation,
the light first had its birth;
this day for our salvation
Christ rose from depths of earth;
this day our Lord victorious
the Spirit sent from heaven,
and thus this day most glorious
a triple light was given.

This day God's people, meeting,
his Holy Scripture hear;
his living presence greeting,
through Bread and Wine made near.
We journey on, believing,
renewed with heavenly might,
from grace more grace receiving
on this blest day of light.

That light our hope sustaining,
we walk the pilgrim way,
at length our rest attaining,
our endless Sabbath day.
We sing to You our praises,
O Father, Spirit, Son;
the church its voice upraises
to You, blest Three in One.

Text: Stanzas 1-2, Christopher Wordsworth (1807-1885), 1862, alt.; stanza 3, Charles P. Price (1920-1999), 1980; stanza 4, *The Hymnal 1982*
Text copyright ©: Stanza 3, Charles P. Price, 1985. All rights reserved. Used by permission. Stanza 4 from *The Hymnal 1982* © 1985 the Church Pension Fund. All rights reserved. Used by permission of Church Publishing Incorporated, New York, NY.

Now the Silence

Now the silence,
now the peace,
now the empty hands uplifted.
Now the kneeling,
now the plea,
now the Father's arms in welcome.
Now the hearing,
now the power,
now the vessel brimmed for pouring.
Now the Body,
now the Blood,
now the joyful celebration.
Now the wedding,
now the songs,
now the heart forgiven leaping.
Now the Spirit's visitation,
now the Son's epiphany,
now the Father's blessing.
Now, now, now.

Text: Jaroslav J. Vajda (b. 1919), 1968

For Further Reading

Dorothy Bass. *Receiving the Day: Christian Practices for Opening the Gift of Time* (San Francisco: Jossey-Bass, 2000). This series of reflections on the sabbath and time understand time as God's gift, not as an adversary to be defeated or mastered. The landmarks of time — the day, the week, the year — are gifts from God that should be embraced. They offer opportunities to engage in regular, patterned practices and rituals that deepen our relationship with God and with one another. Bass weaves together the wisdom of the ages, poetry, and her own personal reflections and experience in this practical and thoughtful exploration of the role of time in human life.

Marva Dawn. *Keeping the Sabbath Wholly: Ceasing, Resting, Embracing, Feasting* (Grand Rapids: Eerdmans, 1989). In this study of the sabbath, Dawn balances thoughtful examination of the biblical, Jewish, and Christian traditions with more personal and practical reflections on the feelings, rituals, and struggles in the discipline of sabbath-keeping. Her overall theme is that observing the sabbath in one's life is not a legalistic duty but a path to true freedom and deep joy.

Abraham Joshua Heschel. *The Sabbath: Its Meaning for Modern Man* (New York: Farrar, Straus & Giroux, 1951). This is a classic of Jewish spirituality. Heschel, an erudite philosopher and theologian, argues that Judaism is a religion of time. It finds meaning not in space and the material things that fill it but in time and the eternity that imbues it. Heschel writes that for Jews, "the Sabbaths are our great cathedrals."

Richard Lowery. *Sabbath and Jubilee* (St. Louis: Chalice, 2000). Lowery explores the rich social, economic, political, and cultural contexts of the biblical world associated with the themes of sabbath and the Jubilee. The resulting themes of social solidarity, economic justice, and God's purposes for creation provide important implications for transforming our modern culture's social, economic, and environmental agendas in new and life-giving ways.

Wayne Muller. *Sabbath: Finding Rest, Renewal, and Delight in Our Busy Lives* (New York: Bantam Books, 1999). Muller's study includes but is not limited to Christian reflections on the sabbath. He seeks to show that some notion of a sabbath — a time of rest and reflection, a recognition of human limitations, rituals that interrupt our routines — may be found in a number of religious traditions and thinkers. Gandhi, for example, affirmed that "there is more to life than merely increasing its speed." Muller's study illustrates the biblical claim that the sabbath is built into the very fabric of creation and addresses a common human yearning for rest and time taken to nurture connections to God, others, and all creation.

Drama and the Sacred: Recovering the Dramatic Tradition in Scripture and Worship

Thomas A. Boogaart

2 KINGS 6

Thomas A. Boogaart

The Marriage

The relationship between the church and the theater has often been compared to a troubled marriage.[1] The two have a long history of breaking up and making up. The early church, for example, separated itself from the decadence and blood lust of Roman theater, while the medieval church embraced drama to express the deep truths of the faith. The so-called miracle or mystery plays were of such high quality that they left a lasting mark on Western culture. After having shunned the theater following the Reformation, Protestants are embracing it once again. This latest period of reconciliation could be dated to 1929 with the establishment of the Religious Drama Society in Great Britain (RADIUS). This society's purpose is "to encourage all drama which throws light on the human condition, especially by means of a Christian understanding." Early on, it gained notoriety with productions such as T. S. Eliot's *Murder in the Cathedral* and Christopher Fry's *A Sleep of Prisoners*. Today it continues to provide drama groups with "scripts that are relevant for churches and communities, Christians and non Christians."[2]

Another significant year in the reconciliation between church and theater was 1977, when the Riding Lights Theatre Company of York, England, was founded. Combining an interest in comic revue and street theater, its founders introduced the "sketch" to many churches in England and America. Perhaps more than any other group, it is responsible for the proliferation of the simple dramas so popular now in many "seeker-sensitive" mega-churches in the United States. Early collections of sketches included *Time to Act, Laughter in Heaven,* and *Red Letter Days.* One of its current productions is *Science Friction,* a dramatic look at the historic opposition between the church and the world of science.[3]

In short, theater companies are proliferating in churches of all denominations and offering their opinions and work, often free of charge, on the Internet.

What are we to make of this burgeoning interest in drama among Western Christians? Is the interest simply utilitarian or something more

1. See Gordon C. Bennett, *Acting Out Faith* (St. Louis: CBP Press, 1986), and Murray Watts, *Christianity and the Theatre* (Edinburgh: Handsel Press, 1986).

2. The quotations and information are taken from the society's Web site, www.radius.org.uk.

3. This information is taken from the company's Web site, www.ridinglights.org.

Resources on the Web

www.radius.org.uk is the Web site for the Religious Drama Society in Great Britain (RADIUS). Click on this site to read about its latest prize-winning drama, *Iscariot,* by Michael Hendy. This play takes Judas to the Day of Judgment and probes the issue of redemption in the face of grievous sin.

www.ridinglights.org is the site connected with the Riding Lights Theatre Company of York, England. Visit this site to learn more about Riding Lights Roughshod, the company's latest attempt "to serve local churches and local communities with high quality, highly mobile theatre."

www.dave-marsh.com is the Web page of the Marsh family. Dave Marsh is an online games producer who became interested in theater at the Willow Creek Church in Illinois. He offers over forty-five "slice of life" dramas on his Web page free of charge. He comments, "These dramas last only 3-4 minutes . . . but create a powerful (and many times humorous) illustration on any given Sunday. I also believe that any church, no matter what size, can use drama effectively, giving God glory, and inspire/convict normal folks like you and I to walk closer to God."

www.drama4church.com is a database program created by Kimberly Creasman and contains descriptions of over 1,300 scripts of quality. She writes, "It grieved me that our Creator has for centuries been represented in the Arts with embarrassing mediocrity. It's time to change that. He has created the Arts to have the power to speak to men and women's souls like nothing else on earth. The experience of live theater is especially powerful in breaking down walls in order to build people up. But only if it is done well. There's the rub."

profound? Are people introducing drama into worship because it works — that is, because it increases attendance and brings young people back to the church? Or are they celebrating drama itself as one of the many art forms that God has given to enrich the human community? I would like to think that it is the latter and that when drama works to attract people, it works for this reason. Drama, after all, is a unique gift to the human community. From the very beginning of time, people have gathered before a "stage" to see the essentials of their lives play out: their depravity and their nobility; their vulnerabilities and their ingenuity; their groveling and their glory; their fascination with and their fear of God. From the very beginning, they have recognized that the life presented on the stage is in a mysterious way a version of their own, and in the process they have become more deeply aware of life's profundity and more fully dedicated to its enhancement.

This increased interest in drama is a good thing and has the potential to invigorate both worship and the community. But it is a good thing only if taken with the utmost seriousness. In his book *Christianity and the Theatre*, Murray Watts bewails Christian ineptitude in the arts:

> The Christian actors and writers of today need to do much more than read the Bible, pray, and then walk on stage hoping for the best. They need to devote themselves to God and to their craft. They will thus honour God by offering the first fruits — the very best — of their abilities. The strange thing is that much Christian exploration of drama, particularly amongst evangelical churches, has fallen well below the standards set by amateur dramatic societies. . . . There is no substitute for apprenticeship to the theatre and a willingness to learn the craft, even from those whose religious beliefs are diametrically opposed to Christianity.[4]

Watts hopes that people so devoted to their craft will produce works of such quality that they will naturally make their way from the church to the streets of the city and the marketplace. True to his Scottish Presbyterian roots, he envisions a time in which the church transforms culture by the sheer virtuosity of its dramatic performances.

Theater in Israel

Christian actors and writers certainly do need to know the current developments and practices of the theater. Their devotion to God should engender a devotion to the theater in all its aspects. One of those aspects is, of

---

4. Watts, *Christianity and the Theatre*, p. 10.

the action moves forward by means of conflict, development, and resolution. On the surface, the conflict is between the various kings in the story: the king of Aram, the king of Israel, and, most importantly, the King of the Universe — the God of Israel (whose presence is not always recognized). The God of Israel possesses a power superior to that of the king of Aram and thwarts his plans. Below the surface, however, the conflict is about the nature of power. The scenes in the play show that the king of Aram as well as the king of Israel use power in a way that contrasts sharply with the way the King of the Universe uses it. The abiding question is whether people — both the characters in the drama and the audience — are capable of seeing the difference between these two uses of power. The issue of *seeing* is closely related to the issue of *power* in the narrative.

Part I: The Conflict

Scene 1

Once when the king of Aram was at war with Israel, he took counsel with his officers. He said,

> *At such and such a place shall be my camp.*

But the man of God sent word to the king of Israel,

> *Take care not to pass this place, because the Arameans are going down there.*

The king of Israel sent word to the place of which the man of God spoke. More than once or twice he warned such a place so that it was on the alert.

Scene 2

The mind of the king of Aram was greatly perturbed because of this; he called his officers and said to them,

> *Now tell me who among us sides with the king of Israel?*

Then one of his officers said,

> *No one, my lord king. It is Elisha, the prophet in Israel, who tells the king of Israel the words that you speak in your bedchamber.*

He said,

> *Go and find where he is; I will send and seize him.*

He was told,

> *He is in Dothan.*

So he sent horses and chariots there and a great army; they came by night, and surrounded the city.

Part II: The Development

Scene 1

When an attendant of the man of God rose early in the morning and went out, an army with horses and chariots was all around the city. His servant said,

> *Alas, master! What shall we do?*

He replied,

> *Do not be afraid, for there are more with us than there are with them.*

Then Elisha prayed:

> *O Lord, please open his eyes that he may see.*

So the Lord opened the eyes of the servant, and he saw; the mountain was full of horses and chariots of fire all around Elisha.

Scene 2

When the Arameans came down against him, Elisha prayed to the Lord, and said,

> *Strike this people, please, with blindness.*

So he struck them with blindness as Elisha had asked. Elisha said to them,

> *This is not the way, and this is not the city; follow me, and I will bring you to the man [one] whom you seek.*

And he led them to Samaria. As soon as they entered Samaria, Elisha said,

> *O LORD, open the eyes of these men so that they may see.*

The LORD opened their eyes, and they saw that they were inside Samaria.

PART III: THE RESOLUTION

When the king of Israel saw them he said to Elisha,

> *Father, shall I kill them? Shall I kill them?*

He answered,

> *No! Did you capture with your sword and your bow those whom you want to kill? Set food and water before them so that they may eat and drink; and let them go to their master.*

So he prepared for them a great feast; after they ate and drank, he sent them on their way, and they went to their master. And the Arameans no longer came raiding into the land of Israel.

Analysis: Power and Kings

Powerful people swim in power like fish swim in water. Power is ubiquitous and therefore invisible. There is always electricity in the wires, always gasoline in the tanks, always natural gas in the lines, always pressure in the water pipes, always money in the bank account, always courts to judge disputes, and always police to enforce the law. Always! Always! For us in the West, power is eternal: it has no beginning and no ending.

But power is not, of course, an eternal reality. Power is created: it has a source. Despite the appearance of ubiquity, power comes from some place, and we are dependent on that place. The electricity in the wires of my house comes from a power plant; that power plant burns coal. The coal comes from a mine in West Virginia. The mine in West Virginia originated when vegetation accumulated over eons and was compressed in the earth's crust. The vegetation grew by absorbing the power of the sun. The sun came into existence. . . . And so the genealogy of power continues, at least for Christians, until we arrive at God, the source of all things.

45

Powerless people know that power has a source and that apart from that source there is cold, hunger, abuse, and death. Most people in the past and most people living today have struggled to survive. The people of Israel and Aram certainly struggled, and their kings were essential for their survival. The king was a source of power. His wisdom, his knowledge, his judgments, and his campaigns went forth from the throne room like electricity from a power plant. Everyone was wired to him. This vital connection is reflected in passages like these:

> In the light of a king's face there is life,
>   and his favor is like the clouds that bring the spring rain.
>
> (Prov. 16:15)

> Give the king your justice, O God,
>   and your righteousness to a king's son.
> May he judge your people with righteousness,
>   and your poor with justice.
> May the mountains yield prosperity for the people,
>   and the hills, in righteousness. . . .
> May he be like rain that falls on the mown grass,
>   like showers that water the earth.
>
> (Ps. 72:1-3, 6)

A king in Israel and Aram verified his authority and justified his position by being the provider. People have always associated sovereign power with the One who could multiply the loaves and fish. Jesus demonstrated his messianic status by doing exactly that. In this regard, the Lord's Prayer has a significance we regularly miss. It is essentially a pledge of allegiance to the Father/king. It begins with the affirmation "your kingdom come, your will be done, on earth as in heaven," and ends, "for the kingdom, the power, and the glory are yours, now and for ever." In exchange for this pledge of allegiance, the people request from their king three things: protection ("Save us from the time of trial, and deliver us from evil"); pardon ("Forgive us our sins"); and provision ("Give us today our daily bread").

The king acted to supply what was necessary to sustain his people. His chief responsibility was to guarantee the supply of food and to wage either defensive or offensive war whenever it was threatened. The close connection between war and food in the ancient world is implicit in the structure of the Hebrew language. The word for "waging war" (*nilcham;* nifal, passive/reflexive) and the word for "bread" *(lechem)* have the same root letters. This connection suggests that the people of Israel understood war fundamentally as a means of "securing bread for oneself." As we shall see below, our narrative plays upon the connection between war and bread, the grim cycle of killing and eating, and suggests a way that this cycle can be broken.

The drama in 2 Kings 6, which we see in Part I, Scene 1, begins with these words: "Once when the king of Aram was at war [*nilcham*] with Israel," or, quite literally, "Once when the king of Aram was securing bread for himself at the expense of Israel" (author's translation). The king convenes his officers for counsel, and together they target the Israelite city to be raided. However, the king's plans are thwarted by an unnamed man of God who warns the king of Israel. In short, the first scene of this story sets the stage for the conflict. There are three kings, three armies, and three kingdoms in this short drama: the king of Aram; the king of Israel; and the King of the Universe, whose presence at this point has not been fully realized. These kings will contend with each other for supremacy. In this contention, the audience will learn which of them is supreme, and in the process uncover the truth about power.

The King of Aram

The king of Aram is a "materialist" in the sense that he acknowledges the reality of what he can see, what he can count, and what he can measure. He believes that power and ultimately life reside in amassing material in any form. In this drama he has amassed a "great army" and uses his horses and chariots to amass food and other resources. He plans numerous raids on the cities of Israel, for the king of Israel had to defend himself "more than once or twice."

In Part I, Scene 2, we see that the success of Israel's defense angers the king of Aram. His heart is stormy *(sa'ar)*. His army returns to him empty-handed, and their empty hands are a direct challenge to his sovereignty and fitness for office. In all the Scriptures, Isaiah 55:10-11 provides the simplest and clearest definition of sovereignty. Assuming the voice of God, the prophet says,

For as the rain and the snow come down from heaven,
    and do not return there until they have watered the earth,
making it bring forth and sprout,
    giving seed to the sower and bread to the eater,
so shall my word be that goes out from my mouth;
    it shall not return to me empty,
but it shall accomplish that which I purpose,
    and succeed in the thing for which I sent it.

The word of a true sovereign does not return empty, and his soldiers do not return empty-handed. Frustrated, the king of Aram stops to consider the reason for his failure. He assembles his officers and says to them, "Now tell me who among us sides with the king of Israel?" This question confirms his materialist orientation. He knows that the words spoken in his council have been passed on to the king of Israel, and he knows exactly who was present at the meeting. The king draws the only conclusion that is rational to him: one of his officers is a traitor. He can see no other explanation. He has no comprehension of a presence beyond a material presence.

However, one of his officers suggests that there is another way to see things: "No one, my lord king. It is Elisha, the prophet in Israel, who tells the king of Israel the words that you speak in your bedchamber." As incredible as it must have sounded under the circumstances, the officer dares to suggest that there was someone at the meeting whom no one saw. This someone is not only present in the king's council room but also in his bedroom. Elisha is a man of God, and his God is present everywhere. There is nothing said and done that is not heard and seen. The ubiquitous God of Israel told Elisha what the king had said, and Elisha told the king of Israel.

Perhaps reporting a rumor and probably not realizing the full theological significance of his words, the officer in essence invites the king to accept a view of reality in which the material and spiritual worlds are tightly interwoven. His interpretation of what happened at the fateful meeting implies that there is more to the world than what meets the eye. His words imply that everyone is subject to the God of Israel, even kings. The king does not have the power to draw a circle around himself and exclude God. There are no secrets and no secret meetings. All human councils and all human hearts are open to the Holy One of Israel. God is an ex officio member of every human congregation, wherever two or three are gathered.

Apparently the officer's invitation is not accepted. Habits of the heart are difficult to break. Reaffirming his materialist orientation, the king says, "Go and find where [Elisha] is; I will send and seize him." Under the cloak of darkness, he sends horses and chariots, a great army, to surround the city of Dothan. This action raises a simple question in the minds of the audience: If the God of Israel was present at the king's first war council and overheard his plans, why would God not be present at this last one? Secrecy cannot veil his plans, and darkness cannot cloak his troops. The king of Aram literally and figuratively operates in the dark; he cannot see God.

Part II, Scene 1, takes up the theme of ubiquity and develops it further. We move to the house of Elisha in Dothan. The servant rises early in the morning, leaves the house, and sees that the city is surrounded. In despair, he cries to Elisha, "Alas, master! What shall we do?" Elisha answers like a mathematician teaching a student addition and subtraction: "Do not be afraid, for there are more with us than there are with them." He invites his servant to count and then compare the relative power of the two sides in the conflict. But the servant is afraid, because he has already counted: it is two against thousands.

The servant needs to learn the mathematics of the kingdom of God, a mathematics that can account for the spiritual as well as the material world. Elisha prays, "O LORD, please open his eyes that he may see." Elisha is not referring to material eyes; the servant's lens and retina are not faulty. He is referring to his spiritual eyes. When God opened these eyes, the servant saw that "the mountain was full of horses and chariots of fire all around Elisha." Now lens and retina see farther and more clearly than ever before. Elisha lives in Dothan, and at the same time he lives on the mountain of God. Elisha is surrounded by horses and chariots of flesh, and at the same time he is surrounded by horses and chariots of fire. The servant sees that the spiritual and material worlds are tightly interwoven. Elisha has no fear because he is surrounded and protected by a circle of fire.

The King of Israel

Although the kings of Aram and Israel contend with each other, they share a view of power. The king of Israel is also a materialist. In the final scene of this three-part drama, Elisha leads the Aramean army into the city of Samaria. The king of Israel sees this as an opportunity to rid himself of his

An Approach to Biblical Narrative

The following approach is the result of over twenty years of work with the Is-raelite dramatic tradition. This summary should help the interested reader to replicate, if not improve upon, the kind of work I have done.

1. Textual Analysis

a. Determine the beginning, middle, and end of the narrative. Most biblical narratives were probably short readings originally, usually five to seven minutes long. They were probably then linked together into longer, more complicated readings where themes and patterns of behavior could be carried forward.

b. Develop an understanding of the range of meaning of the words. An-cient languages like Hebrew grew by expanding the meaning of estab-lished words. A single Hebrew word may need dozens of English words to convey its possible meanings.

c. Use your imagination. A story is read and is therefore a living reality. To hear a story entails first seeing it in your mind's eye and then entering it. You stand first outside the story, examining its structure, and then inside it, experiencing its world. Form a mental picture of all movements, ges-tures, actions, and descriptions in the story. Ask yourself why the story-teller chose to relay them and what they contribute to the meaning.

d. Every story has a group of words that are repeated often. Identify every word that is used three or more times. Repetition is emphasis: ask your-self what each successive occurrence of the word adds to the meaning of the story. Pay close attention to small changes in the repeated phrases.

e. Dialogue is central to Hebrew storytelling. Note the shifts in the story be-tween third-person narration and dialogue. Themes introduced and re-peated in dialogues are often significant.

f. All references to God or the Lord are significant. Note where they occur in the story and who is using the name of the Lord. Note where God is an agent in the story and the nature of God's presence.

g. Ask yourself whether the storyteller is withholding significant informa-tion and why she or he is doing that.

2. *Plot Analysis*

a. Divide the story into scenes. A shift in place, time, or character will mark a new scene. In Hebrew storytelling, third-person narration introduces dialogue, and these together constitute a scene. Identify the main characters and minor characters in the story. In Hebrew storytelling, there will never be more than three main characters and never more than two of them engaging each other at one time.

b. The characters all have a particular way of viewing the world and orienting themselves in it. In biblical storytelling, point of view always touches upon God's relationship to the world and is thus an incipient theology. In addition, the narrator has a particular way of viewing the world that may or may not be different from that of the characters. Identify these multiple "theologies." In hearing the story, you enter the world that has been created by the narrator. You walk along with the characters. Along the way, listen carefully to what they say, watch what they do, and pay attention to what the narrator says about them. You learn to know them as you would learn to know a friend. Your listening skills and observing are crucial for friendship and for exegesis.

c. Define the conflict. There may be an external conflict: one character may be trying to gain control over another. There may be an internal one: the main character may be torn in different directions. Often the external and the internal conflicts are related. Name the conflicting emotions and values. In Hebrew storytelling, the conflict always touches upon God's relationship to humanity and the world, and the story seeks to unveil the true nature of the relationship.

d. Explain how subsequent scenes develop the conflict. Repetition signals development. What changes in the attitudes and circumstances of the main characters are discernible? Do certain actions, movements, and gestures reinforce the development of the conflict?

e. Explain where and how the conflict of the story is resolved. At what point is the tension relieved? Depending on the nature of the conflict, it may be the point at which ignorance is replaced by knowledge, danger by safety, weakness by strength, the absence of God by the presence of God.

enemies and secure the kingdom. He cannot imagine any other reason for Elisha's actions. Dead men tell no tales, and they "no longer [come] raiding into the land of Israel." He asks, "Father, shall I kill them? Shall I kill them?" The power the king knows and trusts is the power of the sword.[9]

The king submits to the authority of Elisha by virtue of asking him what he should do. But he is surely unprepared for the answer. Elisha pronounces a direct and unambiguous "No!" to the sword, to the way of killing, to the idea that one has the right to kill one's enemies. Elisha punctuates the "No!" with these words: "Did you capture with your sword and your bow those whom you want to kill?" The meaning of this rhetorical question needs a little unpacking. That the army of the king of Aram has been captured is eminently clear from the circumstances. But it is equally clear that it has not been captured by a sword and bow. The power demonstrated in bringing the Aramean army to stand helpless and bewildered before the Israelite army is not material power, worshiped in the image of a sword.

Elisha's rhetorical question invites the king to reconsider his understanding of power. In effect the prophet says, "The sword and bow that played no role in the beginning of the struggle will also play no role at its end. Sword and bow are the way of the king of Aram; they are apparently your way too. But sword and bow are not the way of the King of the Universe." In other words, Elisha repeats to the king of Israel his earlier words to the Aramean army: "This is not the way!"

The King of the Universe

In this and all biblical dramas, the narrators strove with all the gifts at their disposal to portray the character of God who was present in events. It was an audacious undertaking and fraught with difficulty. The most obvious

---

9. The king of Israel calls Elisha "Father," thus identifying him with God. The king understood God to be his "Father" and himself to be a "son." He and all the kings of Israel claim divine sonship:

> I will tell of the decree of the LORD:
> He said to me, "You are my son;
>   today I have begotten you.
> Ask of me, and I will make the nations your heritage,
>   and the ends of the earth your possession. . . ."   (Ps. 2:7-8)

difficulty was that a particular portrayal of God could become so fixed in the minds of the audience that it could become an image. The audience could then mistake the image that the narrator had created for the Creator and so reduce God to something that could be carried around and used at one's convenience. Images do not have to be graven to be craven. History has taught us that when a people makes its own image of God and carries it proudly around, bloodshed soon follows. More than any other people, Israel was aware of the dangers of idolatry: "You shall not make for yourself an idol, whether in the form of anything that is in heaven above, or that is on the earth beneath, or that is in the water under the earth" (Exod. 20:4). The difficulties that the narrators faced are exactly those that systematic theologians of all ages have faced. Dr. Hendrikus Berkhof began his book *Christelijk Geloof* with these lines from Alfred Lord Tennyson's *In Memoriam:*

Our little systems have their day;
    They have their day and cease to be;
    They are but broken lights of thee,
And thou, O Lord, art more than they.[10]

One reason why it is so important for actors and writers today to study biblical drama is to learn how the ancient playwrights sought to portray God and how they avoided a trivializing idolatry. Such a study will be demanding because, on the one hand, the church has generally not realized that narratives offer a dramatic portrayal of God and therefore good material on the subject is not readily available. On the other hand, the portrayal of God in narrative is a thing of exquisite beauty. Like all great art, the narrative must be experienced, and that experience overflows the vessels of rational analysis.

After what I have just said, it may not be wise to attempt to analyze the portrayal of God in 2 Kings 6:8-23. There is more to be experienced in the narrative than I am able to put into words, but I offer some words as tokens of appreciation. The narrator of 2 Kings 6:8-23 has crafted the script in such as way that three persons in succession are presented with the opportunity of seeing the God of Israel: the king of Aram, the servant of

10. Hendrikus Berkhof, *Christelijk Geloof* (Nijkerk: G. F. Callenbach, 1973); the lines from Tennyson's *In Memoriam* are from the introduction, lines 16-20.

Elisha, and the king of Israel. Furthermore, the narrator has crafted the script in such a way that the audience sees these three people seeing God. The audience shares to a limited extent the privileged knowledge of the narrator, knowing some things the characters do not know. In all this the narrator has created different levels at which the drama proceeds: those of the characters, the audience, the narrator, and God. All these levels intersect each other in the presentation, and this interaction creates the rich matrix from which the portrayal of God emerges.

God is ubiquitous. The narrator portrays God as both in the scenes and behind the scenes. God is both in a particular time and place and in every time and place. Three times Elisha called on the Lord to act, and three times the Lord acted in a particular way to change the course of events. The Lord opened the eyes of the servant, struck the Aramean army with blindness, and opened the eyes of that same army when they were in Samaria.[11] Yet the narrator makes clear that the Lord is not limited to a particular time and place. The king of Aram heard that God was present at his council meetings, and the servant of Elisha discovered that God was present in Dothan. While the narrator does not present God's ubiquity and particularity as a theological conundrum, he or she does indicate the former is hard for humans to grasp. Both the king of Aram and the servant of Elisha struggle in this regard.

God is irresistible. The narrator portrays a God who is omnipresent, or ubiquitous, as I have just stated. A God who is omnipresent is also omniscient — God knows the words the king of Aram speaks in his bedchamber. A God who is omnipresent and omniscient is also omnipotent. All this is to say that the narrator presents a God who cannot be resisted. Three times in this short narrative a king attempts to close a circle — in other words, three times a king attempts to create a space in which he alone has sovereign sway. First, the king of Aram attempts to close out the world with a secret council; second, he sends his horses and chariots to surround the city of Dothan and to seize Elisha; third, the king of Israel surrounds the Aramean soldiers in Samaria and wants to kill them. In each case, God breaks into the circle and thwarts the intention of the king. This

11. When God acts in a particular way in the narrative, the narrator does not dwell on it. This is odd, in a way, because opening people's eyes or striking them with blindness would have been miracles, mighty acts of God. But in this narrative, they merely contribute to the movement of the whole. The narrator renders the character of God not in particular acts but in the movement of the whole narrative.

drama suggests that there is no place where either kings or commoners stand on their own, where their will exclusively determines the course of life, where they bind the world in the chain of their command.

God is countercultural. The narrator uses repetition to guide the audience toward the truth about God in the world. One of the obvious repetitions in this script is horses and chariots *(susim werekeb)*. The narrator presents the world as two-tiered, heaven and earth, with horses and chariots in both realms. Yet these horses and chariots have entirely different constitutions: flesh and fire. This repetition captures the essence of the conflict in this drama. Despite God's desire, the way of heaven is not yet the way of the earth. First the king of Aram, then the servant of Elisha, and finally the king of Israel express in one way or another their belief in the power of the flesh — that is, a great army equipped with horses and chariots, swords and bows. All three characters fail, at least at first, to understand the meaning of horses and chariots of fire. The way God exercises power in the world runs counter to the way the kings and their subjects exercise it.

God is gentle. In contrast to what the kings of Aram and Israel do, everything the King of the Universe does in this drama mitigates violence, calms anxiety, and protects human life. In the opening scene, God reveals the plans of the king of Aram to Elisha, thereby thwarting his power, and minimizes the suffering of the people of Israel. Later, God acts to reduce fear by opening the eyes of Elisha's servant and to reduce carnage by closing the eyes of the army of Aram. This army experiences a dramatic reversal of fortune. Rather than seizing Elisha and leading him back to Aram, they are blinded by God and led by Elisha to Samaria. The reversal of roles is significant because with Elisha now the commander in chief, the army will neither be harmed nor bring harm to others.

The contrast between the gentle ways of the King of the Universe and the violent ways of the kings of the earth is highlighted by the narrator with the repetition of the Hebrew word for "strike" or "kill" *(nakah)*. Twice the term is used in connection with the army of the king of Aram. Elisha uses the term when he asks God to "strike this people with blindness." The king of Israel uses the term when he sees the helpless Aramean soldiers: "Shall I kill them? Shall I kill them?" Unlike the king of Israel, Elisha did not want the army killed, only immobilized, so he could prevent a battle and lead them on the way to a deeper truth. The stroke of the King of the Universe and the stroke of the king of Israel are as different as the nature of their kingdoms.

55

God is provident. The ultimate manifestation of gentle power is in the drama's final scene. There Elisha tells the king of Israel that instead of killing the Aramean army, he is to "set food [bread] and water before them so that they may eat and drink; and let them go to their master." With the mention of "bread" *(lechem),* we have come full circle. The story began with the king of Aram "securing bread for himself at the expense of Israel" *(nilcham).* Now the king gets bread and water without a fight.

One cannot read this drama in 2 Kings 6 without making a connection to the ending of Psalm 23:

You prepare a table before me
    in the presence of my enemies;
you anoint my head with oil;
    my cup overflows.
Surely goodness and mercy shall follow me
    all the days of my life,
and I shall dwell in the house of the LORD
    my whole life long.

In 2 Kings 6 a table is prepared in the presence of one's enemies. The table of the king of Israel is a manifestation of the table of the King of the Universe, the table envisioned in Psalm 23. The army of Aram and the army of Israel are both guests at this table. Taken together, 2 Kings 6 and Psalm 23 offer a portrait of the hospitality of the King of the Universe. This table is full to overflowing. This King provides. The people do not have to squabble and fight each other for scarce resources. Food and drink are freely given. This providence reconfigures the boundaries between peoples and reconstitutes relationships. Enemies become friends. They sit as family around a table. Ultimate power in this kingdom of God is not a sword but a table, not a well-planned campaign but a well-planned meal, not cut throats but full stomachs. Apparently the king of Israel got hold of the idea, for although Elisha told him to set food and water before the army, "he prepared for them a great feast." And apparently the king of Aram and his army got hold of it too, at least temporarily, for the story closes with these words: "And the Arameans no longer came raiding into the land of Israel."

The peace between Aram and Israel did not last. The stories following this one tell of renewed conflict. Gentle power is vulnerable and unspectacular. Like a flower, it blossoms and withers. A gentle Jesus and a gentle people are tortured and killed. Yet acts of generosity and kindness sow seeds that grow ever so slowly into oaks of righteousness. And strong oaks survive the cold of winter and bud again in the spring. In speaking of gentle power, Henri Nouwen beautifully summarizes the knowledge that we are to appropriate in this drama:

> Life is always small. It is always vulnerable. It never shouts or screams. It always needs protection and guidance. Saying "yes" to it means being willing to look at the small life that seeks to be born in your heart, in your body, in your mind, among people. Death is always glamorous. Death shines; it is always big and noisy. Death goes bang, bang! Because life is very small, you can never see it happening. Have you ever seen a tree actually grow? Can you see a child grow? Growth is too gentle, too tender. Life is basically hidden. It is small and begs for constant care and protection. If you are committed to always saying "yes" to life you must become a person who chooses it when it is hidden.[12]

God is incarnate. As we have said, the narrator presents God as ubiquitous. And although the word is not used, he or she presents God as Spirit or Wind. Like the wind, God cannot be seen, but God's influence on events can be. God strikes an army with blindness, and their blindness has consequences. A ubiquitous God has no specific form, and the narrator, it would seem, is not in danger of presenting an image that could be turned into an idol. But to present God as only ubiquitous would not be true to Israel's experience. It would lead, ironically, to a rarefied form of idolatry, a kind of spiritism where God has no distinct personality and can be joined only in some out-of-body experience. Israel did not experience God as out of this world. God loved the world, and God's kingdom embraced it.

This embrace of the world is seen in the person of Elisha, who is identified as an *'ish ha'elohim* — that is, a man/God. The narrator leaves us to ponder the mystery of this communion of the divine and the human, this incarnation. "Man/God" is a common title in Scripture and is found in close proximity to another one, *nabi'*, or "prophet," which suggests that they are synonyms. Elisha is clearly more than human in the narrative. He

---

12. Henri Nouwen, *Be with Me, Lord: Prayers and Reflections for the Advent Season* (St. Louis: Creative Communications for the Parish, 1998), pp. 5-6.

sees God in ways that others like his servant do not. He converses directly with God, receiving information about the council of the king of Aram and making requests of God. He speaks with the authority of God when he commands the king of Israel to set food and water before his enemies. But he is also less than God. He is limited by time and place and subject to the will of others. And while in this particular drama Elisha is a near-perfect incarnation of the divine will, in other dramas, prophets are not. They allow people to venerate them as an image of God and misuse their status for personal gain.

Elisha is a man/God — that is, an incarnation of God. He shows people the way; he points to a God who is gentle and provident, who has prepared a table to which all are invited. Elisha prepares us Christians to see the unique man/God who will also call us to the table and tell us to love our enemies.

A Call to Apprenticeship

I began this chapter by quoting Gordon C. Bennett, who said that the "Hebrews made little use of drama." The opposite is true. I hope that my analysis of 2 Kings 6:8-23 is enough to convince aspiring actors and writers within the church that they are not imposing an art form on Scripture and on the church. Quite the contrary — they are heirs of a tradition. The better they understand the characteristics and techniques of Israelite "theater," the better they will carry it forward. In some cases they may want to produce these "sketches" as they exist in Scripture; in some cases they may want to embellish them; in some cases they may want to take off in new directions in the spirit of the Israelite dramatists. I echo the words of Murray Watts: "There is no substitute for apprenticeship to the theatre."[13] I would add only this: apprenticeship to theater includes apprenticeship to Scripture.

13. Watts, *Christianity and the Theatre,* p. 10.

O Worship the King, All Glorious Above!

O worship the King, all glorious above,
O gratefully sing God's power and God's love;
our shield and defender, the Ancient of Days,
pavilioned in splendor, and girded with praise.

O tell of God's might, O sing of God's grace,
whose robe is the light, whose canopy space.
The chariots of heaven the deep thunderclouds form,
and bright is God's path on the wings of the storm.

The earth with its store of wonders untold,
Almighty, Thy power hath founded of old;
hath 'stablished it fast by a changeless decree,
and round it hath cast, like a mantle, the sea.

Thy bountiful care what tongue can recite?
It breathes in the air, it shines in the light;
it streams from the hills, it descends to the plain,
and sweetly distills in the dew and the rain.

Frail children of dust, and feeble as frail,
in Thee do we trust, nor find Thee to fail;
Thy mercies how tender, how firm to the end,
our maker, defender, redeemer, and friend.

Text: Robert Grant (1779-1838), 1833, alt.

As We Gather at Your Table

As we gather at your Table,
as we listen to your Word,
help us know, O God, your presence;
let our hearts and minds be stirred.
Nourish us with sacred story
till we claim it as our own;
teach us through this holy banquet
how to make Love's victory known.

Turn our worship into witness
in the sacrament of life;
send us forth to love and serve you,
bringing peace where there is strife.
Give us, Christ, your great compassion
to forgive as you forgave;
may we still behold your image
in the world you died to save.

Gracious Spirit, help us summon
other guests to share that feast
where triumphant Love will welcome
those who had been last and least.
There no more will envy blind us
nor will pride our peace destroy,
as we join with saints and angels
to repeat the sounding joy.

Text: Carl P. Daw Jr. (b. 1944), 1989
Text copyright © 1989 Hope Publishing Company, Carol Stream, IL 60188. All rights reserved.
Used by permission.

For Further Reading

Robert Alter. *The Art of Biblical Narrative* (New York: Basic Books, 1981). What makes this book especially interesting from my perspective as a theologian is Alter's sense that narrative was the genre particularly suited to presenting the tenets of monotheism. He argues that narrative was uniquely able to capture the conflict between a single God whose will determines the course of events and a recalcitrant humanity.

Erich Auerbach. *Mimesis: The Representation of Reality in Western Literature* (Princeton: Princeton University Press, 1953). Anyone who is interested in reading more on biblical narrative should begin with "Odysseus' Scar," Chapter One of Auerbach's book. This chapter opens the door to a new world of interpretation. All who came later followed in the direction that he pointed. He laid bare the techniques and the passion of Israelite storytellers, and thereby challenged the reigning assumption among biblical scholars (most trained as historians, by the way) that storytellers were proto-historians. His remarks on the passion of storytellers suggested — although he did not say this — that they were preachers and that their context was worship.

Meir Sternberg. *The Poetics of Biblical Narrative: Ideological Literature and the Drama of Reading* (Bloomington: Indiana University Press, 1987). This book is a trove of insight into narrative, but what is particularly interesting and novel is Sternberg's suggestion at various points in the book that the narrator functions in ways similar to the prophets. I think he is right about this. This idea helps us to locate the narrator in Israelite society and forces us to break out of long-established patterns of thinking, especially about prophecy in Israel.

Isaiah in Christian Liturgy: Recovering Textual Contrasts and Correcting Theological Astigmatism

John D. Witvliet

Isaiah 42:10

It is a simulating and instructive assignment for a student of Christian worship to reflect on a particular biblical book. Normally, those of us who work as liturgical theologians or congregational worship leaders approach the Bible as a goldmine of resources. We learn skills both to identify which biblical texts are most pastorally useful for a given occasion and to preach or sing these texts clearly and accessibly. We also learn skills for offering a balanced diet of scriptural themes over time, either by working with established lectionaries or by developing informal, unofficial lectionaries of our own. But often we are tempted to strip texts from their contexts in ways that distort their meaning or rhetorical force. One strategy to overcome this temptation is to ask atypical but important questions. Have we as worship leaders been faithful stewards of a given part of Scripture (e.g., the book of Isaiah)? How can we more faithfully present and interpret a given part of Scripture in worship? What themes and strategies can we learn from the text to complement or chasten our most comfortable ways of working? In communities shaped by the conviction that God's Word is sharper than a two-edged sword, these questions should not be atypical. They should be staples of congregational worship-committee agendas and seminary worship courses.

What follows, then, is a liturgist's approach to the book of Isaiah.[1] Because the task is impossibly large, what follows is an illustrative essay that (a) isolates a main rhetorical device of the book (rhetorical contrast) and a main theological theme (idolatry), (b) develops the significance of these dimensions in conversation with some leading students of Isaiah, and then (c) proposes very practical strategies for leading worship in ways that are

---

1. Of the few essays that explore the relationship of Isaiah and worship, most address the theology of worship but don't ask how our textual study might inform our work in leading worship. Representative examples include Christopher T. Begg, "The Peoples and the Worship of Yahweh in the Book of Isaiah"; J. J. M. Roberts, "Contemporary Worship in the Light of Isaiah's Ancient Critique"; and Roy F. Melugin, "Isaiah in the Worshiping Community." All three essays are found in *Worship and the Hebrew Bible: Essays in Honour of John T. Willis*, ed. M. Patrick Graham, Rick R. Marrs, and Steven L. McKenzie (Sheffield: Sheffield Academic Press, 1999). See also J. H. Eaton, *Vision in Worship: The Relation of Prophecy and Liturgy in the Old Testament* (London: SPCK, 1981).

An earlier version of this essay appeared in *Calvin Theological Journal* 39 (2004): 135-56. I am grateful for the assistance of Joyce Borger in conducting extensive background research for this essay and to Ron Rienstra, Carrie Steenwyk, and Carl J. Bosma for helpful comments on earlier drafts of this essay.

faithful to these aspects of the text. The goal is to connect scholarly work on the book of Isaiah with the week-in, week-out practice of worship, to demonstrate both that patient scholarly work can bear rich fruit in the practice of liturgy and that liturgy can be pastorally enriched by patient scholarly reflection on the biblical text.

Recovering Textual Contrasts

Like Rembrandt, Not Kinkade

Isaiah is a workhorse of Christian liturgy, ranking with the Psalms as the most frequently cited Old Testament book in worship.[2] The great *Sanctus* of Isaiah 6:3 is both the heartbeat of traditional Eucharistic prayers and the inspiration of countless worship songs for churches that never use a traditional Eucharistic prayer. The canticles of Isaiah 12 have been a staple of traditional daily and Sunday liturgies for centuries and the basis of several recently written Scripture songs. In times of tragedy, Isaiah 43:1-7 and 44:6-8 are among the first texts to which pastors turn. Holy Week worship nearly always draws on Isaiah 50:4-9; 52:7-10; and 52:13–53:12. And it is almost inconceivable to imagine planning Advent worship without Isaiah 7:14; 9:2-7; 11:1-9; 35:1-10; 40:1-11; 60:1-3; and 61:1-3.[3]

Indeed, the connection between Isaiah and Advent worship is particularly strong (thanks in no small measure to the legacy of Handel's *Messiah*). Imagine the first Sunday in Advent in just about any city in North America. Congregations that follow the lectionary hear readings from Isaiah 2:2-5 and 64:1-9. Other congregations likely hear parts of Isaiah 9:2-7; 11:1-19; or 40:1-11. In one congregation a folk musician sings, "They shall

---

2. Craig A. Evans, "From Gospel to Gospel: The Function of Isaiah in the New Testament," in *Writing and Reading the Scroll of Isaiah: Studies of an Interpretative Tradition*, Supplement to Vetus Testamentum 70, Formation and Interpretation of Old Testament Literature, 2 vols., ed. Craig G. Broyles and Craig A. Evans (Leiden: Brill, 1997), 2:651.

3. For other examples, see the historical survey offered in John F. A. Sawyer, *The Fifth Gospel: Isaiah in the History of Christianity* (Cambridge: Cambridge University Press, 1996); Christopher R. Seitz, "Isaiah in New Testament, Lectionary, Pulpit," in *Word without End: The Old Testament as Abiding Theological Witness* (Grand Rapids: Eerdmans, 1998); and William Holladay, *Unbound by Time: Isaiah Still Speaks* (Cambridge: Cowley Publications, 2002).

mount up on wings like eagles." In another, the choir sings the old spirituals "Hush, Hush, Someone's Calling My Name" and "We're Marching to
Zion." And in another, an operatic tenor sings, "Comfort, Comfort Now
My People," and the congregation responds, "Lo, how a Rose e'er bloom-
ing . . . Isaiah 'twas foretold it, the Rose I have in mind. . . ." Indeed, Isaiah is
the church's poet-of-the-month every December.

But now notice the common disposition of these texts. All of them,
even the ones that acknowledge pain and suffering, are the texts in Isaiah
that feature the most rhapsodic poetry and boundless hope. With the exception of the Servant Song of Isaiah 52:12–53:12, they are the happy texts,
the oasis points for anyone attempting to read Isaiah in a single sitting.
Purely for the limited purposes of this essay, I would like to group these
texts into a very nontechnical category called "The Pretty Texts of Isaiah."[4]
Outside of conferences on Isaiah, it could well be that over 85 percent of all
sermons and other liturgical texts based on Isaiah are from these texts.[5]

But for anyone studying the book with attention to literary form and
rhetorical technique (or for anyone simply reading through the book),
these pretty texts are not the whole story. They leave out vast stretches of
prophetic judgment and warning, and diatribes against all forms of disobedience, hypocrisy, superstition, and injustice. A more accurate view of
the book of Isaiah might be to compare it to a Rembrandt painting, where
vast stretches of darkness, shadows, and judgment are dramatically punctuated by glorious shafts of light and grace.

Indeed, much of the rhetorical force of the book is generated by its
textual contrasts. Nearly all the "pretty texts of Isaiah" are juxtaposed with
texts of prophetic warning and critique. For example, in the first major
collection of Isaiah, Isaiah 1–12, the announcement "The people who
walked in darkness have seen a great light" (Isa. 9:2) erupts out of the "distress and darkness, the gloom of anguish" of Isaiah 8:22. The shoot that

4. Consider working through the book to isolate the texts that function most regularly
in worship and preaching. My own suggestion is that the vast majority of references are limited to about twenty texts: 1:18; 2:4; 6:1-8; 7:14; 9:2-7; 11:1-9; 12; 25:1-10; 35:1-10; 40:1-11; 42:1-9;
43:1-7; 52:7-10; 52:13–53:12; 55:1-13; 60:1-3; 61:1-4; 64:8; 65:17-25; 66:12-14.

5. For example, 86 percent of the sermons in the Hekman Library Sermon Index at Calvin College and Calvin Theological Seminary come from these "pretty texts." My goal for
this essay is to imagine ways of more faithfully using these texts. What is also needed is some
thoughtful and creative work that explores how we can best use the sustained passages of
darkness, the "non-pretty texts," in faithful and pastoral ways.

goes out from the stump of Jesse (Isa. 11:1) appears after we see in video clip-like fashion that "the Sovereign, the LORD of hosts," is about to "lop the boughs with terrifying power" (Isa. 10:33). The very fact that our Advent texts of choice — Isaiah 7:14; 9:2-7; and 11:1-9 — come from alternating chapters and that the chapters in between are almost never read should be a clue that we are missing something.

In the second part of Isaiah, chapters 40–55, the contrast is equally stark. For example, Isaiah 42:1-4, with its rapturous opening lines "Here is my servant, whom I uphold," gains clarity and urgency because of the end of Isaiah 41, with its stinging critique of idolatry (41:29). Similarly, Isaiah 49:1-6 emerges from chapter 48's indictment of Israel's obstinate opposition to God.

But in worship, we love to dwell in the light. We filter out the little poetic diamonds that work well as song lyrics and preaching texts and set aside their textual neighbors — a natural enough impulse for pastorally minded preachers and liturgists, but one that may be, in the end, dishonest and even counterproductive. Just as some source and form critics have often excised the servant songs from the context of Isaiah 40–55, so too liturgists are highly practiced at mining Isaiah's textual diamonds without attention to context.

What is worrisome about this is the likelihood that most of the pretty texts of Isaiah end up functioning like mere truisms. We read and sing them in ways that communicate right and accurate things, but with such familiarity that they are perceived to be routine. Often, after one of these pretty texts from Isaiah is read, preached, or sung, the collective response from worshipers is, in effect, "Tell us something new" or "So what?" In Advent, we hear "He tends his flock like a shepherd" with the same hermeneutic that we use to read a Hallmark card. We sing "Comfort, Comfort Now My People" while worrying about how long to cook our Christmas hams or about which gift to return to the shopping mall. Suspicions of this tendency are confirmed for preachers and worship leaders every time we know a given service or sermon is pregnant with gospel comfort, but all that worshipers want to talk about after the service is the weather. In these cases, Isaiah functions to reinforce rather than challenge the sentimental Christmas we so cherish.

Much of the problem here has to do with the mechanics of how worship is planned and led, how people are invited to sense worship's beauty and power, and how worshipers are invited to prepare for worship. But at least a small part of the problem does have to do with how the text is handled. And thus the problem needs to be addressed not only in classes and books on worship but also in classes and books in Old Testament studies.

In short, there are three basic problems with how we often handle the text. First, we too narrowly limit our liturgical interests to the pretty texts. Second, we too easily lift these texts out of context. And third, we too often read or sing these texts as if we were reading a greeting card rather than the soaring, God-breathed poetry they are. In sum, our worship services, even when they are filled with the best poetry Isaiah has to offer, are often more like the art of Thomas Kinkade than that of Rembrandt: all light, no shadows.[6]

There are many times, of course, when pastoral sensitivity demands that we dwell in the light. When Isaiah 65 is read at the funeral of a baby, when Isaiah 35 is read with confident hope in a worship service in a nursing home, or when we sing "How Firm a Foundation" in the middle of a war, the context of our lives provides the shadows that help us perceive the power and beauty of Isaiah's light. In times like these, we do not take these words lightly. We cling to them.

But in the ebb and flow of our busy lives, on the first Sunday of Advent, in the middle of the Christmas shopping season and the start-up of the basketball season, these same pretty texts wash over us. We hear them but cannot remember them. And if we have heard them, we have often heard them and maybe even spoken them a little sentimentally, kind of like a pious well-wishing to assure us of a comfortable life. The whole experi-

---

6. For more on Kinkade as the "painter of light," see Randal Balmer, "Kinkade Crusade," *Christianity Today*, 4 December 2000, pp. 49-55. The contrast between Rembrandt and Kinkade is worth further reflection in light of our approach to any of the prophets. As Balmer reports, Kinkade describes the missional goal behind his work: "I love to create beautiful worlds where light dances and peace reigns. I like to portray a world without the Fall" (p. 51). He dismisses the critics who charge that his work is sentimental by arguing, "High culture is paranoid about sentiment, but human beings are intensely sentimental" (p. 55). However, Balmer gently concludes, "The art of Thomas Kinkade offers an oasis, a retreat from the assaults of modern life, a vision of a more perfect world. Who wouldn't like to catch a glimpse of that world from time to time, to picture life before the Fall? But we live and move and have our being in a fallen world, and it is our lot as human beings to negotiate that world. Kinkade's paintings furnish little guidance for that enterprise" (p. 55). The spirit behind Kinkade's art and the use of Isaiah in worship (in many styles) strike me as remarkably similar.

ence easily inoculates us from encountering the true force of the texts. Poetry becomes platitude.

The problem with all this is not just aesthetic. It is deeply pastoral. For when these texts function only in a pretty, greeting-card sort of way, we miss their tenacious, life-giving force. Further, in greeting-card worship services in any style, we miss out on hearing, along with the pretty texts of Isaiah, the stinging indictments of superstition, idolatry, and disobedience that their contexts often present with such force. And these indictments are not merely tiresome rants. They too are life-giving — life-giving warnings. They keep us from doing things we should not do for our own spiritual health. At stake is our ability to hear the most important spiritual remedies for the most persistent spiritual diseases we face.

The Critique of Idolatry in Isaiah 40–55

Of all the contrasts that Isaiah draws — the contrasts between light and darkness, obedience and disobedience, hope and despair, Israel's exile and Israel's return — one of the most dramatic and memorable is the contrast between true and false gods in Isaiah 40–55.[7] Isaiah 40–55 works the contrast between idolatry[8] (aiming at the wrong target) and true worship (aiming at the right one), often with rhetoric that features biting sarcasm and mocking irony that is so derisive it almost feels irreligious.[9]

Contrast is the primary rhetorical device for achieving this aim. As Hendrik Carel Spykerboer notes, the prophetic oracles in these chapters of Isaiah "fulfill a very special function in the book as they demonstrate by way of contrast the incomparability and uniqueness of Yahweh and serve to undergird [Second Isaiah's] message that Yahweh, who is the only real God and holy one, can and will save his despondent and doubtful people."[10]

7. On the bipolarities of Isaiah, see John N. Oswalt, "The Book of Isaiah: A Short Course on Biblical Theology," *Calvin Theological Journal* 39 (2004): 54-71.

8. Cf. Isaiah 40:18-26; 41:1-7; 41:21-29; 43:8-15; 44:6-20; 45:15-25; 46:1-13; and 48:5, 14.

9. This concern for true worship is, by the way, one of the themes that provides continuity among the three major sections of the book we know as Isaiah (see, for example, Isaiah 1 and Isaiah 58).

10. Hendrik Carel Spykerboer, *The Structure and Composition of Deutero-Isaiah, with Special Reference to the Polemics against Idolatry*, Th.D. Dissertation, Rijksuniversiteit of Groningen (Meppel: Krips Repro B.V., 1976), p. 185. In this context Spykerboer offers an im-

Similarly, Richard Clifford observes, "The lively sketches of people fashioning and worshipping their idols function to heighten contrasts in the preaching of Second Isaiah."[11] Specifically, the chapters are built around the sturdy refrain "I am the LORD, and there is no other," which is frequently offered in juxtaposition to stinging critiques of the lifelessness of the gods and the folly of the idol fabricators.[12] Viewed as a whole, the chapters feature an alternation of sardonic warning and elevated poetry, a kind of "large-scale antithetic parallelism."[13] The texts not only critique the false gods and idols but also give particular attention to the idol-fabricators, the sin of generating or making or "creating" idols. As Knut Holter observes, "Nowhere else in the Old Testament is idol-fabrication depicted in more gloomy colors, and nowhere else are its consequences pointed out more negatively."[14] As a whole, these chapters constitute one of the most compelling commentaries on the first and second commandments in the Bible.

Importantly, Isaiah 40–55 offers not only prophetic critique against idolatry and idol fabrication but also three specific resources to fight idolatry: positive assertions about God's character and his powerful acts, songs of praise, and messianic images and metaphors that Christians have freely interpreted as clues to the identity and mission of Jesus Christ. These three resources are powerful tools for preaching and leading worship in ways that can invite congregations to fight contemporary idolatry.

1. Positive Assertions of Divine Character,
Offered in Stark Rhetorical Contrast

First, these chapters offer not only a frank dismissal of idols but also many positive assertions of God's character and actions. In the first polemic against the nations and their gods (40:18-26), for example, God is called "the Holy One" (40:25) — indeed, "the Holy One of Israel" is Isaiah's fa-

---

portant warning: "The four polemics against idolatry (40:18-20, 41:7, 44:9-20, 46:5-7) . . . are intimately rooted in their context and cannot be separated from it" (p. 185).

11. Richard J. Clifford, "The Function of Idol Passages in Second Isaiah," *Catholic Biblical Quarterly* 42 (1980): 464.

12. Cf. Isaiah 41:4; 42:6, 8; 43:11, 15; 45:6-8; 46:9; etc.

13. Richard J. Clifford, "Isaiah, Book of (Second Isaiah)," in *Anchor Bible Dictionary*, ed. David Noel Freedman (New York: Doubleday, 1992), 3:496.

14. Knut Holter, *Second Isaiah's Idol-Fabrication Passages*, Beiträge zur biblischen Exegese und Theologie (Frankfurt am Main: Peter Lang, 1995), p. 16.

vorite name for God. Moreover, after this polemic and in response to Israel's complaint that the Lord has ignored her rights (40:27), Isaiah 40:28 asserts emphatically that "the LORD is the everlasting God, the Creator of the ends of the earth" — the ultimate trump card in comparing the God of Israel with false gods and idols.

Most of these assertions are presented directly as straightforward declarations rather than as narratives from which they need to be inferred. Often they are presented as divine speech, the first-person words of God. In the trial speech of 41:21-29, the Lord introduces himself as "the King of Jacob" (41:21). Of particular interest is the use of the divine self-predication "I am the LORD," which, as we noted above, occurs frequently in connection with polemical statements against the gods. Consider, for example, Isaiah 42:8:

> I am the LORD, that is my name;
>> my glory I give to no other,
>> nor my praise to idols.

Or listen to the powerful self-predication in 44:6 that introduces the longest polemic against the gods (44:6-20):

> Thus says the LORD, the King of Israel,
>> and his Redeemer, the LORD of hosts:
> I am the first and I am the last;
>> besides me there is no god.

Chapters 40–55 also contain many positive affirmations about God's actions. In the first polemic against the nations and the gods (40:18-26), for instance, we learn this from 40:22-23:

> It is [God] who sits above the circle of the earth . . . ;
> who stretches out the heavens like a curtain,
>> and spreads them like a tent to live in;
> who brings princes to naught,
>> and makes the rulers of the earth as nothing.

God's governance over the nations is also emphasized in the third polemic against the nations and their gods (41:21-20). According to 41:25, the Lord "stirred up one from the north" to tread "on rulers as on mortar" (cf. 10:6). Moreover, according to 41:27, the Lord gave to Jerusalem "a herald of good tidings." Furthermore, in the fourth polemic (43:8-15) we hear the LORD's powerful claim that, unlike the gods, he has "declared and saved and proclaimed" (43:12). In addition, after the long polemic in 44:6-20, God calls Israel back to himself because he has made her, has swept her sins away, and has redeemed her (44:21-22). And in the scathing critique of the Babylonian gods (chap. 46), God emphasizes to those who are far from deliverance (46:12) that he will bring about what he has planned (46:11) and that he brought deliverance and salvation near (46:13). Throughout the polemical speeches against the gods, therefore, the reader encounters straightforward assertions about God's character and God's actions.

These chapters do not merely complain about idolatry. They also complement the complaint with similarly compelling, positive assertions about God's character and actions in oracles of salvation (41:10, 14; 43:1-7; 44:1-5) and announcements of salvation (41:17-20). Thinking in terms of Rembrandt's work, they not only portray the shadows but also depict the shaft of light that reveals nothing less than the true God, the maker of the universe. We need to see the same contrast in worship and preaching today.

2. Songs of Praise

Second, consider the psalm-like songs of praise that occur throughout these chapters.[15] According to Claus Westermann, these songs of praise are generally the end-piece of a section and call for a decision.[16] A clear example is the summons to praise in Isaiah 42:10-13:

> Sing to the LORD a new song,
>   his praise from the end of the earth!
> Let the sea roar and all that fills it,
>   the coastlands and their inhabitants.
> Let the desert and its towns lift up their voice,
>   the villages that Kedar inhabits;

---

15. Cf. Isaiah 42:10-13; 44:23; 48:20-21; 49:13; 52:9-10; and 54:1.

16. Claus Westermann, *Isaiah 40–66: A Commentary,* Old Testament Library, trans. David M. G. Stalker (Philadelphia: Westminster Press, 1969), p. 19.

let the inhabitants of Sela sing for joy,
    let them shout from the tops of the mountains.
Let them give glory to the LORD,
    and declare his praise in the coastlands.
The LORD goes forth like a soldier,
    like a warrior he stirs up his fury;
he cries out, he shouts aloud,
    he shows himself mighty against his foes.

This powerful summons invites everyone to give glory to the Lord (42:12), the one who refuses to give his glory to idols (42:8).

Significantly, the context of the prophetic critiques of idolatry helps us sense what to emphasize as we hear them — and as we sing them ourselves. Often we naturally approach a song of praise with a kind of blank-slate reading. We express our praise as "*Sing* to the Lord a new song" (as opposed to simply speaking our praise) or "Sing to the Lord a *new* song" (as opposed to singing an old song). However appropriate those interpretations might be in other contexts, here the force of context conveys, rather, "Sing to the *Lord* a new song" (as opposed to singing to idols or false gods). These are hymns offered as polemical statements; they are offered against the gods even as they are sung to Yahweh. When we sing "Praise God, from whom all blessings flow," we are also saying "Down with the gods from whom no blessings flow."

The polemical function of praise has been memorably described by Walter Brueggemann: "The affirmation of Yahweh always contains a polemic against someone else. . . . It may be that the [exiles] will sing such innocuous-sounding phrases as 'Glory to God in the highest,' or 'Praise God, from whom all blessings flow.' Even those familiar phrases are polemical, however, and stake out new territory for the God now about to be aroused to new caring."[17] When we sing our pretty songs of praise, it is as if we are singing "Take that, you false gods!"

17. Walter Brueggemann, *Cadences of Home: Preaching among the Exiles* (Louisville: Westminster John Knox Press, 1997), p. 128. For more on this theme, see Brueggemann, *Israel's Praise: Doxology against Idolatry and Ideology* (Philadelphia: Fortress Press, 1988). The polemical function of praise songs is nothing new in the Christian tradition. The body of Christian hymnody that is most polemical may well be the Trinitarian hymns of the fourth century, such as the *Te Deum* ("Holy God, We Praise Your Name") and "Of the Father's Love Begotten," which were weapons against Arianism.

Brueggemann's insight helps awaken a latent dimension of our doxology. At root, what he is probing is the experience of ordinary worshipers and their own interior conversation during the worship. Commenting on Psalm 146, Brueggemann suggests, "In naming the Name [of Yahweh, vv. 7b-9], the psalm under its breath debunks and dismisses every other name: The Lord [not Baal] sets the prisoners free; the Lord [not Saddam Hussein] opens the eyes of the blind. The Lord [not the free market system or Western government] lifts up those who are bowed down; the Lord [not the church organization] loves the righteous. The Lord [not my favorite political persuasion] watches over the strangers, upholds the orphan and the widow."[18]

3. Messianic Illumination

Third, Isaiah 40–55 offer images that help us understand Christ. The ultimate antidote to idolatry in the Christian faith is Jesus Christ: the exact representation of God's being, the true icon of divine glory. The Christian doctrine of revelation begins with creation, God's general revelation; is focused through special revelation, the gift of Scripture; and is most acutely attentive to the person and work of Jesus Christ, as illuminated by both the Old and the New Testaments. Isaiah, in giving us imagistic language to understand Jesus Christ, provides some of Bible's most forceful idolatry-fighting resources. Specifically, these chapters give us a compelling vision of Christ's identity as one who expresses power in weakness. And they confirm that Christ's mission includes not only redemption from sin but also the extension of justice and righteousness.[19]

The messianic dimensions to these chapters are especially important because of their frequent Christian liturgical use in festivals of the liturgical year: Christmas, Holy Week, Easter, and even Pentecost. These celebrations, as they invite us to meditate on Christ's character, are some of the best

18. Walter Brueggemann, *The Psalms and the Life of Faith*, ed. Patrick D. Miller (Minneapolis: Fortress Press, 1995), p. 127; see also p. 118.

19. Thus Richard Beaton argues that Matthew's quotation of Isaiah 42:1-4 "was employed by Matthew to validate a particular view of Jesus as royal messiah, namely, that he was the Spirit-endowed, compassionate servant of the Lord whose words and deeds evince the justice anticipated with the advent of the messiah and the inauguration of the Kingdom of God" (*Isaiah's Christ in Matthew's Gospel* [Cambridge: Cambridge University Press, 1992], p. 192).

idolatry-fighting occasions we have available to us. They challenge poorly conceived views of divine character and hone our theological imaginations.

In sum, the recipe for fighting idolatry in Isaiah's day and in ours is fourfold: (1) name the sin and its consequences; (2) present a compelling alternative to idol worship with a splendid image of God as given by Scripture; (3) praise this God with determined and intentional songs of praise; and (4) constantly challenge and refine our theological imaginations by focusing on the person of Christ as illuminated by both the Old and the New Testaments. Here are four worthy goals for any worship service, and four worthy criteria for worship worth reviewing at any Monday worship-committee review session.

Correcting Theological Astigmatism as an Antidote to Idolatry

The Contemporary Distaste for Talk of Idolatry

The problem, of course, is that we do not have much interest in hearing about idolatry in contemporary culture, or even contemporary church culture. Despite the fact that idolatry is the most obvious form of false worship, there are very few sessions at most worship conferences entitled "How to Avoid Idolatry in Your Church." Part of the problem is that we assume that the kind of idolatry that plagued ancient Near Eastern culture simply does not trouble us; we do not seem to have physical idols in the way that this culture did. Part of the reason we avoid the topic is that we prefer not to dwell on sin at all. And part of our lack of interest is that we remember worship services that focused on idolatry as being guilt-inducing, works-righteousness promoting, and altogether depressing.

Of course, the warning against idolatry is life-giving. It is a form of wisdom. Like all true wisdom, we neglect it at our own peril. For anyone who works to plan and lead worship, idolatry needs to be a regular matter of concern. Even when our culture (and church culture) protests — even when it seems to be saying, "Do not prophesy to us what is right; speak to us smooth things, prophesy illusions, . . . let us hear no more about the Holy One of Israel" (Isa. 30:10-11) — the first item in the job description of any preacher, worship leader, musician, and anyone who would lead God's people in worship ought to be to work diligently against the sin of idolatry and to work for its opposite: a deeply nuanced understanding of the beauty of God and subsequent loving devotion to this God.

Theological Astigmatism as a Type of Idolatry

Part of what can help us approach this faithfully, I would argue, is to consider the multiple forms of idolatry and to discern which forms are particularly vexing in contemporary life. The obvious form of idolatry is, as the Heidelberg Catechism concludes, "having or inventing something in which one trusts in place of or alongside of the only true God" (A. 95). Thus, money, sex, and power are appropriately the usual targets in many sermons on idolatry.

But there is another form of idolatry that needs our attention, one that Isaiah is very well-suited to address: the idolatry of false or distorted conceptions about God. This idolatry might be thought of as a kind of theological astigmatism or misapprehension in which we misperceive God's character, even when our worship is drenched in orthodox theological language.

This type of idolatry was described by Zacharias Ursinus. In his exposition on the Heidelberg Catechism, Question 94, Ursinus distinguishes seven forms of obedience that the first commandment enjoins. Then, for the first form of that obedience ("the knowledge of God"), he goes on in a moment of scholastic zeal to articulate seven corresponding types of disobedience. Of these, the second is simply clinging to "errors or false notions of God," including the sin of those — that is, of all of us — "who profess that they know the true God; but yet depart from him and worship instead of him, an idol which they make for themselves, because they imagine the true God other than he has made himself known in his word."[20] In his commentary on the Heidelberg Catechism, Karl Barth is even more explicit about contrasting idolatry with the worship of the Triune God: "Every conception and every presentation of a God who is not this three-in-one God, however beautiful and profound it may be, can only set up an idol, a false image of God."[21] Otto Weber argued against any reli-

---

20. *The Commentary of Dr. Zacharias Ursinus on the Heidelberg Catechism*, trans. G. W. Williard (Grand Rapids: Eerdmans, 1954), p. 509.

21. Karl Barth, *Heidelberg Catechism Today* (Richmond: John Knox Press, 1964), p. 57.

gious devotion to God apart from Jesus Christ and the work of the Holy Spirit, referring dramatically to "the struggle against the idolization of Yahweh himself."[22] This is also why the most recent Roman Catholic Catechism comments on the first commandment not only with a protest against polytheism and pagan religion, but also against irreligiosity, atheism, and agnosticism.[23]

More recently, Herbert Schlossberg warns, "Since ours is not so much a pagan (which is to say pre-Christian) society as it is a post-Christian one, the dangers are all the more serious. The forces of idolatry do not urge us to worship Zeus but rather use the language that for many centuries has been associated with the Christian church."[24] This is the type of idolatry that Charles Spurgeon worried about, expressed in his concern that too many churchgoers "are merely stolid, unthinking, slumbering worshippers of an unknown God."[25] This is theological astigmatism, in which we find ourselves attending to the God of Scripture, but in a blurry, ill-formed, and distorted way.

Among the particularly vexing forms of contemporary theological astigmatisms are the sentimentalization of the gospel on the one hand and certain forms of triumphalism on the other. The first, the privatization or sentimentalization of the gospel, ignores God's longing for justice. How often have we heard the pretty texts of Isaiah ("Comfort, comfort now my people," "Here is your God," "I will be with you when you go through the waters"), and almost never heard expressed at the same time the divine

22. Otto Weber, *Foundations of Dogmatics,* vol. 1, trans. Darrell L. Guder (Grand Rapids: Eerdmans, 1981), pp. 358-59. Similarly, John Barton argues, "[There is] a tendency to treat merely human ideas of divine reality as though they were God himself. The recognition that idolatry really consists in making gods for ourselves and putting our trust in them is the great breakthrough in Israel's thinking about the matter, and I have suggested that it may be to Isaiah that we owe it" ("'The Work of Human Hands' (Psalm 115:4): Idolatry in the Old Testament," *Ex Auditu* 15 [1999]: 71). For a similar concern, see James M. Houston, *The Heart's Desire: Satisfying the Hunger of the Soul* (Vancouver: Regent College, 2001), pp. 30-53.

23. *Catechism of the Catholic Church* (New York: Image, 1995), 561-72.

24. Herbert Schlossberg, *Idols for Destruction: Christian Faith and Its Confrontation with American Society* (Nashville: Nelson, 1983), pp. 322-23. For more on this theme, see David Bentley Hart's commentary on the first commandment, "God or Nothingness," in *I Am the Lord Your God: Christian Reflections on the Ten Commandments,* ed. Carl E. Braaten and Christopher R. Seitz (Grand Rapids: Eerdmans, 2005), pp. 55-76.

25. Charles H. Spurgeon, "Degrees of Power Attending the Gospel," sermon no. 648 in *Metropolitan Tabernacle Pulpit,* vol. 11 (London: Passmore & Alabaster, 1866), p. 496.

concern for righteousness and justice that comes along with them? This is why Leslie J. Hoppe defines idolatry as "forgetting that the God whom Israel worshipped was a God who takes the side of the oppressed, demands justice for the poor, and liberates slaves," and why Thomas L. Leclerc argues that "In the context of the prophet's polemic against injustice, it [the "path of justice"] serves as a distinguishing and distinctive feature of YHWH's identity."[26] Isaiah can correct our theological astigmatism by making sure that justice attaches to our vision of divine character.

Second, Isaiah's positive theological vision and critique of idolatry challenge a kind of triumphalism that pictures God as a God of raw-fisted power, a kind of divine Rambo.[27] As classical Christian theology consistently asserts (based in part on Isaiah), God is an omnipotent Creator. But God exercises power in particular ways and toward particular ends. God's power and love are in no way in opposition. In Isaiah the image of God as divine warrior is strikingly juxtaposed with the image of God's suffering servant — challenging our interpretation of each. Isaiah gives us a beautiful and compelling vision of God as a being of power-expressed-in-redemptive-love. It is a vision that constantly challenges our preconceived, culturally shaped views. Paraphrasing a long-standing claim of traditional theological prolegomena, C. Stephen Evans has observed with understated eloquence that "our intuitions about what is perfect may not be altogether trustworthy."[28] We need the biblical text to constantly hone our idea of God and strip away both our implicitly and explicitly cultivated little idols. Isaiah is particularly well-suited to the task, correcting theological astigmatisms of all types.

This theological corrective lens should not be thought of as a luxury, reserved only for people with the time and interest to read books on the Old Testament and worship. It is deeply needed by all sorts of modern worshipers, from religious seekers to longtime worshipers (and leaders) whose faith has grown tired in part because they carry with them distorted

---

26. Leslie J. Hoppe, "Isaiah 58:1-12: Fasting and Idolatry," *Biblical Theology Bulletin* 13 (April 1983): 44-47; and Thomas L. Leclerc, *Yahweh Is Exalted in Justice: Solidarity and Conflict in Isaiah* (Minneapolis: Fortress Press, 2001), p. 129. See also W. A. M. Beuken, "Mišpat: The First Servant Song and Its Context," *Vetus Testamentum* 22 (1972): 1-30.

27. See Millard Lind, "Monotheism, Power, and Justice: A Study in Isaiah 40–55," *Catholic Biblical Quarterly* 46 (1984): 432-46.

28. C. Stephen Evans, *The Historical Christ and the Jesus of Faith: The Incarnational Narrative as History* (Oxford: Clarendon Press, 1996), p. 134.

theological ideas. And it is deeply needed by all those who may be staying away from the church because they want to avoid a God that they misconstrue and misconceive. Part of what the church can give to a longing culture is a fully balanced biblical view of God, one that is so luminous that it challenges and critiques the implicit idolatry of that culture.

Practical Strategies for Subverting Idolatry in Preaching and Leading Worship

Worship as an Arena for Fighting Idolatry

All of this becomes pressing when we realize that public worship is one of the most important arenas for seeking to obey the first and second commandments. Part of the deep purpose of common worship is to fit us for the spectacles of Scripture, to work at correcting persistent theological astigmatisms. Seven days a week, twenty-four hours a day, we live in a culture (and sometimes even a church culture) that tempts us to think of divine life as sentimental love or raw-fisted power, and a thousand other subtle heresies. Worship is a place that says to the world, missionally, "You who are weary from chasing these false gods, come away. Come away to the One who will give you rest."

Here is where pretty words fail us. Here is where we need to draw rhetorical contrasts in ways that point to the compelling beauty of God's character. Yet we often proceed with platitudes. We sing three pleasant songs, skip the confession of sin, hear a nice solo, make sure the sermon is packed with delightful anecdotes, and eagerly move toward coffee time. In the process, the praise songs lose their polemic. Grace and truth lose their beauty, and the evangelistic magnetism of worship loses some of its pull. Like the controls on my old television, the contrast knob doesn't seem to work, and all those vivid colors of Isaiah become pastels.

Anti-Idolatry Strategies in Worship

So now, practically, how do we use the resources of Isaiah 40–55 — their critique of sin, positive theological assertions, polemic doxology, and Christological focus — to fight both explicit idolatry and this kind of theological astigmatism? For starters, we work the contrasts that these texts teach us, contrasts that help us perceive the life-giving beauty of the gospel according to Isaiah. Contrast is nothing new to thoughtful worship planning, of course. The majority of historic Sunday liturgies began with the contrast between the plaintive cry of "Kyrie eleison" and the exuberant acclamation *"Gloria in Excelsis Deo"* — a contrast only somewhat captured in the movement from confession to assurance.[29] Consider how more effective rhetorical contrasts might be achieved in some routine aspects of worship planning.

1. *Choosing and Delimiting Texts*

First, we need to consider which verses we choose to read and present in worship. Courses in both lectionary and nonlectionary homiletics teach us to limit the text by its literary unit. We want one tree in the forest. However, dealing strictly with literary units often means that we miss textual contrasts. Whenever possible, read the preceding paragraph or pericope before the chosen text. If that is not possible, develop a simple one-sentence introduction that is either printed and read or spoken right before the reading. Before hearing the life-giving words of Isaiah 40, a reader might say, "The word of the Lord from Isaiah 40: In contrast to false gods, the true Creator God gives strength and hope. Hear now the word of the Lord." In worship that is less formal, a reader or preacher might say, "Think for a moment of the darkest moment in your life. When Israel heard the words you're about to hear, life was darker still. Now hear the word of the Lord." This is not to suggest that worship (even Scripture reading) should be overly didactic. A two-sentence to three-sentence limit is a wise guideline in many cultural contexts. The practice helps people hear what the text accomplishes in its literary context.

Consider the following suggestions for introductions and reading delimitations:

---

29. Many of our favorite musical examples also operate this way. In the *Messiah*, Handel set up the glory of the Hallelujah chorus with the biting words "Thou shalt break them in pieces like a potter's vessel." After that dour declamation, the great chorus is exhilarating.

	Typical Reading	Alternative Reading
40:9	O Jerusalem . . . say to the cities of *Judah,* "Here is your God!" (This implies a contrast between Judah and the nations.)	O Jerusalem . . . say to the cities of Judah, "*Here* is your God!" (This implies "not over there, with the false gods.")
42:1	Here is my *servant,* whom I uphold. (This implies a contrast between servant and something else.)	[No,] *here* is my servant, whom I uphold. . . . I have put my Spirit upon *him.* (This implies that the contrast is between the servant and the "empty wind" [41:29] of the false gods.)
44:24	Thus says the LORD, your Redeemer, who formed you in the womb: I am the LORD. (This implies, "I am the LORD as opposed to something else.")	Thus says the LORD, your Redeemer, who formed you in the womb: *I* am the LORD, who made all things, who *alone* stretched out the heavens, who *by myself* spread out the earth. . . . (This implies that God, as opposed to the idols, is maker and upholder of all things.)
52:7	Your God *reigns.* (This implies that the relevant contrast is "Your God is not merely interested in you — he reigns.")	How beautiful upon the mountains are the feet of the messenger who announces *peace,* who brings *good* news, who announces salvation, who says to Zion, "*Your* God reigns." (This implies that the relevant contrast is "Your God reigns as opposed to the other gods.")
57:15-16	For thus says the high and lofty one who inhabits eternity, whose name is *Holy:* I dwell in the high and holy place, and also with those who are contrite and humble in spirit, to *revive the spirit* of the humble, and to *revive the heart* of the contrite. For I will not continually accuse, nor will I always be angry; for then the spirits would *grow faint* before me, even the souls that I have made. (These are all appropriate ways of stressing the good news of this text, but without the implied contrasts between this God and other gods.)	For thus says the high and lofty one who inhabits eternity, whose name is Holy: *I* [in contrast to those measly gods] dwell in the high and holy place, *and also* [here is a surprise] with those who are contrite and humble in spirit, to revive the spirit of the humble, and to revive the heart of the contrite. For I will not continually accuse, nor will I always be angry; for then the spirits would grow faint before me, even the souls that I have made.

As these examples indicate, what we need is an Old Testament scholar to prepare a "reading commentary" of Isaiah — a guide to help us understand which words need to be emphasized so that our reading of the book matches our exegesis of the text. Until we have such a resource, may every exegete of the text think about ways not only of developing a sermon outline but also of reading the text with loving care.

3. Contrastive Rhetoric in Preaching

The contrasts between light and dark, folly and wisdom, the gods and God that are so dramatically depicted in the alternating rhetoric of the middle chapters of Isaiah naturally suggest the same kind of rhetoric for preaching today. We need preaching rhetoric that works the principle of contrast. Consider, for example, Fleming Rutledge's memorable Advent sermon, "Advent Begins in the Dark," or Gardner Taylor's "Shadow and Light."[30] The titles themselves convey the contrast. More important is the rhetoric of the body of the sermon. Imagine a sermon that works up quite a bit of rhetorical force in piling up dramatic contrasts:

> The world loves to worship the stuff it has made, but the church proclaims a God who made us. The world lives to worship ideas it has thought up, but the church points to a vision of God far greater than we could ever imagine on our own. The world says that God's power is simply raw-fisted power, but we proclaim a God who redeems through suffering love. The world advises you to take glory for yourself, but the church says to give away the glory of God — to show it to the nations for the purpose of God's mission in the world.

The musicality and rhythmic flow of the rhetoric will inevitably work better in some cultures than others. But however the sentence structure develops, the principle of contrast is worth considering. In general, the rhetoric of sermons is lacking when true claims are made because it does not give a sense of what harder things the softer, "prettier" message displaces.

---

30. Fleming Rutledge, "Advent Begins in the Dark," in *The Bible and "The New York Times"* (Grand Rapids: Eerdmans, 1996), pp. 25-30; Gardner Taylor, "Shadow and Light," in *The Words of Gardner Taylor,* vol. 1, NBC Radio Sermons, ed. Edward Taylor (Valley Forge, Pa.: Judson Press, 1999), pp. 116-19.

This is especially important when we think of the evangelistic opportunities that we find in nearly all preaching and worship contexts. Worship and preaching are so significant because they give us opportunities to correct misapprehensions of God's character that prevent people from joyful worship and abundant Christian living. It is a worthy exercise for nearly every sermon and service plan to imagine the most effective pastoral kind of astigmatism-correction that worship can provide. Consider a few rough drafts of sermon introductions on the themes of this essay (designed here more to convey the idea than the wording that would best express it):

> There are those of you who say that the Christian faith has little to do with the conditions and relationships that people live with every day. Well, the problem here is not with the Bible but with the way people misuse the Bible. The God we worship today loves justice. Listen!
>
> Have you stayed away from church because you are tired of hypocritical religious people? It turns out that the God we worship today hates hypocrisy, too.
>
> Were you ever taught to be afraid of God, like a kid in a thunderstorm? Well, the God of the Bible is big enough to make a thunderstorm. But this God tells us not to be afraid. Listen!
>
> Are you exhausted as you arrive here today, living as if life is a hamster's treadmill? The God we worship today doesn't call us to spiritual life on an endless treadmill, chasing after things that won't satisfy. The God we worship today invites us to a way of life that truly satisfies.

Any one of these introductions would need to be reworked for a particular sermon, but they suggest the kinds of contrast that can help sermons and the services that surround them move beyond truism.

4. The Elements of Worship

Just as important as these homiletical moves are the moves that give shape to the liturgy that surrounds the sermon. Contrastive rhetoric, used in ways that address theological misapprehension, can be prominent throughout worship. Consider the following examples for several elements of worship:

CALL TO WORSHIP

Introductory lines:

Seasonally nonspecific: If you come to worship today exhausted from chasing after the world's gods, hear this invitation of Jesus: "Come to *me,* all you who are weary, for *I* will give you rest."

Seasonally specific: Christmas: All year long our world has told us that things get done with power and money. Today, in striking contrast, the Christian church looks at the baby Jesus and hears the words of Isaiah: "Get you up to a high mountain, O Zion, herald of good tidings; . . . do not fear; say to the cities of Judah, 'Behold, *here* is your God!'" O come, let us adore him.

Scripture texts: Psalm 96, Psalm 115

SONGS AND HYMNS OF PRAISE

Introductory lines:

Every song of praise we sing to God is a song against everything else we would make into a god.

In church we don't waste our breath praising a false god. We worship the One who made us, who loves us, who has redeemed us in Christ. Come, let us worship God.

Scripture text: Psalm 95:1-7

Songs that Draw Contrast/Name Idolatry

"Cast every idol from its throne; the Lord is God, and he alone: to God all praise and glory." ("Sing Praise to God Who Reigns Above," J. J. Schütz)

"We bow our hearts, we bend our knees; O Spirit, come make us humble. We turn our eyes from evil things; O Lord, we cast down our idols. Give us clean hands, give us pure hearts; let us not lift our souls to an-

gregations may be more willing to linger more deeply in Advent longing and Lenten repentance.

Summary

Among its many prevailing themes, Isaiah's trenchant anti-idolatry campaign is among the most pastorally significant for contemporary ministry. Worship is a key arena for rehabilitating practices that correct idolatries of all kinds. When we prepare sermons and the worship services that surround them, we would do well to learn not only from the themes of a given part of Scripture (e.g., Isaiah's anti-idolatry campaign) but also from the strategies they employ (e.g., rhetorical contrast between idolatry and true worship, luminous assertions of divine character, and songs of praise that are experienced as polemic against false gods). The point of giving renewed attention to this theme is not to make worship more dour or depressing. In fact, just the opposite: the point is to help worshipers perceive the resplendent and luminous beauty of the God revealed in Scripture and to offer worship in spirit and in truth.

Sing Praise to God Who Reigns Above

Sing praise to God who reigns above,
the God of all creation,
the God of power, the God of love,
the God of our salvation.
My soul with comfort rich he fills,
and every grief he gently stills:
To God all praise and glory!

What God's almighty power has made,
in mercy he is keeping;
by morning glow or evening shade
his eye is never sleeping.
And where he rules in kingly might,
there all is just and all is right:
To God all praise and glory!

We sought the Lord in our distress;
O God, in mercy hear us.
Our Savior saw our helplessness
and came with peace to cheer us.
For this we thank and praise the Lord,
who is by one and all adored:
To God all praise and glory!

Let all who name Christ's holy name,
give God the praise and glory.
Let all who know his power proclaim
aloud the wondrous story!
Cast every idol from its throne;
the Lord is God, and he alone:
To God all praise and glory!

Text: Johann Jacob Schütz (1640-1690), 1675; trans. Frances Elizabeth Cox (1812-1897), 1864, alt.

Lift Up Your Heads

Lift up your heads, eternal gates, Alleluia!
See how the King of glory waits, Alleluia!
The Lord of Hosts is drawing near,
the Savior of the world is here. Alleluia!

But not in arms or battle dress, Alleluia!
God comes, a child, amidst distress, Alleluia!
No mighty armies shield the way,
only coarse linen, wool, and hay. Alleluia!

God brings a new face to the brave, Alleluia!
God redefines who best can save: Alleluia!
not those whose power relies on threat,
terror or torture, destruction or debt. Alleluia!

God's matchless and majestic strength, Alleluia!
in all its height, depth, breadth, and length, Alleluia!
now is revealed, its power to prove,
by Christ protesting, "God is love!" Alleluia!

Text: John L. Bell (b. 1949), "Lift Up Your Heads," Choral Octavo G-5494 (Chicago: GIA Publications, Inc., 2002)

Text copyright © 2001, Wild Goose Resource Group, Iona Community, Scotland. GIA Publications, Inc., exclusive North American agent, 7404 S. Mason Ave., Chicago, IL 60638 (www.giamusic.com; 800.442.1358). All rights reserved. Used by permission. Original text: "Lift Up Your Heads, Ye Mighty Gates," written by George Weissel (1590-1635), 1642, translated by Catherine Winkworth (1827-1878), 1855, adapted by John L. Bell, 2002

FOR FURTHER READING

Walter Brueggemann. *Israel's Praise: Doxology against Idolatry and Ideology* (Philadelphia: Fortress Press, 1988). This is one of the most sustained treatments of how biblically conceived praise always functions as both an affirmation of divine worthiness and a protest against earthly powers — a theme that also permeates several of Brueggemann's subsequent books.

F. Russell Mitman. *Worship in the Shape of Scripture* (Cleveland: Pilgrim Press, 2001). A sustained argument for doing what this essay practices — to imbed our exegetical work not only into preaching but also into the preparation and shaping of every aspect of a worship service.

John F. A. Sawyer. *The Fifth Gospel: Isaiah in the History of Christianity* (Cambridge: Cambridge University Press, 1996). Sawyer surveys several uses of the book of Isaiah, including in worship, preaching, theological disputes, and choral music.

Clayton J. Schmit. *Public Reading of Scripture: A Handbook* (Nashville: Abingdon Press, 2002). A short but comprehensive look at how to present Scripture in worship in ways that do justice to the particular rhetorical shape of each text.

www.reformedworship.org. A Web site that features several hundred articles on all aspects of worship planning, and also several model worship services that reflect both historic patterns of worship and contemporary improvisations that are guided by scriptural and pastoral concerns, in a similar vein to those described in this chapter.

No Explanations in the Church:
Two Sermons on the Prophets

ELLEN F. DAVIS

JEREMIAH 4

Preaching as Seeing

There is a sign on the wall as one enters the precinct of the Church of the Agony at the foot of the Mount of Olives, the traditional site of Gethsemane. It reads "No Explanations in the Church." The prohibition is, of course, directed at tour guides. It is intended to preserve the silence that wondrously pervades the achingly beautiful and (in times happier than the present) heavily trafficked sanctuary. But the prohibition on explanations in the church has, it seems to me, a different and much broader applicability. Specifically, I propose that it is a helpful observance for preachers. Just as chatty tour guides would get in the way of the message that Antonio Barluzzi's magnificent architectural design silently conveys, so also preachers can obscure the very thing they are bent on making plain — namely, the biblical text.

For most Christian preachers, the perceived need to explain is most acute with the Old Testament. So much of it seems unattractive in presentation, harsh to the taste, altogether indigestible in its present form. If the Old Testament is to be used at all, then surely the first thing necessary is explanation. Yet I am convinced that explaining the text is not a necessity but rather a dangerous temptation, and the reason preachers should not succumb to it derives from the nature and purpose of worship itself. A fundamental aim of worship is that we should see what is not ordinarily visible to us — because we are not really looking, or our vision is unfocused, or we don't know how to interpret what we are seeing, or, perhaps, because we are not spiritually well enough to see and understand. What we are meant to see is the hand of God at work in the midst of our world and our own lives. So preaching is first of all the vehicle whereby the eyes of the heart are trained to see differently and more clearly both our present circumstances and the possibilities for our lives — to see that what we call "reality" has dimensions we have not seriously tried to imagine since we were children.

Preaching, then, should nurture and instruct the imagination. Yet in order for that goal to be something other than frivolous — and sadly, preachers who aim at being imaginative often settle for being merely entertaining — it is necessary to consider the distinctively *theological* function of the well-instructed imagination. Here I propose that the single most important function of the imagination is to enable us to know God truly — though not, of course, wholly — and to act on that knowledge. The biblical texts themselves are addressed to our imaginations, and therefore preachers serve their congregations best when they do not try to explain the text but rather "let it loose" to do its work of creating more profound theological insight and new moral vision in the church.

A good starting point for this argument about the function of the imagination is Garrett Green's suggestion that "imagination" may be the best equivalent in modern English for what the biblical writers mean when they use the words *lev* (Hebrew) and *kardia* (Greek) — that is, "heart." Explicitly and implicitly, the biblical writers speak to the heart; they offer poetic images, storied memories, visions of a future radically different from the present. Thus they nurture and direct the imagination, nudging it, passage by passage, to embrace a more expansive view of reality, equipping it linguistically and conceptually to "imagine God."[1]

The medieval theologians who crafted the great poem that is the Eucharistic liturgy gave central prominence to the "heart," by which they too meant the biblically and theologically informed imagination:

> "Lift up your hearts."
> "We lift them up unto the Lord."
> "Let us give thanks unto our Lord God."
> "It is meet and right so to do."[2]

Significantly, this exchange constitutes the hinge between Word and Sacrament. The forceful priestly imperative occurs just after the Scriptures have been read and their narrative summary (from Genesis through Acts) has been recited in the Creed. With hearts thus equipped, the congregation is called upon to elevate them toward God. The pivotal placement of the *Sursum Corda* signals that directing the biblically shaped imagination toward God is the central movement of all Christian worship.

Yet the logic of the liturgy demands that lifting up our hearts must mean something more than achieving the kind of intellectual dexterity we generally call "imaginative thinking" — a mental skill essential for performing certain jobs well: writing science fiction, for instance, or advertising copy. But this is not the kind of heightened imagination for which the

---

1. Garrett Green, *Imagining God: Theology and the Religious Imagination* (San Francisco: Harper & Row, 1989), pp. 109-10.

2. *The Book of Common Prayer* (New York: The Church Hymnal Corporation, 1979), p. 333.

liturgy calls, and the crucial difference lies in the extent to which the imagination is grounded in reality. An imaginative *mind* may be capable of constructing elaborate fantasies that do not purport to represent real human possibilities. But the elevated *heart* for which the liturgy calls is nothing less than the re-orientation of the whole person to the One who is most real.[3] Therefore, the Eucharistic prayer that follows points toward the remaking of our lives in this world. In the precise and descriptive language of the old Eucharistic rite, we offer "our selves, our souls and bodies, to be a reasonable, holy, and living sacrifice" to God.[4] The movement is from inner to outer aspects of our person: our actions, the shape of our lives follow our affections and thoughts, the pictures we form in our hearts. All these are part of the "sacrifice" (literally, "making holy") that enables us to be drawn into the life of God. In short, the God-directed imagination is far more than the occasional gift of certain poetically minded individuals, a resource perhaps for one's private spirituality. An elevated "heart" is the essential equipment of every Christian, the vital organ of the life of faith. Therefore it must be firmly connected to the realities of this world and at the same time wholly oriented to God.

However, it must be admitted that many people consider those two things to be in tension, if not outright contradiction: on the one hand, being grounded and wisely invested in the world, and on the other, being wholly disposed toward God. Moreover, the church, including its preachers, has largely accepted that seeming contradiction as a reality and made the necessary accommodation. The church's accommodation takes the form of promoting "spirituality" as an inward-looking disposition. The kind of religion with which we are comfortable, and which our culture as a whole accepts — from Christians and non-Christians alike, and even from "spiritually minded" non-believers — is a religion of personal salvation. Maybe the direct question "Are you saved?" sounds gauche to many of us. Nonetheless, we generally prefer to confine our religious conversation, including preaching, to the sphere of personal growth and relationship (including our relationship with Jesus) and leave the world to itself.

However, Dietrich Bonhoeffer, facing probably the greatest moral cri-

---

3. Dietrich Bonhoeffer's observation is apt: "The 'heart' in the biblical sense is not the inward life but the whole man in relation to God" (*Letters and Papers from Prison* [London: SCM Press, 1953], p. 118).

4. *The Book of Common Prayer*, p. 336.

sis of modernity, identified as the church's "cardinal error" its promotion of Christianity "as a religion of salvation."[5] Of particular relevance to the topic of this volume was his further observation that it is precisely this error "which divorces Christ from the Old Testament and interprets him in light of the myths of salvation."[6] In other words, theology and preaching (like the myths of salvation) become preoccupied with deliverance from death, whereas the Old Testament itself "speaks of *historical* redemption — i.e., redemption on this side of death." Reading the Old Testament reminds us that "the world must not be prematurely written off."[7] Writing from a Nazi prison in a confinement that would lead to his execution within the year, Bonhoeffer reflected upon the changed theological perspective that circumstances had forced upon those who participated in the Christian resistance against Hitler:

> Is it not true to say that individualistic concern for personal salvation has almost completely left us all? Are we not really under the impression that there are more important things than bothering about such a matter? (Perhaps not more important than the matter itself, but more than bothering about it.) I know it sounds pretty monstrous to say that. But is it not, at bottom, even Biblical? Is there any concern in the Old Testament about saving one's soul at all? Is not righteousness and the kingdom of God on earth the focus of everything, and is not Romans 3.14ff., too, the culmination of the view that in God alone is righteousness, and not in an individualistic doctrine of salvation? It is not with the next world that we are concerned, but with this world as created and preserved and set subject to laws and atoned for and made new. What is above the world is, in the Gospel, intended to exist *for* this world — I mean that not in the anthropocentric sense of liberal, pietistic, ethical theology, but in the Bible sense of the creation and of the incarnation, crucifixion, and resurrection of Jesus Christ.[8]

The irony that Bonhoeffer sees — and the acute moral danger for the church — is that a focus on salvation has allowed God to be "driven out of

5. Bonhoeffer, *Letters and Papers from Prison*, p. 112.
6. Bonhoeffer, *Letters and Papers from Prison*, p. 112.
7. Bonhoeffer, *Letters and Papers from Prison*, p. 112.
8. This is an excerpt from a letter, dated 5 May 1944, to Eberhard Bethge, Bonhoeffer's best friend and fellow theologian (*Letters and Papers from Prison*, pp. 94-95).

the world" and retained only "in the sphere of the 'personal,' the 'inner life,' the private life."[9] Obliquely, Bonhoeffer is directing us toward the practice of what has been called (with reference to Bonhoeffer's theology) "worldly preaching"[10] — the kind of imaginative yet realistic speech that reckons squarely with the concrete and often pressing circumstances of our lives, with the reality of evil threatening us from the outside as well as from within. That is, he is calling upon Christians to reckon with public evil as well as with private sin, with the public evils in which we are complicit as well as those by which we are victimized. Such a theological perspective forces us to see God as "a very present help in trouble" (Ps. 46:1, KJV) and at the same time as the Judge who presses us to moral decision. So it is not enough for Christians to accept the Gospel assurance and praise God as the One who opens for us the way to eternal life if we do not also hear God's demand that we set aside selfishness and fear in order to participate generously in God's work of bringing forth justice in history (Isa. 42:3). It seems that this is the kind of one-sided reading of the Bible that Bonhoeffer had in mind when he said, "We still read the New Testament far too little on the basis of the Old."[11]

There are no better exemplars of such "worldly preaching" than the Old Testament prophets themselves. Moreover, to return to the point with which this essay began, the prophets engage the moral imagination not by explaining, but by showing. They show what the world looks like through God's eyes. They show us our own badly compromised moral situation, and they show God's anguished response: mingled pain and anger and yet also — strange to say of God — hope, hope that is not quenched even by the many disappointments that God suffers in history, and determination to save.

Most of this essay itself takes the form of showing rather than explain-

---

9. Bonhoeffer, *Letters and Papers from Prison*, p. 116.

10. The phrase is not, I believe, Bonhoeffer's own. However, it does capture his conviction that Christians and Christian theologians must see themselves as "wholly belonging to the world" (*Letters and Papers from Prison*, p. 92). Bonhoeffer's lectures on preaching from the Finkenwalde Seminary were published under this title: *Worldly Preaching: Lectures on Homiletics,* ed. Clyde Fant (New York: Crossroad, 1991). Shirley C. Guthrie articulates an understanding of a "worldly spirituality," based on the same conviction that Christian life is "in and for the world," in *Always Being Reformed: Faith for a Fragmented World* (Louisville: Westminster John Knox Press, 1996), pp. 77-91.

11. Bonhoeffer, *Letters and Papers from Prison*, p. 93.

ing my own view of how contemporary Christian preachers might learn from the biblical writers how to develop a more probing practice of "imaginative preaching." The two sermons (my own) that follow both focus on prophetic texts. They treat mostly "hard words" of the Prophets, passages that a preacher might normally wish to avoid — and that lectionaries often omit. (As an Episcopalian, I normally preach from a set lectionary. However, each of these sermons was preached at a special service — i.e., a service supplemental to the regular daily offices and Sunday Eucharistic services for which readings are prescribed — so I was free to choose the biblical readings.) Although I wrote and preached these sermons considerably before the present essay had taken shape in my mind, I see in retrospect that they anticipate its general direction to an extent that surprises me now. Particularly, I am struck by the strong visual element in each sermon — something of which I was not aware in the original writing or even in choosing them for inclusion here. The verbs "look," "see," and "gaze" occur thirty times in the first sermon, and twenty-three times in the second. (There are also numerous references to "eyes" and "vision.") Thus the sermons tacitly represent the prophets as people who see differently than we normally do, and whose way of seeing must inform our own, if we are to live faithfully in the world. In other words, both sermons imply that the prophetic books are shaping the church's imagination precisely as the faculty of theological and moral insight.

A second way in which these sermons anticipated the argument of the present essay is in grounding theological claims in concrete historical experience, including contemporary experience. The perspective is "worldly": I am trying to see both the created world and the human situation as the prophets saw them, although I stretch that worldly perspective to include our contemporary experience. Seeing as the prophets saw means, of course, witnessing to the presence of radical evil in our own society, recognizing the fundamental ways we habitually set ourselves against God. Both these sermons, then, are about sin, although in somewhat different ways. The first, preached at a service for "Earth Day," deals with the highly politicized sin of ecological destruction. The second, preached toward the end of Lent, treats sin in less immediately topical terms — although the prophetic lament over the sins of Jerusalem never loses its shocking freshness.

A note on how readers may use the sermons that follow in reflecting on their own preaching practices, practices either long-established or now under development: Each of the sermons is framed by comments that aim at tracing how I arrived at this particular interpretation of the text for this occasion in the church's life — that is, at this worship service, with this congregation, at this time in the church year, within this larger cultural context. In each case it is the interpretation of the text and its application to our Christian life that I offer as worthy of consideration. The sermons are not presented as rhetorical models. While I choose my words with care (and I am a manuscript preacher, so what you read here is what was spoken from the pulpit), rhetoric is not an area in which I am competent to teach or think in any depth. I am an Old Testament scholar, and the focus of my teaching is how the church may draw upon and be guided by the biblical text in its ministries. Therefore, I hope that what readers will find useful here is a certain style of imaginative engagement with the text. More specifically, I hope these sermons will suggest ways in which we may submit our imaginations to the text and follow it, perhaps into areas we might never have expected to find ourselves going. Genuine submission to the text is a distinctly countercultural concept in an academic culture that promotes a hermeneutics of suspicion. Yet as preachers, *under*-standing the text (as some of my students have put it) in the truest sense is essential if we are to be trusted to speak God's Word in the first instance, and not simply to rehearse our own personal passions.

One final prefatory comment: the Prophets are hard to hear. Sometimes what they show us about our situation, as it appears in God's eyes, is almost unbearable. An arrogant preacher can wield them like a hammer over a congregation. Yet, when properly handled, their honest disclosure can come as a relief. They can create "an opening of hope" (Hos. 2:15), the kind of resilient hope that rises in us when we are at last freed from our delusions. Therefore, preaching the Prophets requires delicacy — not timidity, but precision and accuracy in applying the text to the life of the congregation, as well as loving solidarity with the congregation in hearing the challenge of the text as addressed to us. The Apostle Paul's instruction to the church in Philippi is apt for this task: "May your gentleness be known to all people. The Lord is near" (Phil. 4:5). The nearness of the Lord is a word of both warning and encouragement. We stand together, awaiting Christ's coming in both judgment and mercy. Sensing the nearness of the Lord, we can afford to be gentle. Indeed, we can scarcely afford to be anything else.

First Sermon: Costly Vision

Preached on 17 April 2001

The Setting: This sermon was preached to my students (and their families) at the Virginia Theological Seminary (Episcopal). The evening worship service marked the conclusion of a week of events and discussion focusing on the ecological crisis and leading up to Earth Day. However, the sermon also takes account of the church calendar, which exercises a shaping influence on all Anglican worship. Earth Day regularly falls during the Easter season, and so I felt a certain salutary pressure to preach the "hard news" of Jeremiah's message explicitly in the context of the Resurrection. Jeremiah therefore appears here as a Janus-faced prophet who looks backward to the creation of the world and forward to a new and unbreakable covenant. Christians, of course, see that prophetic promise fulfilled in Jesus Christ. Yet, bearing in mind Bonhoeffer's dictum that "We still read the New Testament far too little on the basis of the Old," it is equally important to see that Jeremiah's stringent vision cautions against a facile understanding of resurrection hope.

The Sermon

Jeremiah 4:22-26

[Thus says the LORD:]
My people are stupid;
me, they know not.
They are foolish children;
they are not discerning.
They are wise in doing evil,
but good, they do not know how to do.
I see the earth, and here — it is without form and void;
and the heavens — and their light is gone.
I see the mountains, and here they are, rocking;
and all the hills palpitate.
I see, and here, there is no human being,
and all the birds of the heavens have fled.
I see, and here, the farmland is now the wasteland,

and all its cities are pulled down because of the LORD,
because of his hot anger.[12]

Jeremiah 31:31-37

Look, days are coming, says the LORD, when I will cut with the house of
Israel and the house of Judah a new covenant. Not like the covenant
which I cut with their ancestors in the day when I seized them by the
hand to bring them up from the land of Egypt — my covenant which
they broke, though I was their husband, says the LORD. For this is the
covenant which I will cut with the house of Israel after those days, says
the LORD. I will put my Torah *inside* them, yes, on their hearts I will
write it; and I will become their God, and they shall become my people.
No longer shall a person teach neighbor or kinsman, saying, "Know the
LORD!" Rather, all of them shall know me, from the littlest to the greatest, says the LORD. For I will forgive their iniquity, and their sin I will no
longer recall.

No one should ever have to see what Jeremiah saw. What other prophets had foreseen and warned about, and hoped against hope would never
happen, Jeremiah saw with his own eyes. He saw Jerusalem laid in ruins by
Nebuchadnezzar's raging army; he heard her panting and moaning like a
woman: "*Oy li,* woe is me, for I am fainting before killers" (4:31). And he
saw more. As our passage this evening attests, Jeremiah's vision widened —
against his will, surely — and he saw the whole earth laid waste:

I see the earth, and here — it is without form and void
     [*tohu vabohu*];
and the heavens — and their light is gone.

(4:23)

"I see the earth. . . . I see the mountains; *ra'iti,* I see, I see" — Jeremiah
speaks in chapter 4 as one who has learned to see as God sees. He has shed
his illusions, his blinders, his false optimism. And now, with eyes wide
open, he sees the terrible inverse of what God saw in the first week of the
world. He sees the undoing of creation, step by step: human beings —

---

12. Unless otherwise indicated, this and all biblical citations in the sermon are the author's own translations.

vanished; birds of the air — all fled; fertile farmland stripped of vegetation, reverted to wilderness; lights out in the heavens. Jeremiah's prophetic vision is like a film running backward until it gets to the very first frame — *tohu vabohu* (Gen. 1:2), waste schmaste, absolute chaos — and clicks off.

No one should ever see what Jeremiah saw. Yet as twenty-first-century Christians, we are obliged to see it. Five years ago I went to AMERC, the Appalachian Ministries Educational Resources Center, in Berea, Kentucky. I went because a friend whose judgment I trust said, "You must go. There are things you need to see." So with a small group of faculty from various seminaries and Christian colleges, I toured the mountains. I learned a little about the culture of the mountain people — very little, I'm sure. But more importantly, in that week I learned something about my own mainstream urban North American culture. To my astonishment, I learned that the people of Appalachia pay no small part of the cost of my lifestyle. Other states pay the state of Kentucky to let us dump our garbage there. It is possible that some of the wood for my new house in Durham comes from their mountains, which are being methodically stripped of their forests. And then the bare mountains are themselves "removed" — that is, blown to bits — to take out the coal veins that cannot be reached by conventional mining methods.

We visited the office of a mining company, heard the manager's presentation, and then spoke briefly with a few miners who worked in the deep mine, with tunnels and coal carts. Then, under close supervision, we were permitted to enter the removal area. Maybe they let us in because we were professors and thought to have a purely "academic" interest, or maybe because we were church people and assumed to be harmless. Somehow I did not really get it as we rode up the mountain, until we came around to the far side — or what should have been the far side, except it wasn't there anymore. They'd blown it away completely, de-created that segment of the Appalachians — the oldest mountains on this continent, aren't they? — the place where God began work on this quadrant of the globe.

The shuddering, wordless horror I felt is what I imagine one must feel standing within the gates of Auschwitz, witnessing an evil so absolute, it is all but unimaginable. Yet the perverted human imagination had conceived it and brought it into being. Evil so stark it is in any ordinary terms unspeakable, and then I realized that Jeremiah had spoken of it:

105

I see the mountains, and here they are, rocking;
and all the hills palpitate.
I see, and here, there is no human being,
and all the birds of the heavens have fled.
I see, and here, the farmland is now the wasteland.

(4:24-26)

No one should see mountains exploding in Kentucky so that we may defer for a few more years the inevitable, yet initially costly, conversion to sustainable forms of fuel. No one should see the hills of West Virginia blown apart, then the infertile rubble shoveled together into vast tracts incapable of sustaining any form of life — though they will do for building shopping malls. Malls in the place of mountains — no one should ever see that; but the people of Appalachia do see it, and many of them currently depend upon it for a living. They are caught up with us in an extractive economy that is increasingly tragic and desperate, for it seems to leave us, in the immediate, no choice but to destroy what God's hands have made. Of course, the destruction is not random. It happens first, and worst, not in the backyards of the powerful but in the homelands of the poor: in the hollows of West Virginia and Kentucky, in tropical rain forests, on the tundra of Alaska and Siberia. In response to the common defense that we really have no choice, God's judgment is clear:

My people are stupid;
me, they know not.
They are foolish children;
they are not discerning.
They are wise in doing evil,
but good, they do not know how to do.

(4:22)

It would be easier to preach on this subject if Earth Day fell during Lent. Then I might feel justified in announcing that the situation is grim, which is true enough, and be done with it. But by the providence of God, Earth Day falls within the Easter season. So my job is to consider this question: What, in this situation, does it mean for us to claim Christ's resurrected life as our own? Because this subject is so emotionally, economically, and politically charged, the danger of delusion and self-delusion is great.

So I'm going to begin with what resurrection hope does *not* mean in our present ecological crisis.

Resurrection hope does *not* mean that things are not as bad as they seem. It does not mean that we may expect to be shielded from the worst effects of our selfishness — although, if we are honest, probably every one of us nurtures at least some hope of that. But resurrection hope does not mean protection for us as long as we remain committed to self-serving goals. Nor does it mean that piles which once were mountains will again sustain life. I do not believe that we can in good resurrection faith pray that they will, so long as we continue to show contempt for the work of God's hands. Those mountains are dead, and we killed them. If realistic resurrection hope is to take root in us at all, then it will begin with that recognition. As the biblical prophets repeatedly insist, hope will take root in the place that judgment has prepared. When we are able to see ourselves in the same way that God sees us — that is, when we can accept God's judgment on ourselves and our actions — then real hope can strike root and begin to grow.

Jeremiah's message, which accords fully with the message of the Gospel, is that things are every bit as bad as they seem, and for the simplest of all reasons. As usual, the prophet puts it to us straight:

> The heart is more perverse than anything,
> and it is sick beyond what anyone can know.
>
> (17:9)

The human heart is sick beyond what anyone can know. Yet together, Jeremiah and the Gospel affirm that the heart can be regenerated. That is the resurrection hope and the source of all righteous joy — not that God will miraculously undo the destruction we have accomplished, but that by the grace of God, we can turn back to God and never stray away again.

That hope of a thoroughly regenerated heart is what Jeremiah expresses in his vision of "a new covenant":

> Not like the covenant which I cut with their ancestors in the day when I seized them by the hand to bring them up from the land of Egypt — my covenant which they broke, though I was their husband, says the LORD. For this is the covenant which I will cut with the house of Israel after those days, says the LORD. I will put my Torah *inside* them, yes, on their

hearts I will write it; and I will become their God, and they shall become my people. (31:32-33)

I propose that when God speaks here of a new covenant, the vision has the same global scope as the earlier vision of destruction. Just as Jeremiah looks back to the first week of the world and witnesses the undoing of God's whole creation, so this vision of the new covenant also looks back into primeval history. It recapitulates the moment when God made an eternal covenant with Noah and his seed, but also "with every living thing that is with you" (Gen. 9:12) and even "with the earth" itself (9:13).[13] In other words, because the devastation that Jeremiah sees is total, all-encompassing, then so also must the covenantal restoration be total. We are starting over from scratch. Therefore, God can say of Israel, "I will *become* their God, and they shall *become* my people." The covenant written on our hearts means that God at last finds a way to overcome our sick-heartedness, so that we humans might be, for the first time in the history of the world, fully in communion with God.

Likewise, I believe that the new covenant means that we might be, for the first time in the history of the world, fully in community with the other creatures of God, even and maybe especially the nonhuman creatures whom our sin-sick hearts have neglected or despised. A new covenant written on our hearts means that we might for the first time take our proper place as fellow creatures with everyone else whom God has made in love: with every mountain, with the soil and the trees that clothe it, with the animals and the birds that are at home on its slopes, no less than with the people who are at home in its hollows.

Jeremiah's twin visions of devastation and restoration are pushing us toward this comprehensive understanding of covenant, but it is only Jesus Christ who can bring us Gentiles into it — or, more accurately, Jesus Christ brings it into us, inscribing it on hearts that without him could not receive the imprint. And in him, the universal, minutely inclusive scope of

13. The immediate reference in the passage cited is, of course, to the Sinai covenant. However, the argument that the prophet's vision extends back to creation is supported not only by the book of Jeremiah itself, but also by the fact the book of Exodus in numerous places picks up the language and themes of the creation account, implying that the Sinai covenant stands in essential continuity with creation and the covenant established through Noah. See Terence Fretheim, *Exodus: Interpretation: A Bible Commentary for Teaching and Preaching* (Louisville: John Knox Press, 1991).

this new covenant is fully revealed, for Jesus Christ is nothing other than "the firstborn of all creation" (Col. 1:15). "In him all things in heaven and earth were created" (1:16) — and further, "in him all things hold together" (1:17). "In him all things hold together" — the letter to the Colossians[14] is speaking here of global reconciliation, "every creature under heaven" receiving the Gospel hope (1:23) and coming together in "peace" (1:20) — that is, every creature joined in community with every other creature, and all of us, as one, reconciled to God. That is what it means to say that God in Christ is even now "making peace through the blood of his cross" (1:20).

Jeremiah's prophetic vision and Colossians' apostolic one persuade me that the church's most important work in the twenty-first century is to commit itself fully to Christ's work of making peace among all creatures, human and nonhuman. Yet, it is through the blood of the *cross* that peace is being made. That astonishing statement makes it clear that we are talking about sacrifice — that is, about making our lives holy, and doing it at some cost to ourselves. It's going to cost us to commit ourselves to Christ's work of reconciliation; it will cost us our false hopes, our old heedless habits of consumption. It will require from us, as individuals and even more as a society, a large investment of scientific imagination: How can we act on the world without undoing creation? It will require from us (and here, I believe, the church in industrialized regions must lead the way) restraint, a willingness to do with less, because we recognize that the gratification of our desires currently extracts too high a price from others. "Sacrifice" and "restraint" are dirty words in a culture committed to ever-more-aggressive and rapacious economic strategies. My prayer is that the church will in this decade, at this crucial juncture in creation history, be the voice that articulates the blessing that always — always — attends genuine sacrifice. This we know for sure: Where true sacrifice is offered — when human life is made holy, at some cost to ourselves — there God creates abundance, giving life and more life, against the odds and beyond all calculation.

That is the substance of the resurrection hope that the church is charged first to believe, second to practice, and third to proclaim in the midst of an industrial culture committed to degradation and death. May our risen Lord give us understanding and courage to hold fast to that hope in which we are, even now, being saved (Rom. 8:24). Amen.

---

14. The second Scripture lesson read at the service was Colossians 1:11-20.

Guidance from the Text

In preaching a sermon as politically and economically charged as this one, the issue of submitting our imagination to the guidance of the text is especially crucial. Indeed, the central issue in the text has to do with the health and faithfulness of the human imagination. Following Jeremiah, I contrast the works of a perverted imagination ("The heart is more perverse than anything . . .") that have brought us to this present crisis with the vision of a heart regenerated by God, which makes it possible for us to choose a "lifestyle" of sacrifice and restraint — that is, a life of reconciliation with God and our fellow creatures.

The scope of Jeremiah's vision provides the hermeneutical key for the sermon. I found that I could not be faithful to the vision of the book by confining myself to a single passage.[15] I must admit that, when I reread Jeremiah 4 again, some time after witnessing "mountaintop removal," I felt (as I still do) that it may well represent our present situation. Yet because it was the Easter season, I was constrained to look beyond that simple (and unconsoling) reading of our situation before God, to Jeremiah's message of new life for a people who, it seemed, were irremediably alienated from God. However, the fact that Jeremiah 4 was now lodged firmly in my mind meant that I preached the familiar words of Jeremiah 31 in a different way than I might otherwise have done — if, say, I had begun planning a sermon with the events of Easter primarily as the central theme. It now seemed to me that the "gospel" of Jeremiah 31 must be preached in such a way that the image of destruction in Jeremiah 4 would not be erased from our minds.

The relation between the two passages within the book of Jeremiah is indeed something like the relationship between the Old and the New Testaments, at least as most Christians think of them: bad news followed by good news. (In fact, there is plenty of "good news" in the Old Testament,

15. For the purposes of preaching, I bracket the question of whether these passages from chapters 4 and 31 both originate with the prophet himself or whether, as is likely, the latter is the addition of a Deuteronomistic editor. What I am articulating is the vision offered by the whole book of Jeremiah, which is in its present form authoritative for the church's life. I take that vision to be closely related to the vision of the sixth-century prophet by that name, although I allow for the possibility and likelihood that his vision was extended and his message amplified by the circle that preserved his words and produced what we know as his book.

and plenty of divine judgment of sin in the New Testament.) Of course, our tendency is to skip over a passage like Jeremiah 4 — indeed, probably relatively few Christians have ever heard it — and return repeatedly to the passage that comforts us. But I am reminded of Dietrich Bonhoeffer's comment on the shift that took place in his own theology during the first months of his imprisonment:

> My thoughts and feelings seem to be getting more and more like the Old Testament, and no wonder, I have been reading it much more than the New for the last few months. . . . It is only when one loves life and the earth so much that without them everything would be gone, that one can believe in the resurrection and a new world. It is only when one submits to the law that one can speak of grace, and only when one sees the anger and wrath of God hanging like grim realities over the head of one's enemies that one can know something of what it means to love them and forgive them. I don't think it is Christian to want to get to the New Testament too soon and too directly. *You cannot and must not speak the last word before you have spoken the next to last.* We live on the next to last word, and believe on the last, don't we?[16]

As Bonhoeffer suggests, it is not "Christian" — because it is not sufficiently worldly — to rush past the word that accuses us in order to get to the soothing word. In the sermon offered here, "the next to last word" of Jeremiah 4, which I hear as a challenge to our political and economic practices, is the indispensable preface to our rightly hearing "the last word," the gospel of a costly reconciliation with God.

Second Sermon: Lament over Jerusalem

Preached on 24 March 1999

The Setting: As this essay is written, the second Intifada in Jerusalem is now far into its second year, and most of the world is watching the daily news with ap-

---

16. Bonhoeffer, excerpt from a letter written on the Second Sunday of Advent, 1943 (italics mine), in *Letters and Papers from Prison*, p. 50.

prehension. Right now, a sermon on the prophetic lament over Jerusalem as "the city of blood(shed)" reads as though it were motivated by the headlines and had a primarily political agenda. In fact, however, it was in the first instance the liturgical season and in the second a particular class assignment that gave rise to this sermon. The season was the latter part of Lent, nine days before Good Friday 1999. The class was a semester-long seminar in "The Gospel Narrative in Art," taught at Virginia Theological Seminary. As a final assignment, the students were to design a worship service of meditation on the Passion of Christ, using the visual arts along with music and Scripture readings; they invited me to be the homilist.

As the students, their teacher (printmaker and sculptor Margaret Adams Parker), and I worked with various visual images of the Passion, the idea for the sermon presented itself to me as something like a visual image: I saw Jesus standing clearly in the line of the biblical prophets, lamenting over Jerusalem even as he faced his own death in the city that had already killed so many of those whom God had sent. The design of the service traced this line. After an opening prayer, we heard readings from Jeremiah, Zephaniah, and Zechariah. As each was read, an artistic image was displayed on a screen in the front of the sanctuary: for example, the reading from Jeremiah (8:18–9:3) was accompanied by Emil Nolde's stark 1912 woodcut entitled *The Prophet*. The prophetic readings were followed by a hymn ("O Sacred Head, Sore Wounded"), psalms of lament (Pss. 55:4-14; 94:16-22), and finally by Jesus' own lament over Jerusalem (Matt. 23:37-39), the words with which the sermon itself begins.

THE SERMON

> Jerusalem, Jerusalem, the city that kills the prophets and stones those who are sent to her! How often have I desired to gather your children together as a hen gathers her brood under her wings, and you were not willing! (Matt. 23:37)[17]

We are approaching Golgotha, but we are not there yet. Nine days from now, we will move to that barren ground outside the city, but tonight we are still within her walls, in the very heart of Jerusalem. These are our

17. Unless otherwise noted, the biblical citations in this sermon are slightly modified from the New Revised Standard Version, which was used for all readings in the worship service.

Lord's last days in the city that is the geographical center of Israel's imagination, the focal point of so much hope, so many visions, so much grief and tumult: Jerusalem, *'iyr haddamim,* "the city of blood[shed]" (Ezek. 22:2), as Ezekiel calls her, that generates so much opposition to God. "Jerusalem, Jerusalem, the city that kills the prophets . . ." — it is here that Jesus rises to take his place in the line of murdered prophets, the very next one to die because he tells the truth about what he sees in Jerusalem. And what does Jesus see in the city? What all the prophets who testified and died before him saw. Zephaniah, for instance:

> Ah, soiled, defiled, oppressing city!
> She has listened to no voice,
> she has accepted no discipline.
> In the LORD she has not trusted,
> and to her God she has not drawn near.
>
> (Zeph. 3:1; author's translation)

"She has listened to no voice." Time and again, God has sent her prophets; and they have been disbelieved, mocked, imprisoned, deported, killed. "To her God she has not drawn near." How often would God have gathered her people in, as a brood-hen gathers in chicks against the cold, against fear, against the fox. But they went their own ways, to their destruction.

Now, in these final days in the city, the last and greatest of the prophets takes his place in the long line of those who lament over Jerusalem. Tradition has it that Jesus stood on the Mount of Olives, to the east, just opposite the Temple. There he would often spend the night after a day of teaching in the city. Today a small church, shaped like a teardrop, stands on the site; it's called *Dominus Flevit,* "the Lord wept" (cf. Luke 19:41). Jesus wept bitterly, just as Jeremiah had before him:

> My joy is gone; grief is upon me;
> my heart is sick.
> Hark, the loud cry of my poor people from the far corners
>   of the land:
> "Could it be that the LORD is absent from Zion?
> that her King is gone from her?"
>
> (Jer. 8:18-19)

Jeremiah, it seems, is the first prophet to utter the terrible suspicion that God may no longer be present in Jerusalem.

"Could it be that the LORD is absent from Zion?" Like most big questions in the Bible, it is not possible to answer that one finally, yes or no. The question cannot and should not be answered definitely because it is an opening into a bigger problem — one of the deepest problems of the Bible, and surely one of the most painful. This problem: How is it that God's radical holiness can be found in the same place that radical evil is also found — in the same city, even, as we know from personal experience, in the same heart? That is the terrible mystery that moves Jesus to tears as he stands gazing at Jerusalem.

He weeps because he knows what prophets and psalmists have said for centuries about Jerusalem. Yes, God is in the midst of her. Yet our Holy God cannot abide in the presence of evil. So Habakkuk: "Your eyes are too pure to see evil, and to look upon wrongdoing — you cannot" (Hab. 1:13). It's a statement not of God's moral squeamishness but rather of the absolute incompatibility between evil and the presence of God. It's like oil and water: you can't mix them and expect the mixture to be stable (cf. also Ps. 94:20). That is the simple metaphysical fact that lies at the heart of centuries of lament over Jerusalem. God cannot long abide in the presence of evil, and so God must leave the city of blood.

Ezekiel is the prophet who witnesses to that clearly, unforgettably. Ezekiel sees the glory of the LORD rising up, a luminous cloud, out of the Holy of Holies. He actually sees the divine glory depart from Jerusalem, abandoning "the bloody city" to her enemies, Nebuchadnezzar's army. The vision is agonizingly protracted. It extends over four chapters, as though Ezekiel, that painstaking prophet, must tell every single detail because he can scarcely believe what he sees: God is leaving Jerusalem. But there is another reason Ezekiel tells the vision so slowly. It's because God leaves slowly, with awful reluctance. For all the grandeur of the scene — the glory of the LORD mounting up into the air on a great chariot throne, the golden cherubim of the Holy of Holies now become animate — for all that grandeur, you cannot help but feel sorry for God, who is, after all, leaving home. Remember the moment when the chariot throne stops on the Mount of Olives (Ezek. 11:23), just opposite the Temple, the last spot from which you can see Jerusalem, before descending into the eastern wilderness? Like Lot's wife, God turns back once to gaze in yearning sadness at the beloved home, which is consigned to destruction.

And now, six centuries later, Jesus stands in the same place on the Mount of Olives, at the edge of the wilderness; and he weeps. Again, Jeremiah gives us words to amplify the Gospel:

> O that my head were water,
> and my eye a fountain of tears,
> that I might weep day and night for the slain of my poor people!
> O that I had in the wilderness a travelers' lodging place,
> so that I might leave my people and go away from them!
> For they are all adulterers, a band of traitors.
> They bend their tongues as a bow,
> for falsehood and not for truth,
> they grow mighty in the land,
> for they go from evil to evil,
> but me they do not know, says the LORD.
>
> (8:23–9:2, Heb.; 9:1-3, Eng.; author's translation)

"O that I had a lodging in the wilderness, so that I might . . . go away! . . . For my people goes from evil to evil. . . ." God's glory cannot abide in the presence of evil. Ezekiel saw that clearly. Jeremiah saw it, and he wept. Now Jesus, gazing at Jerusalem, confronts that same absolute incompatibility that constitutes the tragedy of this world: between God's presence, yearning to give life and joy, and our persistent evil in God's face. And what we will see and experience over the next nine or ten days is the ultimate consequence of that incompatibility. But note this: What we will see is the very opposite of what Ezekiel saw. For Ezekiel saw God's glory departing over the Mount of Olives toward the wilderness. But now we see God in Christ returning to the city over that same hill, returning to the city to die. God departed the city mounted on a chariot throne. In Jesus the Christ, God enters Jerusalem in deepest humility, mounted on a colt, the foal of an ass. God left, driven out by the oppressive presence of human sin. Now God returns to take all that sin upon him and die on a cross.

The contrast is stunning: God, who once abandoned the bloody city, now enters her to die. As Christians, we believe and proclaim that this change in the divine response literally makes all the difference in the world. Yet one thing we must understand. It is not a difference between the God of the Old Testament and the God of the New Testament. Rather, the prophets already show us that massive, world-tilting shift in how God answers the sins of Jerusalem. The prophets don't explain the shift any more than do the evangelists. But they leave us in no doubt whatsoever that a change has taken place in God's heart. So Zechariah:

> Thus says the LORD of Hosts,
> "I am jealous for Zion with great jealousy,
> and with great fierceness I am jealous for her."
> Thus says the LORD,
> "I shall return to Zion,
> and I shall dwell in the midst of Jerusalem.
> And Jerusalem will be called the city of faithfulness. . . .
> And I shall bring my people [back out of exile],
> and they will dwell in the midst of Jerusalem. . . ."
>
> (Zech. 8:2-3, 8; author's translation)

"I am jealous for Zion with great jealousy, and with great fierceness. . . ." "Fierceness" — the Hebrew word is *chemah* — literally means "heated emotion." And what does God's heated response to Jerusalem mean? Something like this: God's jealous love burns so hot that it melts down the opposition that comes from Jerusalem herself. God's jealousy means that finally God will not take "no" for an answer; the divine Lover will not be refused. And consider this: when that jealousy is fully fired, it is revelatory. It reveals the one simple fact on which all our hope depends: though human sin is real, ghastly real, it is not ultimate. Sin and its ravages belong to the things that are passing away. And what the Prophets show us is that in God's mind, that has already happened; sin has passed away. So Zechariah testifies to God's jealous dream of Jerusalem once more called a faithful city, God and people living together again, and now happily ever after. See what has happened: for a moment at least, Jerusalem's deep, hardened opposition has become immaterial in God's sight. In a hot flash of divine passion, that glacial reality of sinfulness melts; it vaporizes in an instant.

But what does that mean in concrete, historical terms? That question presses us hard, for it is a sad fact that human sin appears to shape our world more powerfully than do God's dreams. Indeed, history often seems to be a cruel distorting-mirror image of God's will for the world. So, through Zechariah, God shares a dream of Jerusalem, the faithful city; and yet five centuries later there is still no visible improvement; and God in Christ returns to the city, not to dwell in peace, but to die in agony. So the Gospel proclaims that Jesus Christ died, taking our sins upon him; and yet twenty centuries later we are still mired in them, and the whole created world groans in agony from the burden.

Yet we say that God's jealousy for Jerusalem makes all the difference in the world. We say that God's hot-burning love, seen most clearly flaming out from the cross — we say that fire is consuming sin and death; in the fullness of time it is melting down those primeval glaciers of opposition to God that now loom so large in our lives. We say that God's jealousy for Jerusalem makes all the difference in the world. Just what difference does it make for us, this evening, this Lent, this time of walking the way of the cross? This difference: As long as we are in this world, it tells us where to focus our attention — not on the ghastly spectacle of human sin, but on the one who is willingly wounded by it. Zechariah shows us where the way of healing lies for our sin-sick hearts, for God's wounded world. Just here: "And I shall pour out on the house of David and on the inhabitant(s) of Jerusalem a spirit of grace and supplication, so that, when they look upon him whom they have pierced, they will mourn over him as one mourns over an only child, and weep bitterly over him, as one weeps over a firstborn" (Zech. 12:10). Look here; look on him, pierced by our sin. Look long and hard, as long as you are in this world; and pray that we may receive God's grace and a steady spirit of supplication, so that we may day by day be transformed by what we see, changed into the likeness of the One on whom we gaze, the One whom we have pierced.

Guidance from the Text

This sermon does not reflect on a specific text (as do almost all my sermons) but rather on an event, the event that stands at the center of the Christian life. This meditation on the Passion differs from most in that it does not focus on the scene at Golgotha and the symbol of the cross. Not wanting to pre-empt Good Friday (which was then more than a week away), I decided to locate the sermon earlier in the Gospel narrative, focusing on Jesus' last days in Jerusalem. Jerusalem, as it is represented in the Prophets and the Gospels, is then the guiding image for the meditation; it provides the unity of theological vision, which in most cases I would find by following a single text.[18]

Jerusalem is here treated not as a political entity but as a spiritual one. It is the place where God's commitment to humanity is most strongly felt, the place where God's love burns hottest, and therefore where God's own suffering is most intense. I examine marks of that commitment and suffering in both Testaments. I hold the two Testaments together by narrowing the geographic focus to one point in Jerusalem: the Mount of Olives. I chose that place first because it is the traditional site of Jesus' lament over Jerusalem (Matt. 23:37-38; cf. 24:3), and then other biblical events that occurred there presented themselves to my imagination. Anyone entering or leaving the city by the eastern route must pass over the Mount of Olives, and suddenly I saw what I had never seen before: the direct inverse relation between God's departure from the Temple in Ezekiel and Jesus' return to Jerusalem to die — both of them divine responses to human sin. An important emphasis in the sermon is that *both* Testaments witness to a shift in God's response, from wrath to compassion. We see it in the Prophets no less than in the account of Jesus' Passion. As all those who preach seriously from the Old Testament know, the popular (among Christians) contrast between "the Old Testament God of wrath" and "the New Testament God of love" is a caricature that breaks down within minutes of beginning to read Israel's Scriptures with care. What regularly happens when a Christian reads the Old Testament with an eye to the Gospel is that the story of God's love in Christ is immeasurably illumined, deepened, and clarified by the long history of God's covenantal relationship with Israel — a history, like the Gospel, of mingled joy and pain on both sides, of wild hope and bitter disappointment, of shaken but unbreakable love.

Like the biblical writers, I make no attempt to explain the shift that I trace here in God's response to our sin, or to explain why Jesus' death does not end the problem of sin once and for all. These things are not subject to rational explanation; and as I suggested at the outset, zeal for explanation bestows the kiss of death on biblical preaching. The main aim of the sermon, like the visual artworks that were displayed throughout the service, is simply to help us to see better, to focus our attention on the mysterious truth that God suffers willingly for our sake.

18. As noted above, the preceding sermon is a slight exception in that I work with two passages from a single book of the Bible.

Touch the Earth Lightly

Touch the earth lightly, use the earth gently,
nourish the life of the world in our care:
gift of great wonder, ours to surrender,
trust for the children tomorrow will bear.

We who endanger, who create hunger,
agents of death for all creatures that live,
we who would foster clouds of disaster,
God of our planet, forestall and forgive!

Let there be greening, birth from the burning,
water that blesses and air that is sweet,
health in God's garden, hope in God's children,
regeneration that peace will complete.

God of all living, God of all loving,
God of the seedling, the snow and the sun,
teach us, deflect us, Christ re-connect us,
using us gently and making us one.

Text: Shirley Erena Murray (b. 1931), 1991
Text copyright © 1992 Hope Publishing Company, Carol Stream, IL 60188. All rights reserved.
Used by permission.

Great God, Your Love Has Called Us Here

Great God, Your love has called us here
as we, by love, for love were made.
Your living likeness still we bear,
though marred, dishonored, disobeyed.
We come, with all our heart and mind,
Your call to hear, Your love to find.

We come with self-inflicted pains
of broken trust and chosen wrong;
half-free, half-bound by inner chains,
by social forces swept along,
by powers and systems close confined
yet seeking hope for humankind.

Great God, in Christ You call our name
and then receive us as Your own
not through some merit, right, or claim
but by Your gracious love alone.
We strain to glimpse Your mercy seat
and find You kneeling at our feet.

Then take the towel, and break the bread,
and humble us, and call us friends.
Suffer and serve till all are fed
and show how grandly love intends
to work till all creation sings,
to fill all worlds, to crown all things.

Great God, in Christ You set us free
Your life to live, Your joy to share.
Give us Your Spirit's liberty
to turn from guilt and dull despair
and offer all that faith can do
while love is making all things new.

Text: Brian Wren (b. 1936), 1973
Text copyright © 1977, rev. 1995 Hope Publishing Company, Carol Stream, IL 60188. All rights reserved. Used by permission.

FOR FURTHER READING

Abraham Joshua Heschel. *The Prophets* (New York: Harper & Row, 1962). Heschel's classic study still offers the best introduction to the thought of the biblical prophets. His profound theological insight and poetic style seem to reflect their own passion for God.

L. Gregory Jones and James J. Buckley, eds. *Theology and Scriptural Imagination* (Oxford/Malden, Mass.: Blackwell Publishers, 1998). This is a collection of seven useful essays that consider various styles of engagement with Scripture, both past (e.g., medieval allegory, Calvin's commentaries) and present (feminist, historical criticism), with an eye to how they do or do not encourage an imaginative opening from within the Bible of new possibilities for Christian theology and identity.

Christopher Seitz. *Word Without End: The Old Testament as Abiding Theological Witness* (Grand Rapids/Cambridge: Eerdmans, 1998). This is an excellent anthology of essays by an important Old Testament scholar, treating major issues in biblical hermeneutics and theology (e.g., the nature of the biblical witness and its authority), as well as practical matters concerning the use of the Bible for teaching and preaching (e.g., "Isaiah in Parish Bible Study").

Finding a Treasure Map:
Sacred Space in the Old Testament

CORRINE L. CARVALHO

1 KINGS 8

But does God truly dwell on earth?
Indeed, not even the heavens, even the highest heavens,
    can contain you,
let alone this house, which I have built.
Yet, may you turn toward the prayer of your servant,
    and to his supplication, O Yahweh, my God,
To listen to the ringing cry and the prayer which your servant
    is praying before you today.
Let your eyes be opened towards this house night and day,
towards the place about which you said "My name will be there!"
so that you might hear the prayer which your servant prays
    towards this place.
May you listen to the supplication of your servant
    and of your people, Israel, who also pray towards this place.
May you hear from[1] your dwelling place, from the heavens.
May you hear and may you have mercy. (author's translation)

1 Kings 8:27-30

Then he brought me to the gate, that is, the gate which faces
    the eastern road.
And, there, the glory of the God of Israel was coming from the east.
Its sound was like the sound of many waters, and the earth
    glowed from his glory.
It was similar to the appearance of the vision which I had seen
when he had come to ruin the city;
the vision was like the vision which I had seen at the river Chebar.
I bowed to the ground.[2]
The glory of Yahweh came to the house through the gate,
    which faced east.
The spirit lifted me up and brought me to the inner courtyard.
And there, the glory of Yahweh filled the house.
I heard someone speaking to me from the house,
although the man was standing right next to me.
He said to me,

---

1. Reading with 2 Chronicles 6:21.
2. The literal translation of this is "I fell on my face," a biblical idiom of prostration.

Son of man, this is the place for my throne and the place
      for the soles of my feet,
where I will dwell among the children of Israel forever. . . .
You, son of man, tell the house of Israel about this house,
      so that they will be ashamed of their sins.
When they measure its dimensions,
then they will be ashamed of all they have done.
Make known to them the design of the house and its arrangements
      both for exits and for entrances,
yes, all of its dimensions, and all of its statutes; all of its dimensions
      and all of its laws.
Write it down for their own eyes,
so that they will preserve all of its dimensions and all of its statutes,
      and carry them out.
This is the law of the house:
upon the top of the mountain and all of its boundaries around it
      is most holy.
Yes, this is the law of the house. (author's translation)

Ezekiel 43:1-7a, 10-12

Looking for a Map

Christians can have a hard time appreciating texts such as 1 Kings 6–8 and Ezekiel 40–48, both of which describe the temple in Jerusalem. One can discern how inherently static and nationalistic they sound. These texts seem to reflect Israel's "chosen-ness" to the exclusion, or at least demotion, of all other peoples. R. Giles perhaps expresses our reaction most clearly when he writes, "The building of the Jerusalem temple was a tremendous feat, but it was apostasy. The Jewish religion thereby was nationalized, centralized, and politicized; it became static."[3] After all, Christ comes to all people, not to a particular nation. Jesus is present across national, ethnic, and class boundaries, and God's presence is surely dynamic.

So if Christianity has such a dynamic sense of God's presence, why do churches today often feel empty, static, even "nationalized"? I often hear

3. R. Giles, *Re-Pitching the Tent: Re-Ordering the Church Building for Worship and Mission*, rev. ed. (Collegeville, Minn.: Liturgical Press, 1999), p. 25.

people express dissatisfaction with "church" today. A colleague bemoans contemporary church architecture. An older parishioner states her annoyance at receiving communion from someone wearing shorts. A seminarian notes he hates "guitar" Mass. It seems we have lost a sense of the sacred. When people today think about a place that feels "holy" to them, they may think about a beautiful place where they have felt close to God. How often do they think of a church building? As a recent book title proclaims, many contemporary churches are *Ugly as Sin*.[4]

Is the desire for a renewed notion of sacred space simply a matter of fashion or aesthetics? Is it just that we yearn for "prettier" churches, "grander" architecture, better musical performances, and a return to the notion of "Sunday best"? Or does this dissatisfaction stem from something else, something deeper, something — dare I say it — theological? Have we lost our map that helps us locate *God's* holy place?

Finding an Ancient Map: The Temple in 1 Kings and Ezekiel

The ancient Israelites knew God's address: the temple in Jerusalem. While this was not God's exclusive or even primary residence, it was the address God gave Israel for divine encounters. If you were to ask the average church member today what they know about this place, they may recall the scene from the New Testament where Jesus "cleanses" the temple. A few may recall that Solomon built the temple and placed the Ark of the Covenant there, while fewer still would know about the sacrifices and pilgrimages that took place in and around the temple. I would guess that only a very few would realize how central the theology of the temple was for ancient Israelites, how often it lies behind both Old and New Testament texts, and how it continues to inform Christian theology. If we want to retrieve a sense of the sacred, perhaps we need to start with these primary biblical texts.

In ancient Israel, the theology of God's presence was also a theology of God's absence. The Israelites had to deal with two aspects of divine presence. On the one hand, this presence was permanent, stable, and reliable

---

4. M. S. Rose, *Ugly as Sin: Why They Changed Our Churches from Sacred Places to Meeting Spaces — And How We Can Change Them Back Again* (Manchester, N.H.: Sophia Institute, 2001).

because it was a manifestation of God, who was also reliable, trustworthy, and true to the covenants made with the people. On the other hand, the Israelites themselves recognized that their own experience of God varied. At some points God seemed closer, more present. For instance, God "appeared" on certain festivals; similarly, certain places were experienced as more sacred, more holy, more infused with God's presence than others. Temple texts reflect these dual sides of the human experience of God's presence for the community. Metaphors, an essential element in any language about God, helped the Israelites negotiate the complexities of God's presence. The predominant metaphor used to convey notions of God's real presence with the Israelites was that of domestic architecture, what today we call the temple.[5]

The domestic background of the temple is evident throughout Israelite temple texts. There is no word for "temple" in Hebrew; instead, the word used most often is *bêt* or "house," and sometimes "palace" *(hêkal)*. The priests who served at the temple were God's "servants," and the sacrifices resembled meals or banquets. The temple was actually a complex of structures, much like rich homes, including courtyards, separate areas for butchering and cooking, and storerooms. The focal point of the complex was the sanctuary building, which housed the object that represented the divine resident's presence. That presence was housed in an inner room that was often windowless, allowing the resident cool rest or sleep. Certainly neither all activities nor all structures within the temple reflected this domestic metaphor, but the temple as "house" remained predominant. God in the temple was like a royal resident in a palace. The walls of the courtyards restricted public access to God. Some priests served God, while others acted as bodyguards and gatekeepers. The quality of items devoted to God was strictly monitored. Items that "came in contact" with God were considered holy.

Throughout the ancient Near East, the presence of divine beings within a temple was represented in a concrete way. The Babylonians depicted their deities with anthropomorphic statues. These statues — or idols, as the Israelites called them — were actualized or made effective con-

---

5. The monograph by M. Haran remains a good introduction to temples in ancient Israel: *Temple and Temple-Service in Ancient Israel: An Inquiry into the Character of Cult Phenomena and the Historical Setting of the Priestly School*, rev. ed. (Winona Lake, Ind.: Eisenbrauns, 1995).

Worship as Sacrifice

Attempts to reconstruct the worship services at the temple run into a wall of silence. The biblical texts simply assume that readers know everything that they need to know about the rituals taking place there. Clearly, temple worship featured music as an essential element, as is evident from narratives that describe ritual activity. In addition, Israelites distinguished between priests and laity. Sometimes these distinctions were maintained by literal walls of separation between the two.

The Pentateuchal laws governing ritual matters further highlight the role of sacrifice in Israelite worship. Most sacrifice consisted of the presentation of edible materials "before" God — that is, placed in front of whatever object represented God's real presence in the temple. Sometimes all or part of this food was burned. At other times the food was simply placed on a table "before" God.

The edible offerings represented a range of foods normally present in a rich person's diet: grains in the form of breads and cakes, fruits and vegetables, oil, wine, and, most prominently, meat. The ritual laws seem most concerned that the right number and kinds of meat products be offered to Yahweh at the right times. The least expensive meat was poultry (usually doves or pigeons). Above that were sheep and goats, and topping the list were bulls. These animals were first slaughtered in a butchering room in the temple precinct, and the blood of the animal was collected. The blood was dashed against the outside altar, which was considered a direct offering to God. The meat was placed on the altar, sometimes in a kettle of water, other times roasted. Sometimes the whole carcass was burned; other times part was burned for God and the rest was eaten by the priests and/or worshipers. This was especially the case for thank offerings, annual pilgrimages, and peace offerings.

Although animal sacrifices may appear primitive to some people today, it is important to remember that most of Israelite worship consisted of this sanctified meal. To be sure, sometimes the only one "eating" was God (in the case of the whole burnt offering), but the food metaphor remained. "Communion" — that is, encountering God — meant meeting God at the table. To lose sight of this means losing sight of the many images of sacrifice found in the New Testament — images that lie at the heart of the Eucharist, our sanctified meal with the Triune God.

veyors of divine presence through an elaborate ritual. In other parts of the Fertile Crescent, especially in the Levant, the gods were not "pictured" by a statue; instead, an empty throne or pedestal was placed in the temple, above which the god was invisibly present. These items that served as the focal point for divine presence are what sociologists call "cult objects."[6]

In the Israelite temple, the ark was an empty throne, or, to be more precise, a footstool for the invisible God. The cherubim, whose wings covered the ark, formed the seat of this throne. In Israelite texts that describe the creation of a sacred space, such as Exodus 25–27:21 and 35:4–40:38, 1 Kings 5:1–8:66, and 2 Chronicles 2:1–7:22, it is the installation of the ark that marks the entry of God into the temple (Exod. 25:10-22; 1 Kings 8:4-11; 2 Chron. 5:7-14). These texts focus on the ark not just as a receptacle for sacred objects, such as the laws of the covenant, but also as the palladium for God.

In Exodus 25:14-15, 1 Kings 8:8, and 2 Chronicles 5:9, even after the ark was installed within the innermost room of the temple, the poles used for transporting the ark remained attached. These poles conveyed the idea that God's presence is portable. In fact, Israelite texts depict the ark traveling with Israel when they lived outside the Promised Land, as in the days of Moses. It could be carried onto the battlefield to signify God's presence with the Israelite army in times of war, as it was in the days of Samuel. It could be moved to another temple, as it was when David brought it into Jerusalem.

The divine resident "picked" the spot for the temple or house. Often the spot was connected with creation or with some divine manifestation. The choice was not arbitrary. The place for the temple was "different" than all other space, its choice making public its own holiness. Because of this, the site for a temple was always sacred space, even if no building stood there. This divine choice reflected the permanent quality of God's presence. Although enemies or natural disaster might destroy a temple complex, a new temple would be built on the same spot. God's choice was eternal, permanent, and reliable. The theology of sacred space reflected both the reliability of God and the power of God to move at will.

Temples were not like churches. Churches serve the needs of a gathered community, while temples served the divine resident. Churches "be-

6. This is a technical term; it in no way implies that ancient religions were "cults" in the modern sense of the term.

come" sacred through ritual activity, while temples *are* sacred. While church architecture does concretize theological concepts, it is no less driven by practical concerns. Temple architecture also had to consider practical concerns, but the ideology of the design was more expressly driven by theological principles. Yet, despite these differences, we see these temple texts struggling with the same problems of divine presence that we do. On the one hand, they speak about the "movement" that takes place when God becomes more manifestly present to the community. On the other hand, they maintain a theology of God's permanent presence with the people. Lastly, they remind us of the serious obligation placed on humans when God is truly present.

Pilgrimage and Prayer: Movements toward Divine Presence

Some Israelite texts reflect the community's movement toward God's presence. Pilgrimage was an important part of Israelite religious life, especially in the Second Temple Period. Israelite males were required to go to Jerusalem once a year for one of the three high holy days. Before the monarchy, the Deuteronomistic Historian depicts the yearly pilgrimage of Samuel's family to the temple at Shiloh. Similarly, Luke 2:41 states that Jesus' family made annual pilgrimages to Jerusalem at Passover. These texts attest to the presence of whole families in these annual pilgrimages. The psalms of ascent (120–134) probably derive from this pilgrimage setting. They attest to the worshipers' anticipation of entry into sacred space. "I rejoiced when they said to me, 'Let us go to the house of the Yahweh!'" (Ps. 122:1, my translation). Worshipers drew nearer to God's presence as they approached the temple.

In the text from 1 Kings, however, the movement between God and the community comes from the divine side, reinforcing the dynamic quality of God's presence. In 1 Kings 8:27-30, the Deuteronomistic historian focuses the reader's attention on the actualization of God's presence through prayer. The passage that heads this chapter comes from Solomon's prayer at the installation of the Ark of the Covenant into the newly built temple of Jerusalem. In this prayer, while the ark represented God's presence within Israel, it was the act of worship itself that made that presence effective for the community.

In this pericope, God is not "contained" in any one place, although, as this passage states, God's primary location is "heaven." The temple is not so much the place where an aspect of God's presence is housed as it is a location toward which prayer is directed. This suggests that God's presence has a dynamic character. While there is a permanent locus for divine presence — that is, above the ark — the ark is also the vehicle by which God becomes "more" present for the praying community. When prayer is directed to the temple, God can choose to be present to that community, implying that, while God is present in the temple, that presence is only partial. Worship may bring "more" of God to the temple — that is, it may actualize God's presence more fully.

Solomon's prayer highlights the partial nature of God's presence. The temple is the place where God's *name* dwells — that is, a particular aspect of God is present for the community in the temple. In some ancient Near Eastern texts, the "name" of a god can be a separate deity. In the Old Testament texts, God's name symbolized God's unique presence for Israel. The concept of a god's partial presence residing in a temple is present throughout the ancient Near East. Mesopotamian hymns note that the gods are not fully present in the temples that contain their statues. This language reflects the common human experience that, although we speak of God as omnipresent, we also "feel" or experience God's presence more fully at certain times and in certain places. While Christian theology focuses on the imperfection of human nature as incapable of fully experiencing God, the ancients used language of partial and portable presence to convey this inability of humanity to fully experience God always and everywhere.

Within the Deuteronomistic history, this image of God's portable presence was reassuring. When the final form of the books of Kings was put together, the temple of Jerusalem lay in ruins, the ark was gone, and God's presence seemed to be a distant fantasy. The Deuteronomistic historian highlights God's partial and portable presence as a response to this devastating loss. This is done in three ways. First, by focusing on the portability of the ark throughout Israel's history, this historian constantly reminds the reader that God can be with them even in exile. Second, the notion that only God's name dwells in the temple undercuts the temple's prestige as the only place where God's presence is contained. If only God's name is in the temple, then other aspects of God's presence extend beyond the walls of this one building. Third, by emphasizing prayer rather than either building or cult object as the means by which God's presence is made real, the historian relativizes the importance of tangible ritual elements and focuses on the actions of the community as essential to making God's presence real. Since the temple is only an earthly parallel to God's "real" home in heaven, this community can pray "toward" the temple, even if the temple has been destroyed. God can hear their prayers and have mercy on them even if the ark no longer exists.

Israelite metaphors that portray God's presence as portable, partial, and actualized by prayer fit well with Christian notions of sacred space. Christian liturgical theology tends to emphasize, on the one hand, the universal nature of God's presence, and on the other, the fact that a community of faith through worship actualizes God's presence. It is not surprising, then, that many introductions to Christian worship, when discussing Old Testament texts, focus on the ark and the wilderness tabernacle, portable symbols of God's presence with the community, as the "best" precursors to Christian worship.

Yet, by concentrating solely on these biblical witnesses to sacred space, we miss the far more dominant theologies of divine presence found throughout the Old Testament. While the partial, portable presence of God is a comforting notion, especially in such a fast-paced world, the biblical texts remind us that there is another side to God's presence. God's presence makes demands on us, requires from us a new way of living. The ripples of holiness extending out from God's presence change all of reality, affect all of our "space."

The Temple and God's Permanent Presence

The text from Ezekiel highlights the importance of every aspect of the temple. While the general notions reflected in temple theology — such as God's reliable presence and the importance of the divine resident within a temple — are easy enough to grasp, more difficult for contemporary Christian readers are the detailed descriptions of the temple buildings themselves. Exodus, 1 Kings, 2 Chronicles, and Ezekiel all include exact measurements for portions of the sacred spaces they describe. Ezekiel 40–48 stresses the importance of each measurement for the house of Israel.

The second passage that heads this chapter comes from the long vision that closes the book of Ezekiel. In the book itself, whose oracles span the years when Jerusalem was besieged and then sacked by the Babylonians, Ezekiel uses the image of God enthroned above the cherubim as a structuring device. The book opens with Ezekiel's initial vision of this image. God tells the prophet to warn the people away from their sins, which have defiled the land. When these sins do not abate, the enthroned Yahweh abandons the city (Ezek. 8–11), leaving the city open to every disaster that will befall it at the hands of the Babylonians. After the fall of the city is related in 33:21, the book switches to oracles of restoration. The final vision of the book, in chapters 40–48, describes a rebuilt temple. Led by an angelic tour-guide, the prophet is told the measurements of the courtyards and the major buildings. In 43:2-4, Ezekiel sees God, riding above the cherubim, re-enter the temple. Once inside the Holy of Holies, God speaks to Ezekiel, telling him that he must convey this very plan to the people of Judah to keep them from sinning again. The vision continues with laws pertaining to sacrifices and personnel. It describes how the presence of this temple reconfigures the apportionment of land to the king and then to the twelve tribes of Israel. At the end of the vision, the prophet is led through a river that springs up underneath the altar and flows down to the Dead Sea, a river so fructifying that it turns most of the Dead Sea to fresh water with fruit tress growing on its banks. The vision maps Israel geographically.

God's presence in Ezekiel is portable. While scholars disagree about God's destination once the city is abandoned, God clearly moves. But that portability is certainly not at the discretion of the community. God's abandonment of the city is not a comforting image, like the tabernacle and ark in the wilderness. This is not the parent accompanying the child into the great wide world, but rather the angry parent leaving the child all alone as punishment. Portable, yes; comforting, no.

God's presence is also partial in Ezekiel. Ezekiel 43:4 states that God's "glory" resides in the temple. Similar to the Deuteronomistic view that God's "name" resides in the temple, this language also asserts that it is some aspect of God that is present in the temple. For the Deuteronomistic historian, the incomplete nature of God's presence left room for a further actualization of that presence. Unlike the book of 1 Kings, however, the book of Ezekiel wants to emphasize the reality of that presence, however partial it may be.

The ultimate permanence of God's presence is stressed in the passage where, once God enters the Holy of Holies, the east gate is locked. "Yahweh said to me, 'This gate will remain closed; it will not be opened, nor will anyone enter through it. Because Yahweh, the god of Israel, has entered by it, it will remain closed'" (44:2, my translation).[7] For Ezekiel, himself a former

---

7. Aquinas, quoting a sermon by Augustine, uses this image of the closed gate as a typology for the perpetual virginity of Mary. Mary, who is the temple that houses Jesus, is

priest of the temple of Jerusalem, the fall of the city led to a theological crisis: Could God's presence in the temple be reliable? Or did God abandon
the city on some fickle whim? Such questions were not unheard of in the
ancient Near East. Mesopotamian laments over the destruction of various
temple cities rarely provided a reason for a god's abandonment of that city.

For Ezekiel, any presence of God was a serious matter, one that made
demands on the community. The most prominent demand was the need
for humans to refrain from defiling sacred space. Within the book of
Ezekiel, sin is defined as defilement. He recognizes a variety of sinful actions on the part of the people of Jerusalem, and the direct result of their
sin is defilement. Defilement stands in opposition to holiness; it is a char-
acteristic of that which is unworthy of being in God's presence. A defiled
object cannot enter sacred space; a defiled Israelite cannot approach the
temple. In Ezekiel, God was forced to leave the city once it had become utterly defiled. The direct and consistent result of sin is removal from God's
presence. To be sure, within the book the build-up of defilement finally
forced God's abandonment of the temple itself. The divine resident must
leave. But this defilement attaches itself to the violator, not to God. So although the movement in the book depicts God's abandonment of Israel,
the ritual theology of the book exposes the reality that it is the sinners who
have removed themselves from God.

The vision of restoration would be ineffective if it did not entail some
radical change in Israel's relationship to the temple and God's presence.
One way the author communicates this difference is by making God's
speech a divine command. God will return to be present once again to Israel, but that return includes new regulations for every single member of
the new nation. Both the architectural plans that the vision includes and

---

closed to all but God. "On the other hand, there is what is said in Ezekiel 'This gate will be
closed,' and 'it will not be opened, so that no man will pass through it, because the Lord, God
of Israel, has entered through it.' Interpreting this in a particular sermon, Augustine says,
'What does it mean, "The closed door in the house of the Lord," unless it means that Mary
will always be intact? What does it mean, "No man will pass through it (Latin *eam*, a femi-
nine singular pronoun)," except that Joseph would not know her? What does it mean, "The
Lord alone enters and exits through it," unless it means that the Holy Spirit will impregnate
her and that the Lord of the angels will be born through her? And what does it mean, "It will
be closed for eternity," unless it means that Mary was a virgin before the birth, a virgin during the birth, and a virgin after the birth?'" (*Summa Theologiae*, III, 28, iii; translation based
on the Latin text in the 1969 Blackfriar's edition).

the laws about personnel and land that follow make clear that the presence of God in the temple maps the location of every single person in the restored nation. The architectural design is governed by the desire to maintain strict separation of sacred and profane realms. Only God enters the sanctuary; only priests enter the courtyard around the sanctuary building; only Israelites worship in the outer courtyard. Among the Israelites, the king stands right at the threshold of the gate that separates the two spheres.

In the description of the territory of Israel that follows, Israel is mapped by the sacred space even outside the context of worship. The temple land is clearly separated from royal land. These two areas, although in the center of the nation, do not even touch each other. Spread out from there, each of the tribes has a strip of land, with six tribes to the north, and six tribes to the south. For Ezekiel, the resolution of the defilement of the temple that led to the city's fall is the prevention of contamination by the defiling citizens. Only if such strict separation between sacred and profane can be maintained will the nation hope to survive. Inherent within this description of the renewed temple and nation is a notion of social hierarchy. Ezekiel scholars have noted that the placement of the tribes in parallel strips reflects social status within the nation. The royal family is accorded a place "above," or, to use Ezekiel's terms, it is given a location more central than that of any of the tribes. But the royal family remains subordinated to the priests — that is, to the clan of which Ezekiel himself was a part. The vision maps Israel socially.

Ezekiel's vision of God's permanent presence within a reconstituted nation, with its nationalistic particularity and social interest, seems unredeemable for Christian theology. Even more than the temple in 1 Kings, the temple in Ezekiel is so unlike Christian churches, that a reader may be tempted to view this as a bit of historical trivia rather than a fruitful theological text.

Reading the Map: Help from Sociology

In order to interpret texts like Ezekiel 40–48 for a contemporary audience, readers may first need to find ways to talk about the common human experience of the sacred. Sociologists such as Mircea Eliade and Clifford Geertz have studied the writings about sacred space found in many cul-

Sanctuary, Holiness, and Refuge

Anyone who has seen *The Hunchback of Notre Dame* remembers the scene where Quasimodo enters the cathedral and claims sanctuary. Less well-known are both the biblical roots of such a claim and its modern application.

In the Old Testament, certain people could claim safety from unjust prosecution by entering into the temple precinct. The legal texts (Exod. 21:12-14; Deut. 4:41-43 and 19:11-13) allowed for certain cities to serve as places of refuge against vigilantism in cases of accidental death or manslaughter. In the historical material (1 Kings 1:50-53 and 2:28-29; 2 Kings 11:1-3), those fleeing political assassination sought safety by fleeing to the temple. Since the shedding of blood defiled a place, the death penalty could not be enacted within temple grounds. There were priests who served as guards (1 Chron. 23:5) and as judges (Deut. 17:8-13; 1 Chron. 23:4) within the temple precincts. While we do not know how the temple judicial system related to the royal one, it would not be a stretch to presume that the temple priesthood had their own way of determining guilt or innocence, and their own means to enforce their decisions. Thus, sanctuary was granted at the behest of the temple priesthood.

In Christian history, the practice of sanctuary continued, although it became part of the clash between church and state especially in the Middle Ages. Again, it was considered sacrilegious to defile a sacred church space with killing or force of arms. Thus a person was often "safe" from forceful arrest within a church. However, they were also essentially imprisoned within the church grounds.

The practice of sanctuary fell out of use for much of the modern period until the 1980s. In March 1982 a Presbyterian minister in Tucson, Arizona, declared his church a "sanctuary" for illegal immigrants fleeing state oppression in Guatemala and El Salvador. This declaration was part of a broader ecumenical effort within the United States to protect political refugees, an effort that came to be known as the "Sanctuary Movement."

tures, pointing out the universal nature of notions of the sacred inherent in such texts. For instance, cultures that retain articulated notions of sacred space often depict these spaces as mapping the rest of the space around them. The concept of sacred space is one that works out of a theol-

Although the United Nations had declared those fleeing from Guatemala and El Salvador to be political refugees, the Reagan administration, which supported the oppressive governments at the time, refused to recognize the UN resolutions. Even though Congress had passed a nonpolitically based definition of refugees, the Reagan administration tended to recognize only those fleeing communist regimes. They declared that those fleeing from Central American rightist governments were merely economic refugees and therefore ineligible for legal entry into the United States.

A large number of Christian and Jewish denominations not only objected to this national policy but also declared that they would employ acts of civil disobedience to address the situation and raise public awareness. Once again, churches claimed the right to judge the ethics of the state. They set up a type of "underground railroad" to help illegal immigrants enter and survive within the country. The U.S. government prosecuted and convicted a number of the leaders of the Sanctuary Movement in 1986, but the movement continued. In 1985 a group of church members filed suit against the government, charging that it was in violation of the definition of refugees enacted by Congress; the government settled the suit out of court in 1990 when it became clear that it would not win.

As the U.S. once again contemplates immigration reform, some churches and religiously motivated individuals stand in protest against the deportation of illegal immigrants. Elements of the Catholic Church in the U.S., for example, which had active members in the Sanctuary Movement, have spoken out publicly against the deportation of thousands of people who, they believe, (1) should have been declared legal residents to begin with, and (2) have proven themselves to be positive members of American society in the many years that they have lived and worked here. Once again, people are talking about granting sanctuary to those facing unjust political persecution.

ogy of the real presence of a divine being. Since we think of reality as tangible — that is, spatially located — sacred space becomes an essential metaphor for real presence. To put it another way: It's not real if it doesn't take up space. That space "taken up" by the divine presence is sacred space.

For ancient Israel, sacred space was primarily a metaphor of the experience of God's presence with the worshiping community. Eliade has outlined the ways in which "the sacred" differs from "the profane," whether that be sacred time, sacred people, or sacred places.[8] All of these things are "sacred" or distinct from ordinary human existence because of the presence of a god who interacts with humanity. For ancient Israel as well as for Christianity, Yahweh is a god who interacts in deliberate and concrete ways with the human community. The "space" within which such interaction occurs is rendered "sacred" by this interaction.

Sociologists tend to concentrate on the human structures within which a particular metaphor functions. Geertz, for instance, notes that elements of culture are semiotic, meaning they provide semantic structures by which communal experience becomes intelligible.[9] Religious metaphors as semiotic, then, both express the experiences of the community and shape that community's experience. To use our tangible example, metaphors of sacred space both communicate the community's experience of God's real presence in its midst and shape the way that community experiences God's presence. Geertz notes that religious elements are not simple communicators — that is, they do not communicate only one thing. Sacred symbols can communicate a variety of complex ideas in multiple ways. We have seen this in our discussion of Israelite notions of sacred space. Images of the temple can express God's presence as well as Israel's social hierarchy.

Since today most Christians profess that God is really present in worship, why do Israelite texts about God's presence within a sanctified space seem so archaic to us? Is it that we do not have meaningful symbols for God's real presence? Do Israelite symbols communicate only human social structures and not communal experience of the divine? What is it about sacred space that our contemporary culture finds void of meaning? While sociology has provided contemporary liturgical theology with new ways to "make sense" of the sacred in general, when it comes to questions of sacred "space" specifically, the results of sociological interpretation can still fall short.

8. See especially Mircea Eliade, *The Sacred and the Profane: The Nature of Religion* (New York: Harcourt Brace, 1959).

9. See Clifford Geertz, *The Interpretation of Cultures* (New York: HarperCollins/Basic Books, 1973), especially chapter 2.

Reading a Map Theologically

When Christian theology turns to Old Testament presentations of sacred space, it seems to encounter another world, something completely foreign. For contemporary Christian worshipers today, sacred space has a different origin than it did for the ancient Israelites, and so the attempt to bring together the ideas of Yahweh residing in the temple with a Christian theology of God's presence may seem like a futile project. In fact, many contemporary studies of Christian liturgy either simply ignore the topic of sacred space as embodied in the Jerusalem temple, or only examine parallels with the ark, the tabernacle, or the synagogue.[10] Yet, as R. F. Melugin offers,

> What we must do, I contend, is to propose models for usage of the ancient text to construct symbolic worlds for communities of faith in modern settings. A symbolic world constructed for a present-day worshipping community must necessarily be a hybrid; it must include both the language that comes from the past *and* a construal of a symbolic world in which a modern worshipping community can be shaped *in the context in which it lives.*[11]

In Israelite temple texts, sacred space was located at a specific site, be it a holy mountain, a mound of earth in the middle of a river, or a sacred grove of trees. For them, sacred space could be mapped; in fact, it generated maps. Sacred space relativized all space around it, and the world was ordered around this sacred space, like guests at a wedding oriented to the bridal table. On the other hand, we create sacred space through ritual. That is, our sacred actions demark a site as sacred, as if we bring to the surface the holiness lurking beneath a commercially designed "worship space." Yet the concept of sacred space is just as theologically important for us today

---

10. For some representative examples, see L. Bouyer, *Liturgy and Architecture* (Notre Dame: University of Notre Dame Press, 1967); M. J. Hatchett, *Sanctifying Life, Time, and Space: An Introduction to Liturgical Study* (New York: Seabury/Crossroad, 1976); R. T. Beckwith, "The Jewish Background to Christian Worship," in *The Study of Liturgy*, rev. ed., ed. C. Jones et al. (London: SPCK; New York: Oxford University Press, 1992), pp. 68-80; and Giles, *Re-Pitching the Tent.*

11. R. F. Melugin, "Isaiah in the Worshipping Community," in *Worship and the Hebrew Bible: Essays in Honour of John T. Willis*, ed. M. P. Graham et al., JSOT Supp. 284 (Sheffield: Sheffield Academic, 1999), pp. 256-57 (emphasis his).

as it was for ancient Israel. Why? As L. P. Wandel notes, "As is evident in all sorts of sources . . . where and how one worshiped God — both liturgy and ethics — were the expression, the outward form, of one's theology, one's understanding of God and His relation to humankind."[12] A theology of sacred space is ultimately a theology of revelation.

The Incarnation changes the dynamic of God's real presence to the people. The Incarnation expresses God's "descent" into human reality, cutting against the need to elevate humanity to find God's presence. Christ remains present to the community through Scripture and the Eucharist, religious elements open to all. This presence does not map, nor does it form areas of separation. Christ's presence is both portable and permanent, partial and perfected. L.-M. Chauvet notes that the difference between Israelite and Christian worship is essentially theological:

> The difference is of the *theological* order. More precisely, it is founded entirely upon the rereading of the whole religious system, a rereading imposed by the confession that Jesus is the Christ. . . . In a word, the difference is *eschatological.*[13]

Without an adequate notion of sacred space, a fuller theology of revelation suffers, and without an adequate theology of revelation, we lose sight of the eschatological reality that informs all of theology.

If we define "sacred space" as the concept that the divine realm is truly present spatially, then the act of Christian worship actualizes this eternally present reality for a community of faith.[14] Within Catholic liturgical theology, divine presence is actualized in multiple ways: in the sanctity of articles transformed by ritual sanctification, in the Word proclaimed in ritual, and in the real presence of Christ in the consecrated host.[15] Catholics view

---

12. L. P. Wandel, *Voracious Idols and Violent Hands: Iconoclasm in Reformation Zurich, Strasbourg, and Basel* (Cambridge: Cambridge University Press, 1995), pp. 6-7. This book shows how theological issues about the location of God's presence lay behind iconoclasm in the Reformation.

13. L.-M. Chauvet, *Symbol and Sacrament: A Sacramental Reinterpretation of Christian Existence* (Collegeville, Minn.: Liturgical Press, 1995), p. 250 (emphasis his).

14. On this concept, see, for example, L. Bouyer, *Rite and Man: Natural Sacredness and Christian Liturgy,* Liturgical Studies (Notre Dame: University of Notre Dame Press, 1963), esp. pp. 151-88.

15. I concentrate on Catholic theology because it is the tradition with which I am most

a church as sacred space. This is symbolized by the lighted lamp indicating the presence of consecrated hosts within the tabernacle, and the arrangement of other blessed items such as the Bible, a crucifix, statues, a baptismal font, and so forth. Blessing oneself with holy water upon entering the space indicates one's willing entry into the symbolic world of sacred space. God is present.

In the celebration of the Mass, that presence is further actualized in the Liturgy of the Word. The full form of every Catholic sacrament includes a reading from Scripture.[16] Catholic liturgical renewal has made the proclamation of the Word more central to sacramental worship. The Triune God is made present in this ritualized reading. For most Catholics, however, it is the liturgy of the Eucharist that marks the full realization of God's presence in their midst. The ritual actions mark the consecration of the bread and wine and their reception in communion as the high points of the ritual acts. The participation of the community in this act by their own consumption of the bread and wine also conveys added meaning to the symbolic actualization of Christ's presence for the community, not just as a collective group but as individual members of the body of Christ.

While what I have described derives from Catholic liturgical theology, many of these same concepts are present in varying forms throughout Protestant liturgy as well. For instance, Luther, although he rejects a theology of transubstantiation, affirms the real presence of Christ in the Eucharist.[17] G. W. Lathrop states, "The intention of the liturgy is to manifest the presence of God."[18] The Presbyterian Church (PCUSA) maintains that Christ is present in the proclamation of the Word:

> The church confesses the Scriptures to be the Word of God written, witnessing to God's self-revelation. Where that Word is read and proclaimed, Jesus Christ the Living Word is present by the inward witness

---

familiar. However, many of these features are present in varying degrees in other Christian traditions.

16. Even within the Sacrament of Reconciliation, part of the penitent's preparation should include the reading of Scripture.

17. See, for instance, *The Babylonian Captivity of the Church*.

18. G. W. Lathrop, *Holy Things: A Liturgical Theology* (Minneapolis: Fortress Press, 1993), p. 18.

of the Holy Spirit. For this reason the reading, hearing, preaching, and confessing of the Word are central to Christian worship.[19]

The doctrine of the Incarnation lies behind the "remembrance" of that presence in the breaking of the bread and the pouring out of the wine.[20] While sacred space, then, is actualized in Christian ritual rather than always present, it remains no less important for contemporary Christian theology than it was for ancient Israel. Only if God can be really present for the community does any of our theology "work."

Finding a Place on the Map:
Sacred Space and Social Hierarchy

As wonderful as a theological approach to sacred space sounds, sociological analysis further reminds us that sacred space re-inscribes social hierarchy. Sociological assessments of ritual note the ways in which public ritual serves the interests of those in power. Ritual mapping communicates social order: those things "closest" to the center of the map have more prestige, honor, holiness. Ritual specialists, such as priests and ministers, draw honor from their connection to this center. In ancient Israel, the temple served the monarchy as a vehicle for social unity and stability. Sociologists note that ritual tends to be conservative and static, so that it preserves social hierarchy. While it is easy to see these elements in Israelite worship, a closer look will show that these same elements of human-social mapping still cling to worship in the contemporary setting.

The higher the articulation of the sanctity of part of the building (the sanctuary), the more the elements around that sanctified spot are experienced as hierarchically arranged. I am a Catholic who can remember those pre–Vatican II days. While the congregation may have been confused about certain theological principles, it clearly knew the difference between the priest and the laity. The ordination of the priest set him apart from the congregation, and even after Vatican II, priests are still perceived as "holier" or

19. Constitution of the Presbyterian Church (USA), Part II, *Book of Order, 2001-2002* (Louisville: Office of the General Assembly, 2001), Section W.2.2001.

20. See, for instance, J. F. White, *Introduction to Christian Worship* (Nashville: Abingdon, 1980), pp. 76-109. For references to works relating to various Christian denominations, see the bibliography in Jones et al., *The Study of Liturgy*, pp. 3-5.

Some Unanswered Questions

1. How can a minister help a congregation to embrace shame or humility in a positive way?
2. How can liturgical aesthetics be appropriately beautiful and at the same time point to something greater?
3. When should church ritual support the state, and when should it stand over and against the state?
4. What is the role of liturgy in relation to social order and stability?
5. What should the relationship be between liturgy and politics?

"religiously better" than the laity. For some people, traditional forms of ritual, especially those that maintain a high notion of sacred space with its hierarchical mapping of social reality, must be rejected as contrary to the inherent Christian message. Christian movements prevalent in the 1970s that sought a return to the "house church," for instance, were in part attempts to reject the structures of privilege in traditional worship services. Similarly, feminist Catholics have noted how traditional Catholic ritual pervasively re-inscribes gender inequality within the church. This hierarchy is "communicated" so effectively that even church documents have trouble communicating a different view. For those who maintain that the patriarchal hierarchy is irredeemably encoded into the hierarchy of ritual space and action, the only alternative is to reconstitute or reject the ritual itself.[21] Even today, while liturgical theologians utilize the fruits of a sociological analysis of ritual *action*,[22] they tend to ignore or downplay sacred *space* as an essential dimension of contemporary worship.[23]

---

21. Similarly, one of the underlying issues in sexual abuse by priests, whether of children, adolescents, or even vulnerable adults, is their hierarchical position ritually represented in liturgy. To ignore the different degrees of power that are always present in relationships between priest (or minister) and congregant is to ignore a reality that ritual itself declares repeatedly.

22. For an excellent review of the intersection of social theory and liturgy, see N. D. Mitchell, *Liturgy and the Social Sciences*, American Essays in Liturgy (Collegeville, Minn.: Liturgical Press, 1999).

23. See, however, newer work by C. Bell, especially *Ritual Theory, Ritual Practice* (New York: Oxford University Press, 1992).

As a "people of the Book," is our rejection of an articulated notion of sacred space really the only solution to the abuse of power and privilege enabled by traditional worship, especially when that "tradition" extends back to the days of the Israelite monarchy? Can we read Ezekiel, for instance, only as a model of worship that must be rejected? Or does his vision call us to rethink what the ritual space is trying to communicate? Walter Brueggemann calls for a renewed use of Old Testament models of worship by Christian churches. He writes, "These were visible, legitimated, acceptable, stable, well-financed religious structures with recognized, funded leadership. *The temple and its priesthood* played a legitimating role in the ordering of civil imagination, and the role of the stable temple for this model of church can hardly be overaccented."[24]

If these texts are primarily expressing a theology of God's presence, how can they serve as a "model of church"? Is the model telling the church that we have to make sure God is "felt" by the congregation? As many of you prepare for ministry, are you sure that every worship service will make real God's presence in the midst of the congregation rather than communicate your own status? How would you ensure this? Do you plan to have services where the people feel some connection to each other so that they leave "feeling good" about themselves, a kind of ritual group therapy? Do you plan to make sure the music is so perfect that Jesus is conjured up in the assembly like Samuel rising from the dead? Or will you keep the right number of candles lit and use more incense to convey a sense of religious mystery? Will you go back to the "good old days" before liturgical renewal? And if you are successful, if you recapture the old ritual, have you also retrieved a social map?

Looking at the Map from a New Location: Privilege, Shame, and Worship

The Old Testament does not give us ritual rubrics. In fact, it does not tell us much about the specifics of the Israelites' own worship services. Instead, it gives a theology of worship by examining what it was the Israelites thought

---

24. Walter Brueggemann, "Rethinking 'Church Models' through Scripture," in *Cadences of Home: Preaching among the Exiles* (Louisville: Westminster John Knox, 1997), p. 100 (emphasis his).

they were doing. The Old Testament invites us to keep that question in the foreground. Are we serving our own ends in worship, re-inscribing our own status? Or do we "bow to the ground" like Ezekiel when we realize God's real presence in worship?

Israelite texts that concentrate on the worshipers' pilgrimage to the temple become fruit for our own thinking about the ultimate end of our quest to "see" God. As a journey through sacred time, pilgrimage to the temple is a metaphor for our pilgrimage through life, especially as a community of faith. In this sense, as Christians pray psalms such as Psalm 122, they place themselves on an eschatological journey, one that moves through time, through salvation history to ultimate salvation. In a discussion of how Catholic churches, especially those serving African-American Catholics, should recall elements of the "hush harbors" from the days of slavery, a committee writes, "They must be spaces that have 'the power to anchor and map our human world and our Christian journey through it.'"[25] Ideally sacred spaces aid this ultimately eschatological journey.

Israelite texts such as the prayer of Solomon also have an eschatological dimension, but here the eschatology is spatial. G. E. Tinker has pointed out that white Christians have too often ignored the importance of spatial eschatology, instead focusing only on temporal eschatology.[26] Spatial eschatology is the realization of the abiding nature of a divine reality beyond our own. Heaven will not be created at the end of time; it exists now and always. Solomon's prayer calls on God to enter human "space," showing prayer and worship as ways to actualize an eschatological reality that is not temporal but spatial. Spatial eschatology is the realization that God *is* present, even if we can experience that presence only within our own confines of time and space. The prayer of Solomon bridges the eschatological notions of sacred space as both a continuous reality and an ultimate goal.

The book of Ezekiel, however, focuses our attention much more on the effect of this presence on human action. Ezekiel concentrates on ritual space as a vehicle for divine communication. The temple plan itself is a primary means of divine revelation. As divine revelation, the sacred space Ezekiel describes is not the result of human effort but a pure gift from

25. "Plenty Good Room: The Spirit and Truth of African-American Catholic Worship," Secretariat for the Liturgy, Secretariat for Black Catholics, and the National Conference of Catholic Bishops (1991), para. 58.

26. G. E. Tinker, "Reading the Bible as Native Americans," in *The New Interpreter's Bible*, vol. 1 (Nashville: Abingdon, 1994), pp. 174-80.

God. Sacred space is graced space. God's graced presence calls for new actions and a new world order; it calls for changes that are structural and enduring. Revelation through sacred space virtually shifts the focal center away from human actions in worship to human response to God's presence.

It is not absurd to realize that if God is truly present to us, then that presence places some demands on us. If we act according to certain rules of protocol around important human leaders, how much more does God's presence demand of our behavior? This is the essential message of the whole book of Ezekiel. Ezekiel defines sin in terms of ritual space and a defilement of that space that violates the divine presence. Likewise, restoration is the re-creation of sacred space, and the "law" that follows is the plan itself. But this law will work because the experience of God's presence is transformative: the transformation in the people is the internalization of shame. "When they measure its dimensions, then they will be ashamed of all they have done" (Ezek. 43:10-11).

Shame is a countercultural notion today. It is something we avoid, something "bad," something that goes against our feel-good-about-ourselves mentality. Does shame have any positive value? In the book *Teaching to Transgress,* bell hooks hints at the link between shame and the knowledge of privilege, although she backs away from seeing these two things as essentially connected. Her essay on the subject raises the question of whether "knowledge of racism" for white women could ever be free of "guilt, shame, or fear."[27] In a discussion about this question I had with colleagues of different racial backgrounds, it became clear that the experience of shame differed for each group. As white women who want to fight against racism and oppression, some of us found shame and guilt to be part of the knowledge one acquires when being transformed away from racism, an integral part of "knowing" our own privilege. Similarly, Ezekiel speaks to a privileged group; as a priest of high status, his theology reflects the experience of the privileged class.

Shame is a prominent theme in the book of Ezekiel, but an elusive one for a contemporary audience. Shame is the recognition of the abuse of privilege that comes from an inadequate recognition of the true goal of worship. Just as a person of privilege today must at some level be ashamed

27. bell hooks, *Teaching to Transgress: Education as the Practice of Freedom* (New York/London: Routledge, 1994), p. 106.

by the ways unwarranted privilege has served to benefit her unjustly, so too the former privilege of Israelite leaders reinforced in ritual devoid of God's presence turns to shame when God returns "before their eyes" to the temple. Ezekiel asserts that God can call those of us who experience social privilege to embrace shame in true worship. Shame is the result of the rejection of privilege that empty ritual, ritual insufficiently cognizant of God's real presence within the worshiping community, can foster. To put it in Ezekiel's terms: Accepting human privilege offered in ritual defiles or removes us from the reality of God's presence. Accepting shame, or the proper demotion of human power called for in worship, takes us into the reality of God's presence.

What Ezekiel calls "shame" is similar to what Christian tradition calls the virtue "humility." On the one hand, shame or humility derives from the recognition of human sinfulness. When we think of sin legalistically, we may only think of shame/humility as an emotional response when we feel guilty. But when we think of sin as part of the human condition, then we can see the reason why Ezekiel envisions the people leading a new life in shame. Shame is the recognition of human limitation.[28] On the other hand, shame or humility derives from the recognition of divine holiness. It is not the feeling that "I am so bad"; it is the knowledge that "God is so good." If we see our own limitations in this light, it is only because we recognize them in relation to something unbound: God. Shame or humility is the human response to God's revealed nature.

Shame is not the driving force behind Ezekiel's theology; the prevailing theological metaphor for the book is God's real presence among the people — an image that has both frightening and fruitful consequences. For Ezekiel, shame is the *fruit,* not the *fright.* Throughout the book of Ezekiel, the prophet maintains that Israel has never done anything to deserve God's regard. In the metaphorical retelling of Israel's history in chapters 16 and 23, Jerusalem is a baby born defiled, wallowing in its own birthblood. When Yahweh sees her, he (as a clear male in this metaphorical retelling) first purifies her before raising her and taking her as his bride. Similarly, in the oracles of restoration that close the book, God first purifies Israel before restoring it. In other words, within this biblical book there is never a time when Israel stands clean and holy before God. Israel's essen-

28. See Cornelius Plantinga, *Not the Way It's Supposed to Be: A Breviary of Sin* (Leicester, Eng.: Apollos/Grand Rapids: Eerdmans, 1995).

tial nature is that of a defiled and defiling creature. What God does for Israel, both in its past and in its restoration, is done solely on God's own behalf. God does not act for any reason other than self-will. God simply chooses to save Israel.

How does the temple plan, the detailed description of the new sacred space, solve the problem of defilement that had been present before the fall of the city? Certainly it does not wipe out human hierarchy or privilege. In fact, this text sees privilege as an essential component to the restoration. For Ezekiel the answer is shame. Human privilege remains, but even in that privileged society all are shamed before the presence of God. The book of Ezekiel defines shame as the community's recognition of its inherent unworthiness. Baruch Schwartz objects to a certain Christian reading of Ezekiel as a theology of grace, in part because the book never speaks of God's love for Israel.[29] But for Christians there remains a parallel between Ezekiel's notion that Israel does not deserve what God has granted, no matter what God's motivation to grant it may be, and a theology of grace — that is, an undeserved gift from God. Just as a Christian who truly recognizes the greatness of God's gift and the undeserving state of human nature cannot live life in the same way, so too Ezekiel envisions a world transformed by Israel's knowledge of its own shame.

What does this mean for those training for positions of religious status — training to be ministers, priests, teachers, and educators — in a nation of privilege such as the United States? Do grander churches and better music serve God, or do they serve us? Are Christian services in the U.S. in which God's presence becomes actualized simply an exercise in re-inscribing our own privileged positions? The danger, of course, is that they can be. We can leave our own worship spaces confirmed in our own "space," not seeing that the whole space has become relativized by God's real presence. The temple texts in the Old Testament call us to recognize sacred space as a grace, not a right. Even a prophet like Ezekiel who expresses God's permanent presence recognizes the danger of taking such presence for granted. God can and has chosen to leave in certain circumstances.

Texts such as Ezekiel 40–48 call us to take up shame and guilt, to understand the positive function of such states. This may be shocking to a

---

29. Baruch Schwartz, "Ezekiel's Dim View of Israel's Restoration," in *The Book of Ezekiel: Theological and Anthropological Perspectives,* ed. M. S. Odell and J. T. Strong, SBL Symposium Series, 9 (Atlanta: Society of Biblical Literature, 2000), pp. 43-67.

contemporary audience; I suspect it was shocking for Ezekiel's audience as well. Sacred space does not just evoke shame; it is defined as the place where we embrace shame. It is a place where we are sucked up into the vortex of sacred reality and tumbled head over heels before God's presence. It is the place where we realize that our grand churches should remind us how feeble human constructs are compared with God's real home in heaven, and how poorly we sing, even at our best, compared with the "choirs of angels." It is the place where we realize that God's presence is permanent, perfect, and universal. It is we who are portable, thinking we can move in and out of that presence; imperfect in our ability to see, know, and experience the terrible reality of God being here among us; particular and partial, unable to see beyond our own experience, our own self-definition, our own metaphors for God.

A colleague once asked me if guilt and shame could ever go away. I answered that I could dream of a perfect world where they would have no useful function, but that I did not believe I would ever see it. I realized later that, of course, I would never see it. To have no shame would mean that there is no privilege. But I know that is an eschatological hope. For Ezekiel, as long as there is a God who gives humans things they do not deserve, a God who gifts us with real divine presence, then humans should feel shame for such a privilege. With Christ comes shame, the internalized self-knowledge that we have been gifted with a real divine presence beyond imagination.

Arriving at the Treasure

Many Christian worship services have rubrics for embracing a theologically fruitful concept of shame or Christian humility. Catholic and Lutheran services place the Kyrie near the beginning of the service. The Lutheran Book of Worship allows for a longer confession of sin, usually before the service. The Reformed Church in America's liturgy places its prayer of confession after an opening hymn of praise; the placement recognizes the worshiping community's sense of its sinfulness in the presence of a holy God (see Isa. 6:1-5). Just before communion, Catholics pray with the Scriptures, "Lord, I am not worthy, but only say the word and I shall be healed." How often are these various acknowledgments of human sinfulness muttered quickly, omitted altogether, or replaced by something that makes us "feel better" about ourselves? As future leaders of the church, we are challenged by Old Testament texts to make meaningful again this part of our ritual heritage. They do not call us to ask, How do we make church "feel holier"? Instead they call us to ask, How do we acknowledge worship as grace, not performance?

Why should Christians read temple texts such as 1 Kings 5–8 and Ezekiel 40–48? The answer is simple. As a community that believes that Christ, through the Incarnation and the Resurrection, is truly present to us, we are reminded by these texts that God's presence transforms reality. That transformation makes demands on us, and failure to recognize the transformative nature of divine presence is a sin. Sin defiles — that is, it forces us to be removed from God's presence. As Ezekiel reminds us, we are incapable of living truly in God's presence on our own because human nature is defiled. Yet, we become able to live rightly not through our own actions but through the initiative of God, the One who chooses to be truly present still and again, the One who locks the door after entering into our profane space, making it sacred. This entrance, begun in the days of Israel and fulfilled in the Incarnation, will perfect us in our ability to "see" God in the eschaton.

How Lovely, Lord

How lovely, Lord, how lovely is Your abiding place;
my soul is longing, fainting, to feast upon Your grace.
The sparrow finds a shelter, a place to build her nest;
and so Your temple calls us within its walls to rest.

In Your blest courts to worship, O God, a single day
is better than a thousand if I from You should stray.
I'd rather keep the entrance and claim You as my Lord
than revel in the riches the ways of sin afford.

A sun and shield forever are You, O Lord Most High;
You shower us with blessings; no good will You deny.
The saints, Your grace receiving, from strength to strength shall go,
and from their life shall rivers of blessing overflow.

Text: Arlo D. Duba (b. 1929), 1984
Text copyright © 1986 Hope Publishing Company, Carol Stream, IL 60188. All rights reserved.
Used by permission.

Love Divine, All Loves Excelling

Love divine, all loves excelling,
joy of heaven, to earth come down,
fix in us Thy humble dwelling,
all Thy faithful mercies crown!
Jesus, Thou art all compassion,
pure, unbounded love Thou art;
visit us with Thy salvation,
enter every trembling heart.

Breathe, O breathe Thy loving Spirit
into every troubled breast!
Let us all in Thee inherit,
let us find the promised rest;
take away our bent to sinning;
Alpha and Omega be;
end of faith, as its beginning,
set our hearts at liberty.

Come, Almighty, to deliver,
let us all Thy life receive;
suddenly return, and never,
nevermore Thy temples leave.
Thee we would be always blessing,
serve Thee as Thy hosts above;
pray, and praise Thee without ceasing,
glory in Thy perfect love.

Finish, then, Thy new creation;
pure and spotless let us be;
let us see Thy great salvation
perfectly restored in Thee;
changed from glory into glory,
till in heaven we take our place,
till we cast our crowns before Thee,
lost in wonder, love, and praise.

Text: Charles Wesley (1707-1788), 1747

For Further Reading

Samuel E. Balentine. *The Torah's Vision of Worship,* Overtures to Biblical Theology (Minneapolis: Fortress Press, 1999). Balentine combines social history and contemporary theology in his re-examination of the way the Pentateuch views proper Israelite worship. He shows how the Israelites themselves used laws about worship to conceptually recreate an ideal world, a vision of an eschatological end that was inherently countercultural.

John G. Gammie. *Holiness in Israel,* Overtures to Biblical Theology (Minneapolis: Fortress Press, 1989). Gammie outlines the basic notions of holiness that permeate so many Israelite texts. He includes in his discussion sacred time, sacred space, and sacred persons.

Tremper Longman III. *Immanuel in Our Place: Seeing Christ in Israel's Worship,* The Gospel According to the Old Testament (Phillipsburg, N.J.: P & R Publishing, 2001). In this introductory book, Longman examines Old Testament texts about Israel's worship for a Christian evangelical audience. The book introduces the main aspects of Israelite rituals and shows where those traditions inform later Christian worship.

Nathan D. Mitchell. *Liturgy and the Social Sciences,* American Essays in Liturgy (Collegeville, Minn.: Liturgical Press, 1999). While this book is not intentionally constructive, it provides an excellent entrance into the ways various social theories impact liturgical theology. Mitchell unpacks the difference between the thought of people like Mircea Eliade and Victor Turner. This book can also be used to find further reading on these topics.

The Hope of the Poor: The Psalms in Worship and Our Search for Justice

J. Clinton McCann Jr.

PSALM 9

J. Clinton McCann Jr.

A Crucial Connection

On September 29, 1987, the *St. Louis Post-Dispatch* reported on its front page the tragic murder of Incarnate Word Sister Patricia Ann Kelly, a tireless advocate of the poor who raised over one and a half million dollars to help the needy pay their utility bills. Not surprisingly, Sister Pat's favorite passage of Scripture was Psalm 9:18: "For the needy will not always be forgotten, and the hope of the poor will not perish forever" (author's translation). Sister Pat knew, at least implicitly, that the Psalms are, in the words of J. David Pleins, "the poets' vocabulary of justice [that] continues to draw out of us a response to suffering and injustice."[1] Because this is true, and because the Psalms have for centuries occupied an important place in Jewish and Christian worship, the book of Psalms is in a unique position to contribute to our search for justice.

To be honest, however, the synagogue and the church have not always recognized the connection between worship and justice. Biblical evidence in this regard is found most explicitly in the prophets. In fact, the prophet Amos issues what sounds like a direct criticism of worship itself, including the use of the Psalms:

> Take away from me the noise of your songs;
>   I will not listen to the melody of your harps.
> But let justice roll down like waters,
>   and righteousness like an everflowing stream.
>
> (Amos 5:23-24)[2]

But Amos and the other prophets were *not* opposed to worship or to the use of songs/Psalms in worship. Rather, what they called for was an appreciation of the connection between worship and justice. Worship without justice is empty, even offensive to God. In other words, genuine worship of the God of Israel will inevitably involve the pursuit and embodiment of what this God wills for the world: justice and righteousness.

In their more faithful moments, the synagogue and the church have

---

1. J. David Pleins, *The Psalms: Songs of Tragedy, Hope, and Justice* (Maryknoll, N.Y.: Orbis Books, 1993), p. 1.

2. See also Isaiah 1:12-18; Jeremiah 7:1-15; Hosea 6:1-6; and Micah 6:1-8.

maintained the connection between worship and justice, as the prophets advocated. The "Directory of Worship" of the Presbyterian Church (USA), for instance, articulates this connection as follows: "The church in worship proclaims, receives, and enacts reconciliation in Jesus Christ and *commits itself to strive for justice and peace in its own life and in the world.*"[3] It is the purpose of this essay to suggest how the Psalms, fully understood, will inevitably contribute to the church's appreciation of the connection between worship and our search for justice.

There is no shortage of psalms that would serve to illustrate this crucial connection. Necessity, however, suggests that we select a few on which to focus. We shall begin with Sister Pat's favorite psalm — Psalm 9 — and its "other half": Psalm 10. (Though these are numbered separately, they were originally a single psalm.) Then we will consider another well-matched pair: Psalms 98 and 100. For each illustrative set, we will comment first on their use (or lack of use!) in Christian worship and on their distinguishing characteristics. We will then suggest some specific implications for the ways these psalms can help us to "present offerings to the LORD in righteousness" (Mal. 3:3).

Psalms 9–10

Psalms 9:7-8, 18-20; 10:1-6, 12-18

9:7 . . . But the LORD sits enthroned forever,
     he has established his throne for justice.
 8 He establishes justice in the world by setting things right;
     he establishes justice among the peoples with equity. . . .
18 For the needy will not always be forgotten,
     and the hope of the poor will not perish forever.
19 Arise, O LORD! Do not let humans triumph;
     bring the nations to justice before you.
20 Strike awe in them, O LORD;
     let the nations know that they are only human.
10:1 Why, O LORD, do you stand far away?
     Why do you hide in times of distress?

3. Constitution of the Presbyterian Church (USA), Part II, *Book of Order, 2003-2004* (Louisville: Office of the General Assembly, 2001), Section W-7.4001; emphasis added.

A Psalms Explosion

The Psalms have been said and sung in worship throughout the centuries. Recently, these "golden oldies" that made their debut in ancient Israelite worship have enjoyed an unprecedented resurgence in popularity. The recent hymnals of several major Protestant denominations, for example, include sections devoted exclusively to the Psalms, and some even include instructions for singing the Psalms. These include the following volumes:

Evangelical Lutheran Worship (Minneapolis: Augsburg Fortress Press, 2006), 335ff.

The United Methodist Hymnal (Nashville: United Methodist Publishing House, 1989), 736-862

The Presbyterian Hymnal: Hymns, Psalms, and Spiritual Songs (Louisville: Westminster John Knox Press, 1990), 158-258

The New Century Hymnal (Cleveland: Pilgrim Press, 1995), 618-731

Chalice Hymnal (St. Louis: Chalice Press, 1995), 726-68

The Psalter: Psalms and Canticles for Singing (Louisville: Westminster John Knox Press, 1993)

2 The wicked arrogantly oppress the poor;
   let them be caught in the schemes they have plotted.
3 For the wicked boast of their own selfish desires;
   those greedy for gain curse and reject the LORD.
4 The wicked say proudly, "God will not investigate."
   They think that there is no God.
5 Their ways prosper all the time;
   your deeds of justice are on high, beyond them;
   they scoff at their opponents.
6 They say in their heart, "We shall not ever be moved;
   we shall never experience adversity." . . .
12 Arise, O LORD God, raise your hand;
   do not forget the oppressed.

In Roman Catholic circles the Psalms have never gone out of fashion. The following collections bear witness to recent publications that have contributed to psalm-singing both inside the Roman Catholic tradition and beyond:

Gather (Chicago: GIA Publications, 1988), nos. 18-63

Forty-One Grail/Gelineau Psalms (Chicago: GIA Publications, 1995)

Michel Guimont, *Psalms for the Revised Common Lectionary* (Chicago: GIA Publications, 2002)

Finally, the following publications, which are not associated with any specific denomination, illustrate the ways in which the Psalms have played a part in the worldwide renewal of Christian worship:

John L. Bell/The Iona Community, *Psalms of Patience, Protest, and Praise* (Chicago: GIA Publications, 1993). See also *Psalms of David, Songs of Mary*, also by Bell, Wild Goose Resource Group, Iona Community (GIA, 1997)

Praise: Hymns and Choruses, 4th ed. (Nashville: Maranatha! Music, 1997). While this collection does not have a psalm "section" per se, it lists 168 titles based on psalms

Renew! Songs and Hymns for Blended Worship (Chicago: Hope Publishing Co., 1995), nos. 103-119 plus sixteen others

13 Why do the wicked reject God,
      saying in their hearts, "You will not investigate"?
14 For you do see trouble and grief;
      you notice in order to take it in hand.
    The helpless turn themselves over to you;
      you are the helper of the orphan.
15 Break the arm of the wicked and the evil ones;
      investigate their wickedness until there is nothing left to find.
16 The LORD is king forever and ever;
      the nations perish from his land.
17 You will hear, O LORD, the desire of the meek;
      you will steady their heart;
      you will give them a hearing,

18   in order to do justice for the orphan and the oppressed,
     so that earthly mortals will no longer terrorize them.

(author's translation)

Although the Hebrew title for the book of Psalms is *tehillîm* (meaning "Praises"), a majority of the psalms are prayers for help that scholars usually call "laments" or "complaints." To be sure, these prayers almost always include a section of praise; but the emphasis is on communicating to God what is wrong in the psalmist's life and/or in the world, as well as asking God to help.

Because the focus in these prayers is upon what is wrong, they are often viewed as "negative" or "depressing." Consequently, they are not often used in worship services. But the failure to use the prayers for help in worship is problematic, or, as Walter Brueggemann puts it, "costly."[4] If we, as individuals and as communities of faith, are not allowed to identify and bring before God what is wrong, then we risk the following "costs": (1) the silencing of victims; (2) the failure to identify injustice and the perpetrators thereof; and (3) the lack of opportunity to pray for and commit ourselves to the pursuit of God's will for justice, righteousness, and *shalom* in the world. In short, if we do not admit that things are not right, we will not commit ourselves to changing anything. Simply to begin to use the prayers for help, like Psalms 9–10, in worship on a regular basis would serve as an acknowledgment of the connection between worship and justice.

Before pointing out how the above "costs" are avoided in Psalms 9–10, it should be noted that the psalmists, even as they lament or complain, never abandon the conviction of God's sovereign claim on the world. As in the songs of praise (see the discussion below on Psalms 98 and 100), God's sovereignty is associated with God's will for justice (see Ps. 9:7-8; Ps. 10:16-18). But clearly, God's will for justice is not being enacted (Ps. 9:18-20; Ps. 10:1-6, 12-14). This situation has profound consequences for understanding God's sovereignty — that is, for comprehending how God exercises power. In short, because God has enemies, and because God's will is regularly opposed, God's sovereignty or God's power simply cannot consist of sheer force. Rather, God's power is sheer love. It may look like weakness (see Ps. 10:4, 13),

---

4. Walter Brueggemann, "The Costly Loss of Lament," *Journal for the Study of the Old Testament* 36 (1986): 61-65. I have described the "costs" in slightly different terms than Brueggemann does.

but the psalmists never fail to trust that the power of love will ultimately prevail (see Ps. 10:14); they are thus energized to resist injustice and oppression.

So may contemporary worshipers be energized and empowered by God to resist injustice and oppression precisely by praying the prayers in the book of Psalms. As suggested above, in so doing, we open the way for victims to speak; we name injustice and its perpetrators; and we commit ourselves to the pursuit of God's will for world-encompassing justice, righteousness, and *shalom.*

Letting Victims Speak

In my experiences of teaching and learning about the Psalms in various congregations, I have discovered that people often perceive the pray-ers of the psalms as "whiners." Almost certainly this is the case because many North Americans have never experienced prolonged or severe victimization, or perhaps because they have been taught not to identify it as such and talk about it publicly. In any case, the prayers for help bring before God and the community of faith the things in the world that are not right. They simply must be heard as the prayers of victims. To be sure, sometimes the pray-ers seem to blame God (see Ps. 10:1); but ultimately they claim God's help against "the wicked" (Ps. 10:2).

Those of us who cannot identify with the degree of hurt and victimization expressed in the prayers for help perhaps can claim the ancient tradition of praying these prayers *for others,* thus giving them voice and claiming solidarity with them. As James L. Mays puts it,

> Could the use of these prayers remind us and bind us to all those in the worldwide church who are suffering in faith and for faith? All may be well in our place. There may be no trouble for the present that corresponds to the tribulations described in the psalms. But do we need to do more than call the roll of such places as El Salvador, South Africa, and Palestine to remember that there are sisters and brothers whose trials could be given voice in our recitation of the psalms? The old church believed that it was all the martyrs who prayed as they prayed the psalmic prayers.[5]

5. James L. Mays, *The Lord Reigns: A Theological Handbook to the Psalms* (Louisville: Westminster John Knox, 1994), p. 52.

As Mays suggests, to pray the psalmic prayers is to recognize that it is *the faithful* who are suffering. The effect of this recognition is to obliterate any comprehensive doctrine of retribution, which would allow the prosperous to claim God's favor and thus to ignore those less fortunate. In other words, praying the psalmic prayers actually opens a logical space for *grace,* which results in solidarity (see below).

It is unclear whether or not the pray-er of Psalms 9–10 is the victim. But, in any case, she or he prays for "the needy" (9:18), "the poor" (9:18), "the oppressed" (10:12), "the helpless" (10:14), and "the meek" (10:17). The prayer itself binds the pray-er to those who are suffering and also opens the way for the victimized to be recognized and for their pain to be acknowledged and articulated publicly.

Naming Injustice and Its Perpetrators

Letting victims speak, as well as speaking on their behalf, is the first step in naming injustice. But Psalms 9–10 do not stop at this. "The wicked" and their behavior are thoroughly exposed (see Ps. 10:1-6); this is often the case in the prayers for help, where "the wicked," "the enemy," and/or "the foe" regularly appear as opponents of God, God's purposes, and God's people.

More so than most, however, Psalms 9–10 expose the mind of the wicked by citing their speech and their thoughts (see 10:4, 6, 11, 13). What results is a portrait of persons who are thoroughly self-centered and accountable to no one but themselves (see also Pss. 3:1-2; 14:1; 42:10; 53:1; 64:5-6; 73:11; 79:10; 115:2). To be sure, this sounds uncomfortably like what passes for "business as usual" or just plain "good sense" in contemporary North America — what will be described below as "the illusion that we are in charge" or "the illusion of power and self-control." By praying these prayers, we may not only be reminded of the plight of the poor and the victimized; we may also be led to consider the possibility that we are complicit in injustice in our own communities and throughout the world.

Praying for and Pursuing Justice

In the North American context, it is often a countercultural activity to admit that we need help and to ask for it. Yet, the psalmists regularly ask God to help them and to help others — for example, "the oppressed" (see Ps. 10:12). We are generally more comfortable with the plea for help when it is framed positively. The obverse side of this request, however, is frequent in the prayers for help — that is, that God, for instance, "Break the arm of the wicked and evil ones" (10:15).

While this request may sound rather violent and vengeful, it is really nothing more than a request that the perpetrators of injustice might experience the destructive consequences that they are inflicting upon others (see Ps. 10:2). Or, in other words, it is a plea for something that most citizens of the United States routinely accept as fair — namely, that the punishment fit the crime. But the issue is not personal revenge. Rather, the intent of the prayer is that things be set right for victims. In short, these violent-sounding prayers are essentially prayers for justice; and by entrusting the situation to God, they actually break the cycle of revenge and violence. Erich Zenger summarizes their effect as follows:

> These are poetic prayers that hold up a mirror to the *perpetrators* of violence, and they are prayers that can help the *victims* of violence, by placing on their lips a cry for justice . . . , [by urging them] to hold fast to their human dignity and to endure *nonviolently,* in prayerful protest against a violence that is repugnant to God, despite their fear in the face of their enemies and the images of enmity.[6]

In essence, therefore, these prayers are requests that God's "will be done, on earth as it is in heaven." Every time we pray the Lord's Prayer, we are requesting that God's sovereignty be recognized ("thy kingdom come") and that God's will for the world be concretely enacted. Every time we pray the Lord's Prayer, we are praying for and committing ourselves to the enactment of God's world-encompassing justice, righteousness, and *shalom.* Thus, when fully understood, the use of the psalmic prayers in worship affirms, as the Lord's Prayer affirms, the inextricable connection between worship and justice.

While the psalmists pray for God's justice in the psalmic prayers, they celebrate the foundation for and world-encompassing scope of God's justice in the songs of praise, to which we now turn.

---

6. Erich Zinger, *A God of Vengeance? Understanding the Psalms of Divine Wrath,* trans. Linda M. Maloney (Louisville: Westminster John Knox Press, 1996), p. 92.

Psalms 98 and 100

Psalm 98:7-9

7 Let the sea thunder, and all that fills it;
the world and all its inhabitants.
8 Let the cosmic rivers clap their hands,
and the mountains sing joyously together
9 in the presence of the Lord, for he comes to establish justice
upon the earth.
He will establish justice in the world by setting things right
and among peoples by showing equity. (author's translation)

Psalm 100

A Psalm of Thanksgiving
1 Raise a joyous shout to the Lord, all the earth!
2 Worship the Lord with gladness;
come into his presence with singing.
3 Know that the Lord is God.
He made us, and we belong to him.
We are his people, the sheep of his pasture.
4 Come into his gates with thanksgiving,
and his courts with praise.
Give thanks to him; bless his name.
5 For the Lord is good;
his steadfast love is forever,
and his faithfulness from generation to generation.
(author's translation)

The Christian church traditionally sings Isaac Watts's metrical version of Psalm 98 at Christmas, the Festival of the Incarnation, to celebrate the divine love that could not help but enflesh itself in the world (see John 1:14). The title by which we know this song is, quite appropriately, "Joy to the World." To celebrate the incredible good news of Incarnation, we sing! Yet, Psalm 98 reminds us that we sing not alone, but in concert "with heaven and nature." By this particular use of the Psalms in worship, we are thus reminded of the profoundly countercultural good news that God will not be content, nor will our own joy be complete, until all creatures and all features of creation participate in the justice, righteousness, and *shalom* that God wills. We remind ourselves, in other words (drawn also from the Gospel of John; see 3:16), that God loves the world!

Perhaps more than any other psalm or song, Psalm 100 has been used in Jewish and Christian worship. As James L. Mays concludes, "Were the statistics known, Psalm 100 would probably prove to be the song most often chanted from within the history that runs from the Israelite temple on Mount Zion to the synagogues and churches spread across the world."[7] In other words, Psalm 100 may be the number-one song of all time! No wonder it was chosen to be sung at the First Assembly of the World Council of Churches in Amsterdam in 1948. Psalm 100 is, indeed, a world-class song!

Psalm 100 is also a song that articulates eloquently the world-encompassing perspective that is typical of the songs of praise in the book of Psalms, a perspective that forms the foundation for the claim that the book of Psalms is quintessentially about God's will for justice in the world. The familiar opening invitation — "Make a joyful noise to the LORD" (RSV, NRSV) — is addressed to "all the earth," and this expansive perspective proves to be typical. The songs of praise regularly invite a worldwide congregation to worship God. Phrases like "all the earth" (Pss. 66:1; 96:1, 9; 97:1; 98:4; and 99:1 as well as 100:1), "all you nations" (Ps. 117:1), and "all you peoples" (Ps. 117:1; see also Pss. 96:7; 99:1) are standard parts of the psalmists' repertoire. The call to worship culminates in the universe-encompassing invitation of the last verse of the Psalter: "Let everything that breathes praise the LORD!" (Ps 150:6; see also Pss. 96:11-12; 98:7-8; 148:1-13, where even some things that don't "breathe" get in on the act).

These remarkably expansive invitations to worship God communicate a critically important theological claim — namely, the God of Israel is the God of all peoples, nations, tribes, clans, and families of the earth. Indeed, this God is the God of all creation; and this God will not properly be worshiped until the whole world is welcome! The substance of the invitation in Psalm 100:1 is not simply to make lots of noise. Rather, to "make a joyful noise" or to "raise a joyous shout" is the appropriate biblical way to greet a monarch (see Pss. 95:1-2; 98:4, 6). In short, God's sovereign claim embraces the whole universe — all people, all creatures, all features of the cosmos; and the whole creation is invited to acknowledge and celebrate God's claim.

---

7. James L. Mays, "Worship, World, and Power," *Interpretation* 23 (1969): 316. Mays cites A. F. Kirkpatrick, *The Book of Psalms* (Cambridge: Cambridge University Press, 1912), pp. 587-88.

Worship Service

Because both "worship" and "serve" are appropriate translations of the Hebrew verb that begins Psalm 100:2, it is fitting that many Protestants ordinarily designate an occasion for worship as a "worship service." Strictly speaking, the phrase may be redundant; but it has the advantage of communicating the reality that worship is essentially a public profession of submission to God and God's purposes for our lives and the life of the world. As such, it is to be expected that there will be a continuity between liturgy and lifestyle. This is precisely the continuity for which the prophets called (see the first two pages of this essay).

The proclamation of God's sovereign claim on "all the earth" is reinforced by the second invitation to praise that begins Psalm 100:2, usually translated "worship" (NRSV) or "serve" (RSV). This word in the book of Psalms always occurs in conjunction with a royal figure, either the earthly king or God as monarch (see Pss. 2:11; 18:43; 22:30; 72:11; 97:7; 102:22). It means "to be a servant" (or even "to be a slave") to a sovereign master — in short, to submit to God's claim on human life and the life of the world. Both "worship" and "serve" are appropriate translations. In fact, the two complement each other, suggesting that submission to God involves both liturgy ("worship") and lifestyle ("serve"). In Walter Brueggemann's terms, praise or worship is "world-making." He explains: "'World-making' is done by God. That is foundational to Israel's faith. But it is done through human activity which God has authorized and in which God is known to be present."[8]

In other words, worship *of* and submission *to* a God who claims all the world's people and who values the whole created order will lead to a particular style of life. And, in a word, this lifestyle is what the Psalms and the rest of the Bible call *justice.*

In this regard, it is crucial to note that Psalm 100 follows a group of so-called enthronement psalms (Pss. 93, 95–99) that explicitly proclaim God's

---

8. Walter Brueggemann, *Israel's Praise: Doxology against Idolatry and Ideology* (Philadelphia: Fortress Press, 1988), p. 11.

reign (93:1; 96:10; 97:1; 98:1) or greet God as "King" (95:3; 98:6). These psalms also explicitly articulate God's royal policy, or God's will, for the world. This is especially the case in Psalm 98:9, which tells what God "comes" to do — namely, "to establish justice upon the earth" (my translation; see also 96:13, and the mention of God's "justice" and/or "righteousness" in 97:2, 6; 99:4). "Justice" here connotes not retributive judgment (as the RSV or NRSV may suggest), but rather the positive creation of conditions that make life possible for all the world's people, creatures, and features.

Lest there be any doubt about what "justice" looks like in concrete terms, Psalm 72 makes it clear that the earthly king was primarily entrusted with enacting God's will in the world. Psalm 72 also makes it clear that justice and righteousness primarily and positively involve attendance to and provision for the "poor" (vv. 2, 4, 12), "needy" (vv. 4, 12, 13), and "weak" (v. 13). Justice will take the form of "judgment" only in the case of "the oppressor" (v. 4), who opposes God's will by perpetrating "oppression and violence" (v. 14). The goal of divine justice, however, is not retribution, but rather the creation of conditions in which the whole cosmos can flourish — in a word, *shalom* (NRSV: "prosperity" in v. 3 and "peace" in v. 7; notice how the features of creation participate in *shalom*).

To "worship" God is to "come into his presence" (Ps. 100:2b); it is to pledge allegiance to God and to God's will for justice, righteousness, and *shalom.* This liturgical activity happens in God's "place" — the Temple in ancient times (see "gates" and "courts" in v. 4), the synagogue, and the church sanctuary. But to keep up with God, one cannot remain simply in God's "place," because God does not simply stay there, either. Notice how the noun "presence" (literally "face") and the verb "come" in Psalm 100:2b echo the language of Psalm 98:9, where *God* "comes" *into the world* "to establish justice upon the earth." God's "place" finally is the entire cosmos, so in Psalm 98:7-9 the whole creation celebrates God's "presence." Those who honor God in worship will continue to honor God in service in the world, which God claims as God's home — in particular, by participating in the universe-encompassing justice, righteousness, and *shalom* that God wills. The particular shape of such participation will be explored in the following sections.

We Are Not Our Own

There are seven invitations to praise in Psalm 100 — three in verses 1-2, one in verse 3, and three in verse 4. The number seven suggests wholeness, completeness, comprehensiveness; God is to be fully praised. The use of seven imperatives is probably intended also to highlight the middle invitation in verse 3 (which the NRSV appropriately sets off from vv. 1-2 and v. 4). The intent to focus attention on verse 3 is also indicated by the fact that it invites not a liturgical celebration but rather a liturgical revelation: "know." All the songs of praise — indeed, all worship — is instructional or revelatory, but Psalm 100 is explicitly so.

What Psalm 100 wants people to know reinforces God's claim on human life. Human life is not self-constituted. Rather, God "made us." The next phrase is traditionally translated "and not we ourselves" or "and we are his." In either case, the intent is captured by the translation "and we belong to him." In short, human life is not an achievement; it is a gift. Almost certainly the most challenging — and for precisely that reason, the most important — affirmation that Psalms 98 and 100 and all the other songs of praise make is that God's claim on our lives and the world is *prior* to our own claims. To worship God is to say, in essence, that God "made us" and that "we belong to him." In short, we are *not* "self-made men" and "self-made women." To worship and serve God means that we will *never* say what passes for self-evident in our culture: "It's my life to live!"

The psalmic way to affirm God's prior claim is to say that God rules the world (see Pss. 93:1; 96:10; 97:1), an affirmation that, according to some scholars, lies at the very heart of the theology of the Psalms.[9] Of course, we humans think that we rule the world, or at least that our nation rules the world. We citizens of the United States of America, for instance, rather like to think of ourselves as a "superpower." But to worship God is to believe and to act otherwise! I sometimes think that the pre-eminent contemporary heresy is what writer Anne Lamott calls "the illusion that we are in charge."[10] This widespread illusion has done and is doing unspeakable

9. See, for instance, Gerald H. Wilson, *The Editing of the Hebrew Psalter,* Society of Biblical Literature Dissertation Series 76 (Chico, Calif.: Scholars Press, 1985), p. 215; Gerald H. Wilson, "The Use of Royal Psalms at the 'Seams' of the Hebrew Psalter," *Journal for the Study of the Old Testament* 35 (1986): 92; Mays, *The Lord Reigns,* pp. 3-11.

10. Anne Lamott, *Bird by Bird: Some Instructions on Writing and Life* (New York: Anchor Books, 1994), p. 181.

harm — in families, in churches, among nations, in nature (see below). To use the Psalms regularly and faithfully in worship might have the transforming effect of, quite literally, putting us in our place. It might school us to submit to God rather than asserting self, and consequently attune us to God's will for world-encompassing justice, righteousness, and *shalom.*

To put it a final way, to worship God is to affirm that "we are not our own." This affirmation echoes 1 Corinthians 6:19, and it is also the title of a contemporary hymn by Brian Wren. (See the full text of this hymn printed at the end of this chapter.) Wren's hymn is not a paraphrase of Psalm 100 or any other psalm (although stanza 4 of the hymn invites the same thing that Ps. 100:4 invites), but it expresses beautifully what the use of the Psalms in worship might regularly communicate.

Gratitude

The second series of three imperatives found in Psalm 100:4 highlights the concept of gratitude. What the worshiper is to bring with him or her is "thanksgiving." This noun occurs also in the title to Psalm 100, and it could be translated "thank offering." Given the content of verse 3, however, the "thank offering" is not to be understood as an animal sacrifice (see Lev. 7:12-15). Rather, it is an offering of the worshiper's whole self and being (see Pss. 50:23; 51:17; see also Pss. 25:1; 86:4; 143:8, where the phrase "To you, O LORD, I lift up my soul" could also be translated "To you, O LORD, I offer my life"). Such submission of the self to God, in liturgy and in lifestyle, is the essence of "praise," which is also mentioned in verse 4. The invitation "Give thanks" represents a verbal form of the Hebrew word translated "thanksgiving." The final invitation to "bless his name" returns to the concepts of sovereignty and submission, since the word "bless" meant originally "to kneel," as in recognition of the claim of another upon one's life.

By simultaneously inviting worshipers to be submissive to God — including God's will for justice, righteousness, and *shalom* — and to "Come into his gates with thanksgiving . . . Give thanks" (v. 4), Psalm 100 suggests another profoundly countercultural conclusion — namely, that God's justice begins with gratitude (see again the fourth verse of Wren's hymn, which brings together "thanksgiving" and "justice"). In other words, God's justice begins with grace rather than merit.

This, of course, sounds downright un-American. Virtually every system and institution in the United States operates on a system of merit, including churches and seminaries — grades, degrees, academic ranks, ecclesiastical titles and hierarchies. Perhaps this is inevitable, maybe even necessary; but it makes it nearly impossible to comprehend grace. Reinhold Niebuhr made the following observation seventy-five years ago after attending a community Thanksgiving service in Detroit: "Thanksgiving becomes increasingly the business of congratulating the Almighty upon his most excellent co-workers, ourselves."[11] This situation is probably even more pronounced today. When gratitude or thanksgiving becomes self-congratulation, then grace becomes an endangered species. What inevitably happens is that the prosperous will pat themselves on the back while admonishing the poor to get a job, or at least to work harder. What is missing is any sense of responsibility to or caring for the other — that is, what is missing is any sense of God's will for world-encompassing justice.

The situation is so extreme that Henri Nouwen said that he literally had to leave the United States to begin to learn about grace and gratitude. He went to Bolivia and Peru, and he discovered that people in Latin America were generally much more thankful, even though they had less "stuff." Nouwen wrote that "slowly I learned . . . what I must have forgotten somewhere in my busy, well-planned, and very 'useful' life. I learned that everything that is, is freely given by the God of love. All is grace."[12]

What Nouwen learned is precisely what Psalm 100 wants worshipers to "know" (v. 3), and it is an urgent lesson. As Nouwen concludes,

> A treasure lies hidden in the soul of Latin America, a spiritual treasure to be recognized as a gift for us who live in the illusion of power and control [see the Lamott quote above]. It is the treasure of gratitude that can help us to break through the walls of our individual and collective self-righteousness and can prevent us from destroying ourselves and our planet in the futile attempt to hold onto what we consider our own.[13]

11. Reinhold Niebuhr, *Leaves from the Notebook of a Tamed Cynic* (San Francisco: Harper & Row, 1929/1956/1980), p. 187.

12. Henri Nouwen, *Gracias! A Latin American Journal* (Maryknoll, N.Y.: Orbis Books, 1983/1993), p. 187.

13. Nouwen, *Gracias! A Latin American Journal,* p. 188.

In other words, God's justice — the existence of a world characterized by caring and sharing rather than acquisitiveness and greed — begins with thanksgiving, the recognition that "All is grace."

To be sure, this lesson should not be as difficult to learn as it seems to be. Both Testaments of Scripture portray a God who graciously loves and repeatedly forgives sinful people. A major affirmation of the New Testament, and one that lies at the heart of Reformation traditions, is justification by grace. That is, God pursues justice, God sets things right in the world, God reconciles *by grace* rather than by punishing the guilty. As Elsa Tamez, a Latin American theologian and New Testament scholar, points out, if Christians in North America actually believed in grace and lived by it, the result would be "solidarity" among generally prosperous North American Christians and those in Latin America and the rest of the world.[14] As it stands now, North American Christians, like North Americans in general, are characterized by a pervasive sense of entitlement accompanied by ignorance of and apathy toward billions of desperately poor and needy persons throughout the world. The use of the Psalms in worship can help us get in touch with what Nouwen calls "the treasure of gratitude," which is, biblically speaking, the foundation of God's "justice."

Then too, of course, one of the central acts of Christian worship is called the Eucharist, which means "thanksgiving." The focus of this liturgical act is God's gift to humankind, manifest and embodied in Jesus Christ. When the Lord's Supper is celebrated according to Jesus' institution, it is clear that God's gift is entirely unmerited and undeserved. This is so because no one *deserves* to be at Christ's table; all *are welcome*. Again, thanksgiving is the foundation for the world-encompassing solidarity that characterizes God's justice. For the Reformed churches, one might even argue that the Lord's Supper is *the* liturgical acting out of the thanksgiving invited by Psalm 100 and the other songs of praise in the Psalter. As Brian Gerrish puts it, "The holy banquet is simply the liturgical enactment of the theme of grace and gratitude that lies at the heart of Calvin's entire theology. . . . It is, in short, a 'eucharistic' theology."[15] It is, in other words, a the-

14. Elsa Tamez, *The Amnesty of Grace: Justification by Faith from a Latin American Perspective*, trans. Sharon H. Ringe (Nashville: Abingdon Press, 1993), esp. pp. 134-54.

15. Brian Gerrish, *Grace and Gratitude: The Eucharistic Theology of John Calvin* (Minneapolis: Fortress Press, 1993), p. 20. See also William C. Placher, *Narratives of a Vulnerable God: Christ, Theology, and Scripture* (Louisville: Westminster John Knox Press, 1994), pp. 137-60; and William T. Cavanaugh, *Torture and Eucharist: Theology, Politics, and the Body of*

ology congruent with the invitation of the Psalms to recognize God's prior and fundamental claim on the life of the world, and to respond with unceasing gratitude in liturgy and lifestyle.

Caring for the Earth

Henri Nouwen's conclusion that gratitude "can prevent us from destroying ourselves and our planet" — along with Brian Wren's invitation to "give to earth, and all things living, liturgies of care" — suggest a final dimension of what it means to participate in the justice, righteousness, and *shalom* that God wills. The use of the Psalms in worship can remind us that God's will for justice really is *universe*-encompassing, embracing not only all peoples but also all creatures and all things. It is of paramount importance that God's presence in the world is greeted, according to the psalmist, by "the sea . . . and all that fills it," "the cosmic rivers," and "the mountains" (Ps. 98:7-8; see Pss. 96:11-12; 148:1-13). It may be an anachronism to label the psalmists "environmentalists" or "ecological activists," but their perspective on creation certainly invites contemporary worshipers to be deeply attuned to and concerned for the whole creation.

As did its opening invitation, the conclusion to Psalm 100 also articulates a universe-encompassing perspective. As is typical for a song of praise, Psalm 100 concludes with a statement of reasons to praise God. The reasons are simple and standard (see Pss. 106:1; 107:1; 117:2; 118:1, 29; 136:1), but profoundly meaningful and important. Given the creation-wide perspective that is present from the beginning of Psalm 100 (as well as the creation-wide perspective represented in Psalm 98 and others of the preceding enthronement psalms and other songs of praise), the adjective "good" in verse 5 recalls the repeated divine assessment of creation in Genesis 1. In this regard, it is noteworthy that contemporary theologians are suggesting the appropriateness of thinking about creation as God's "play." As Daniel L. Migliore puts it,

---

Christ, Challenges in Contemporary Theology (Oxford: Blackwell Publishers, 1998). Cavanaugh argues for what he recognizes will sound like an "odd claim" — namely, "that the Eucharist is the key to Christian resistance to torture" (p. 279). He demonstrates how liturgical, Eucharistic activities by oppressed persons in Chile created the solidarity and courage that allowed them to stand against the repressive, violent, absolutist government of Chile from 1973 to 1990.

We often speak of the creation as a "work" of God. That way of speaking has its place, but it may connote something routine and mostly unpleasant, which is unfortunately the way work is often experienced in human life. It may be more helpful, therefore, to think of the creation of the world as the "play" of God, as a kind of free artistic expression whose origin must be sought ultimately in God's good pleasure.[16]

As Migliore also suggests, when the creation of the world is so conceived, what follows is this: "Creation fittingly expresses the true character of God, who is love."[17]

That the conclusion of Psalm 100 moves from God's goodness to God's "steadfast love" and "faithfulness" is entirely fitting. Actually, the word pair "steadfast love" and "faithfulness" recalls most explicitly not the creation accounts but rather God's grace and mercy shown to sinful Israel following the golden-calf episode in the book of Exodus (Exod. 34:6-7; note also the appearance of this word pair in Ps. 98:3). Not coincidentally, however, the Exodus itself is portrayed as a new creation (note the role of the "wind" or "spirit" in Exod. 14:21, recalling Gen. 1:2; note as well the appearance of "dry land," recalling Gen. 1:9), and this further episode in the book of Exodus amounts to another new creation, resulting from God's gracious love (see the appearance in Exod. 34:10 of the Hebrew verb that is especially used for God's creative activity, which the NRSV translates as "been performed").

To be sure, the creation-wide perspective that leads people to care for the earth is related to the awareness that "we are not our own" and to the psalmic invitation to live with gratitude. The current environmental crisis derives largely from the conviction that we humans are "self-made" and consequently "own" the world and deserve the right to dominate it — what Anne Lamott calls "the illusion that we are in charge" and Henri Nouwen calls "the illusion of power and control." Another hymn by Brian Wren voices eloquently the humble gratitude that the Psalms invite in relation to the whole creation:

Thank you, God, for water, soil, and air,
large gifts supporting everything that lives.

---

16. Daniel L. Migliore, *Faith Seeking Understanding: An Introduction to Christian Theology* (Grand Rapids: Eerdmans, 1991), p. 93.

17. Migliore, *Faith Seeking Understanding*, p. 85.

Forgive our spoiling and abuse of them.
Help us renew the face of the earth.

Thank you, God, for minerals and ores,
the basis of all building, wealth, and speed.
Forgive our reckless plundering and waste.
Help us renew the face of the earth.

Thank you, God, for priceless energy,
stored in each atom, gathered from the sun.
Forgive our greed and carelessness of power.
Help us renew the face of the earth.

Thank you, God, for weaving nature's life
into a seamless robe, a fragile whole.
Forgive our haste that tampers unaware.
Help us renew the face of the earth.

Thank you, God, for making planet earth
a home for us and ages yet unborn.
Help us to share, consider, save, and store.
Come and renew the face of the earth.[18]

Unfortunately, the persistence of "the illusion that we are in charge" makes the use of the Psalms in worship all the more timely, indeed urgent. Peter Raven, Director of the Missouri Botanical Garden and an internationally known botanist and conservationist, recently said that it is "incredibly stupid" for human beings to drive to extinction the very lifeforms on which our own survival depends.[19] And yet we are doing precisely this at an alarming and unprecedented rate. But beyond our own self-interest and survival, worshipers of the God revealed in the Psalms

18. Brian Wren, "Thank You, God, for Water, Soil, and Air," in *Worship and Rejoice* (Carol Stream, Ill.: Hope Publishing Company, 2001), no. 36. Text: Brian Wren (b. 1936), 1973. Text copyright © 1975 Hope Publishing Company, Carol Stream, IL 60188. All rights reserved. Used by permission.

19. Peter Raven, in an address given at an environmental conference held on 25 April 2002 in St. Louis, sponsored by the Missouri Botanical Garden and the Episcopal Diocese of Missouri.

have a simple reason to be proponents of ecological justice: "The earth is the LORD's and all that is in it" (Ps. 24:1), and God wills that the whole creation participate in an unending chorus of praise.[20]

Saturated with Justice

The preceding analysis of Psalms 9–10 and Psalms 98 and 100 and their implications is meant to illustrate that the book of Psalms is, in the words of Paul Westermeyer, "saturated with justice." He continues,

> Justice is on every page of the Psalter. Justice is sung throughout the Psalms. Justice and song lead back and forth to one another, and the whole Psalter with all its concerns for justice leads to the song of praise in Psalm 150 toward which the whole cosmos is moving. The *telos* of praise contains justice within it as a part of its very essence.[21]

In the days following the tragic events of September 11, 2001, a National Public Radio correspondent asked the poet laureate of the United States, Billy Collins, for a literary response. His suggestion was to read the book of Psalms. In a world like ours, beset by violence, victimization, selfishness, greed, ecological catastrophe, and rapidly growing extremes of poverty and affluence, it is perhaps a small but encouraging sign that the book of Psalms is being rediscovered. As it has for centuries, the book of Psalms will remain a primary source for the worship of God that invites us out of a selfish complacency and into the faithful pursuit of God's universe-encompassing justice, righteousness, and *shalom*.

20. See J. Clinton McCann Jr., "Righteousness, Justice, and Peace: A Contemporary Theology of the Psalms," *Horizons in Biblical Theology* 23 (2001): 128-31. See also Terence Fretheim, "Nature's Praise of God in the Psalms," *Ex Auditu* 3 (1987): 16-30, esp. 27-30; James Limburg, "Who Cares for the Earth? Psalm 8 and the Environment," in *Word and World Supplement Series* 1 (1992): 43-52; and James Limburg, "Down-to-Earth Theology: Psalm 104 and the Environment," *Currents in Theology and Mission* 21 (1994): 340-46.

21. Paul Westermeyer, *Let Justice Sing: Hymnody and Justice,* American Essays in Liturgy (Collegeville, Minn.: Liturgical Press, 1998), pp. 29-31.

Heaven Shall Not Wait

Heaven shall not wait
for the poor to lose their patience,
the scorned to smile, the despised to find a friend:
Jesus is Lord;
he has championed the unwanted;
in him injustice confronts its timely end.

Heaven shall not wait
for the rich to share their fortunes,
the proud to fall, the élite to tend the least:
Jesus is Lord;
he has shown the masters' privilege —
to kneel and wash servants' feet before they feast.

Heaven shall not wait
for the dawn of great ideas,
thoughts of compassion divorced from cries of pain:
Jesus is Lord;
he has married word and action;
his cross and company make his purpose plain.

Heaven shall not wait
for triumphant Hallelujahs,
when earth has passed and we reach another shore:
Jesus is Lord
in our present imperfection;
his power and love are for now; and then for ever more.

Text: John L. Bell (b. 1949) and Graham Maule (b. 1958)
Text copyright © 1987, Wild Goose Resource Group, Iona Community, Scotland. GIA Publications, Inc., exclusive North American agent, 7404 S. Mason Ave., Chicago, IL 60638
(www.giamusic.com; 800.442.1358). All rights reserved. Used by permission.

We Are Not Our Own

We are not our own. Earth forms us,
human leaves on nature's growing vine,
fruit of many generations,
seeds of life divine.

We are not alone. Earth names us:
past and present, peoples near and far,
family and friends and strangers
show us who we are.

Through a human life God finds us;
dying, living, love is fully known,
and in bread and wine reminds us:
we are not our own.

Therefore let us make thanksgiving,
and with justice, willing and aware,
give to earth, and all things living,
liturgies of care.

And if love's encounters lead us
on a way uncertain and unknown,
all the saints with prayer surround us:
we are not alone.

Let us be a house of welcome,
living stone upholding living stone,
gladly showing all our neighbors
we are not our own!

Text: Brian Wren (b. 1936), 1987
Text copyright © 1989 Hope Publishing Company, Carol Stream, IL 60188. All rights reserved.
Used by permission.

FOR FURTHER READING

J. David Plains. *The Psalms: Songs of Tragedy, Hope, and Justice* (Maryknoll, N.Y.: Orbis Books, 1993). Organized by traditional form-critical categories, this volume systematically explores what the author identifies as "the question of 'suffering, social justice, and worship' in the Psalter" (p. 1), taking seriously the contemporary global context of pervasive poverty and oppression.

Stephen Breck Reid, ed. *Psalms and Practice: Worship, Virtue, and Authority* (Collegeville, Minn.: Liturgical Press, 2001). Several of the fifteen essays collected in this volume deal specifically with the Psalms in worship, including prayer, song, and preaching. See especially Part II, "Psalms and Practice: Contemplation and Worship," pp. 59-158.

Paul Westermeyer. *Let Justice Sing: Hymnody and Justice,* American Essays in Liturgy (Collegeville, Minn.: Liturgical Press, 1998). After a documentation of the pervasiveness of the theme of justice in twentieth-century hymnody, the volume explores historical antecedents of this reality, including the book of Psalms, the hymns of Luther and Wesley, and African-American spirituals. The volume concludes with an assessment of the significance of the theme of justice in the church's hymnody.

Knowing Our Limits:
Job's Wisdom on Worship

CAROL M. BECHTEL

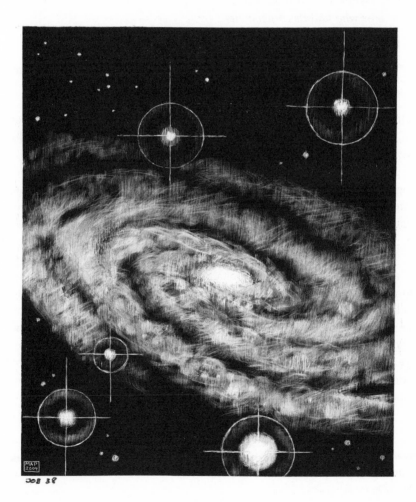

Then the LORD answered Job out of the whirlwind:
"Who is this that darkens counsel
  by words without knowledge?
Gird up your loins like a man,
  I will question you, and you shall declare to me.
Where were you when I laid the foundation of the earth?
  Tell me, if you have understanding.
Who determined its measurements — surely you know!
  Or who stretched the line upon it?
On what were its bases sunk,
  or who laid its cornerstone
when the morning stars sang together
  and all the heavenly beings shouted for joy?"

Job 38:1-7

The book of Job may seem like a strange place to search for wisdom on worship. Stranger still is the section of Job on which this essay will focus. Job 38:1-7 is the beginning of God's enigmatic response to Job's demand for an explanation of his suffering. Over the centuries, many readers of this passage have expressed dissatisfaction with God's reply, pointing out that God effectively sidesteps Job's questions. "Where were you when I laid the foundation of the earth?" seems nonresponsive at best, and callous at worst. Students of pastoral care might well give God low marks for listening skills.

There is a sense, however, in which Job's ancient story is precisely where we need to begin when we talk about what it means for human beings to join creation's chorus in the worship of an almighty God. That is because this Old Testament book cuts straight to the heart of our assumptions about who we are in relation to God and the universe. If we do not get those assumptions straight before we darken the door of God's house, we could well be in danger of "darken[ing] counsel by words without knowledge" (Job 38:2). Chances are, we already have — in which case, God's questions to Job in these essays are directed straight at us!

To paraphrase the book of Job's own extended meditation of where to

Portions of "Reading Job through the Lens of Human Limits" may also be found in a curriculum by this author, *Job and the Life of Faith: Wisdom for Today's World* (Pittsburgh: Kerygma, 1995).

find wisdom (chap. 28): How shall this "worship wisdom" be found? And how shall we go about gaining this kind of understanding?

The first step will be to re-evaluate the book of Job as a whole. What are its central questions? How does the structure of the book itself shape our understanding of what this book is about? Once we have arrived at a theory of the book's theme, what difference does it make for interpretation if we read the rest of the book through that theme's lens?

Next, we will need to apply our learning to the world of worship. Two sections entitled "Worship as Reality Check" and "All Nature Sings" will attempt to focus more specifically on the "where were you" speeches of Job 38–41 while "mining" them for implications relating to worship. That these sections will not be exhaustive goes without saying, since, after all, no one but God fully understands the way to wisdom (Job 28:23). They will, however, be suggestive. Finally, each reader must look to his or her own heart and situation and ask, "How must I reshape my assumptions and actions on the basis of Job's wisdom for worship?"

Reading Job through the Lens of Human Limits

Popular opinion would probably identify the central theme of the book of Job as "the problem of human suffering," or, more broadly, "the problem of evil." While the question of theodicy is certainly important for the book, we might want to rethink this identification of its centrality. There is a sense in which the problem of suffering is only *the presenting problem* in the book of Job. Its central theme has to do with *the limits of human wisdom*. This assertion is based on an analysis of the prologue, which offers critical clues for the interpretation of the whole book.

The Prologue: Chapters 1–2

If we look carefully at the way the book of Job is organized (leaving aside the question of the book's complex literary evolution), there is a kind of "upstairs/downstairs" configuration at work. This is most apparent in the prose prologue (chaps. 1–2), which alternates between scenes that take place on earth ("downstairs"), and those that transpire in the heavenly court ("upstairs").

An Outline of the Book of Job

I. Prologue (chaps. 1:1–2:13)

Upstairs: 1:6-12   2:1-6

Downstairs: 1:1-5   1:13-22   2:7-13

II. Dialogues: Human to Human (chaps. 3–27)

Opening Soliloquy (3:1-26)

Cycle A (chaps. 4–14)

Round 1: Eliphaz (chaps. 4–5)
Job (chaps. 6–7)

Round 2: Bildad (chap. 8)
Job (chaps. 9–10)

Round 3: Zophar (chap. 11)
Job (chaps. 12–14)

Cycle B (chaps. 15–21)

Round 1: Eliphaz (chap. 15)
Job (chaps. 16–17)

Round 2: Bildad (chap. 18)
Job (chap. 19)

Round 3: Zophar (chap. 20)
Job (chap. 21)

Job is introduced downstairs in 1:1-5. Even before the storyteller regales us with the description of Job's great wealth and fine family, he tells us that Job is "blameless and upright, one who fear(s) God and turn(s) away from evil" (v. 1). This is high praise indeed — so high, in fact, that Christians are often quick to raise a mental objection along the lines of Romans 3:23 ("all have sinned and fall short of the glory of God"). We must remember, however, that the narrator is not suggesting that Job is *sinless;* rather, Job is described as *blameless.* (God uses this same word to

Cycle C (chaps. 22–27)

> Round 1: Eliphaz (chap. 22)
> Job (chaps. 23–24)

> Round 2: Bildad (chap. 25)
> Job (chaps. 26–27)*

III. Hymn to Wisdom (chap. 28)

IV. Dialogues: Human and Divine (chaps. 29:1–42:6)

Job's summation and oaths (chaps. 29–31)

Elihu's interjection (chaps. 32–37)

God's response (chaps. 38–41)

> Round 1: God (chaps. 38:1–40:2)
> Job (40:3-5)

> Round 2: God (chaps. 40:6–41:34)
> Job (42:1-6)

V. Epilogue (chap. 42:7-17)

*The dialogue appears to break down here. Some scholars suggest that 27:7-23 contains the "lost speech" of Zophar.

describe him in 1:8 and 2:3.) Given the Old Testament context of this story and the details about Job's offering sacrifices for his children, we should probably assume that his blameless state is the result of scrupulous habits of sacrifice combined with a genuinely righteous character.

Upstairs in 1:6-12, God indulges in what could be characterized as self-congratulatory statements about the loyal Job. This draws the attention of a member of the heavenly court called "the satan" or, more literally, "the adversary." The two make a wager on whether or not Job will "fear God for

Satan in the Old Testament

Readers of the New Testament — and John Milton's *Paradise Lost* — may have difficulty knowing what to make of "the satan" character in the prologue of Job. If we are expecting the "devil" (Matt. 4:1), the "tempter" (Matt. 4:3), the "accuser" (Rev. 12:10), the "ruler of the demons" (Luke 11:15), or the "ruler of this world" (John 12:31), we will be disappointed. And if we insist on superimposing these more malevolent figures on the character of Job, the results will be both confusing and misleading.

Perhaps it will help us to read Job more objectively if we start at the beginning of the Bible and read forward rather than the other way around.

The Old Testament is quite candid about the presence and reality of evil, though it does not speculate much about its origins. Still less does it seek to personify evil. To do so would have been to give it too much credit. All things were seen as being somehow, mysteriously, within God's powerful aegis. This accounts for statements like the one from Job's own lips: "Shall we receive the good at the hand of God, and not receive the bad?" (Job 2:10).

In the story of Balaam and his infamous donkey in Numbers 22, we encounter an angel (or messenger) from God who block's Balaam's path. The Bible says that this angel "took his stand in the road as his adversary" — literally, his *satan* (Num. 22:22). Here we see the word *satan* being used simply as a descriptive noun; it denotes one who gets in the way but not necessarily with evil or malevolent intent.

nothing" — that is, whether Job will live an obedient life if there is nothing in it for him (1:9). God is confident Job will; the adversary is convinced that Job's loyalty will evaporate as fast as his possessions.

Downstairs in 1:13-22, the messengers fairly trip over one another to bring Job the bad news about a series of disasters that have wiped out his livestock, his livelihood, and finally, his children. Job responds with understandable grief. Yet when we expect him to curse God, he worships instead (1:20)! "Naked I came from my mother's womb," he says in words made familiar by many funeral liturgies, "and naked shall I return there; the LORD gave, and the LORD has taken away; blessed be the name of the LORD" (1:21).

In both Job 1–2 and Zechariah 3:1-2 we encounter the word *satan* again. In both these instances it is used with the definite article (**the** *satan*) and refers to a member of the heavenly court. Thus, while it has slightly more specificity than the example in Numbers, it is still a far cry from being a proper noun. Instead, it attaches to a character that is clearly under God's control and whose function it is to inform God about whether humans have been "naughty or nice." The most useful modern analogy might be to a prosecuting attorney.

The one other example of the noun's use in the Old Testament comes from 1 Chronicles 21:1, where the NRSV says, "Satan stood up against Israel, and incited David to count the people of Israel." Interestingly, the parallel passage in 2 Samuel 24:1 credits "the anger of the LORD" as the force that incited David. In light of this parallel and the uses of the word already cited in Job and Zechariah (also from the post-exilic period), it would seem more responsible to translate the noun in the Chronicles passage as simply "an adversary."

The search for "Satan" with a capital "s" does not truly succeed until the literature of the intertestamental period. Here — most probably under the influence of the more dualistic Persian religion, Zoroastrianism — Satan came to be understood as the personification of evil and the leader of the demonic powers. It was also during this period that the snake of Genesis three began to be associated with Satan. (For further information, see the article entitled "Satan" by J. M. Efird in *Harper's Bible Dictionary* [San Francisco: Harper & Row, 1985], pp. 908-9.)

The scene shifts back upstairs in 2:1-6, where the satan and God carry on a conversation very like the one they had before. This time, however, God gives the satan permission to torture Job within an inch of his life, effectively raising the stakes of the heavenly bet. The directive is carried out downstairs in 2:7-12, and Job finds himself inflicted with "loathsome sores . . . from the sole of his foot to the crown of his head" (2:7). Job's wife (whom Augustine uncharitably called "the devil's helpmeet") advises him to "curse God, and die" (2:9). Under the circumstances, her advice seems both practical and understandable. Job, however, refuses to turn against God. The scene closes with Job receiving a pastoral call from his three friends, who sit beside him on his ash heap for seven days and nights, only opening their mouths to weep.

In subsequent chapters, the friends are not so silent, nor Job so patient. But before we move on to the rest of the story, we need to take stock of what the structure of the prologue has suggested about the theme of the book.

What most of us fail to realize is that we as readers know far more than the human characters do. As is so often the case, it helps to ask, "What do the characters know, and when do they know it?" Job and his wife, along with the three friends, are completely clueless about the heavenly wager that's been placed "upstairs."[1] They are, as George Eliot once put it, "well-wadded in stupidity."[2]

Why is this so important? Simply because it sets up the central theme of the book — namely, the limits of human wisdom. Job and the other human characters operate with very limited information. This is particularly obvious when the friends (after their golden silence in the prologue) assume that "somewhere in his youth or childhood, Job must have done something bad." From their perspective, Job's suffering is a consequence of this unknown sin. Their assumption is based on the theology of retributive justice — popular throughout the ages — which assumes a direct correlation between obedience and blessing, sin and suffering. In this instance, however, such logic flies in the face of God's own statements about Job's blameless character (1:8 and 2:3). But remember, *the friends do not hear this statement;* only the readers and the members of the heavenly court do.

Similarly, Job's unnamed wife responds to their joint plight on the basis of limited information. She knows better than anyone that her husband is a good man. Over the years she has watched him get up early to go and make sacrifices for each of their children, as if he could somehow sanctify them in the overflow of his own righteousness (1:4-5). For most of their lives it must have seemed as if God was rewarding Job's righteousness, and that they were enjoying blessings in proportion to Job's exemplary behavior. Now, however, the scales of God's justice seem to have gone completely

1. We as readers may wish we did not know either, as the heavenly wager presents some real difficulties with regard to God's character. Still, Job's author(s) must have felt this was worth the risk. Readers who are troubled by this picture of God can take comfort in the fact that this is not the only book in the Scripture's canon.

2. George Eliot, *Middlemarch*, first published 1871-72 (New York: Penguin Books, 1985), chap. 20, p. 226.

haywire. Has her husband served God so faithfully all these years for this? Knowing Job as she does, she does not seem even to consider the explanation that Job's friends suggest: that Job has brought all this on himself (and on her!) through some secret sin. Failing that explanation, however, she can see, evidently, only one other: that God is not just. This explanation represents the realization of her (and our) worst fears — namely, that the God she knew to be just is in actuality a capricious tyrant. From her limited perspective, then, Job may as well "curse God, and die" (2:9), since an unjust God is not worthy of our trust, our service, or our worship.

Job shares her limited perspective, but not her negative conclusion. He too is faced with the choice of whether or not to trust God in the midst of dire circumstances and limited information. But his response is one of faith. True, he will rail against the apparent injustice of his situation and eventually will demand an explanation (chap. 31); but he does not — here or later in the book — "curse God, and die." His response points beyond despair to another possibility: faith in the face of limited information.

The beauty of Mr. and Mrs. Job's story is that it so closely parallels our own. Though not many of us have experienced a litany of disasters such as theirs, we do share their limited perspective. We too seek to make sense of our lives and losses without benefit of full information. We too are asked to stand in the midst of suffering and choose between despair and faith.

The beauty of the inclusion of the book of Job in the canon is that it gives us a rare glimpse into the heavenly court. We may not be entirely comfortable with what we see there, but at least it helps us to be sure of one thing: *Now we know for sure that human suffering is not always the consequence of some specific sin.* This canonical moment should give us pause every time we hear (or ask) the well-worn question "What did I do to deserve this?" The answer may well be "Nothing." Because of this glimpse, we know that the answer to this question may not be as simple as we had assumed. There may be times when there is more going on than is dreamt of in our theology, and we cannot with any confidence read the traditional equation between sin and suffering in the reverse. In short, the prologue to Job cautions us against claiming to know more than we can within the limits of human wisdom.

But what about the rest of the book? Does it fit with this revised notion of what it is "about"? In what follows we will use the theme of limited wisdom as a lens through which to read the rest of the book of Job.

The Debate with the Three Friends: Chapters 3–28

While Job does not curse God, he does spend the lion's share of chapter three creatively cursing the day of his birth. This outburst is too much for his friends — Eliphaz, Bildad, and Zophar — who spend chapters 4–27 trying to argue Job out of his innocence.

As was already suggested above, a new sense of the book's theme cautions us against giving too much credence to the arguments of Job's friends. The debate that they carry on with their "friend" Job covers almost half the book. Sometimes their arguments are eloquent ("Human beings are born to trouble just as sparks fly upward" — 5:7); sometimes they are arrogant ("Know then that God exacts of you less than your guilt deserves" — 11:6); and sometimes they are downright libelous ("You have sent widows away empty-handed, and the arms of the orphans you have crushed" — 22:9). In the final analysis, however, they are simply wrong. We know this because of our rare glimpse into the heavenly court. If we still have any doubts, however, God's own judgment will put them to rest in 42:7-8. There God announces with crucifying candor: "You have not spoken of me what is right, as my servant Job has. . . . I will accept his prayer not to deal with you according to your folly."

Just when the debate between Job and his friends seems to be deteriorating to the point of incoherence, the book takes a breath. In what has often seemed a non sequitur, the debate is interrupted by a hymn (presumably by the book's narrator) on the inaccessibility of wisdom. In light of our revised description of the book's theme, this makes perfect sense. The inaccessibility of wisdom is precisely the point, and the previous twenty-three chapters have illustrated it. "Where then does wisdom come from? And where is the place of understanding?" verse twenty asks. "It is hidden from the eyes of all living," replies verse twenty-one. Even Death has only heard a rumor of it (v. 22). God, on the other hand, knows well "the way to it" and "knows its place" (v. 23). The chapter concludes with some sage advice on what human beings ought to do in the face of our limited understanding. "Truly," God counsels in verse twenty-eight, "the fear of the Lord, that is wisdom; and to depart from evil is understanding." In other words, reverence for and obedience to God constitute the only wise course of action in light of our limits.

Job Serves a Subpoena: Chapters 29–31

Once again, we as readers know more than the human characters do. While we have been privy to chapter twenty-eight's helpful meditation on the inaccessibility of wisdom, Job and the friends have not. So when Job rises to speak his mind in chapter twenty-nine, he speaks without reference to God's advice at the end of the hymn. Perhaps as significantly, Job speaks no longer to the friends, but directly to God. In chapters 29–31 he summarizes his position and swears a series of scathing oaths with regard to his innocence. The climax of his argument is the ultimatum in 31:35:

> Oh, that I had one to hear me!
> (Here is my signature! let the Almighty answer me!)

It is as if Job has served God with a subpoena, calling God to testify in a court of Job's own choosing. (And in Job's court, God seems to be the accused rather than the judge!) Job throws in one more oath of innocence for good measure and returns to the plaintiff's desk to see what will transpire.

Elihu's Interruption: Chapters 32–37

When chapter thirty-one closes with "the words of Job are ended," we as readers are bracing ourselves for the lightning bolt we assume will ensue. We, after all, know that God does not deserve this, and we worry that Job has finally gone too far, overstepping the limits of both propriety and wisdom.

Instead of a lightning bolt, however, we get Elihu.

The most common response to Elihu's presence at this point in the book is "Elihu who?" He is not one of the original friends. Neither is his presence reflected (positively or negatively) in God's judgment against the friends in the epilogue. Because of this, most scholars assume that Elihu's speeches in chapters 32–37 are an interjection by a later editor who thought he/she could do a better job than the friends of defending the traditional doctrine of retributive justice. It is also the judgment of most scholars that he/she does not.

One of the things Elihu *does* do, however, is represent the youth of the world (32:6). By his own account, he speaks up at this point because his more aged friends have not succeeded in defending either God or orthodoxy. Whatever the original intention of the inclusion of these chapters, they now have the effect of demonstrating that youth does not have the answers either. The most pointed critique of Elihu's words comes from the fact that even God ignores them. God seems to wave away Elihu's arguments like so many pesky mosquitoes. When God's voice thunders out from the center of the whirlwind in chapter thirty-eight, it is a storm directed solely at Job.

God Responds to Job: Chapters 38–41

"Where were you when I laid the foundation of the earth?" God asks in the first of a relentless barrage of rhetorical questions. "Tell me, if you have understanding. Who determined its measurements — surely you know!" (38:4-5).

Perhaps Job is too terrified at this point to ask himself "Is this germane?" Generations of readers, however, have had sufficient presence of mind to ask this very question. "Where were you when . . . ?" is hardly the response we — or Job — are hoping for here. As was mentioned in this essay's introduction, God's apparent disregard for Job's questions has left many readers dissatisfied.

Yet, before we complain too much about what God *does not* say in these chapters, perhaps we should look first at what God *does* say.

First, it is significant that God responds to Job at all. This is surely a measure of both God's grace in general and God's regard for Job in particular. It is a bit like Einstein taking time out to explain the theory of general relativity to his beagle. Like God (in this purely fanciful and obviously flawed analogy), Einstein know that the beagle has not got a prayer of understanding the true explanation. So Einstein gives the faithful beagle what he *does* need and *can,* in fact, comprehend: a reality check. "You are a beagle," he says with admirable patience. "I am a brilliant scientist. I love you enough to take time out for this little talk, but you must know you're out of your league."

It is also significant that God speaks from a whirlwind. This powerful image is often used in conjunction with God's wrath (see Isa. 29:6; Jer. 23:19 and 30:23; Ezek. 13:11, 13; and Zech. 9:14). It is also used in a more positive (but no less daunting) sense in passages describing a dramatic manifestation of God's presence often called a theophany. The whirlwind is the means by which Elijah is taken up to heaven in 2 Kings 2:1 and 11. Ezekiel's vision on the banks of the river Chebar also commences with this same "stormy wind" that whirls out of the north: "a great cloud with brightness around it and fire flashing forth continually" (Ezek. 1:4).

Perhaps what the image of the whirlwind conveys most powerfully in all of these contexts is the utter uncontrollability of God. Anyone who has ever experienced a tornado or a hurricane can testify to the sense of human helplessness in the face of overwhelming and unpredictable force. This is precisely the sense that Job (and we) need to feel as we listen to the voice that booms out of the whirlwind.

God's words in both divine speeches (38:1–40:2; 40:6–41:34) are laced with no small amount of sarcasm. God demands to know where Job was when God created any number of natural wonders. It a list that Ellen Davis calls "a cosmological and zoological tour-de-force,"[3] and it is not arranged at random. There is a kind of relentless rhetoric to God's review of creation. God starts with the land, the sea, the constellations, and the weather, then moves on to caress the memory of any number of creatures, from the wild ass to the famously idiotic (albeit fast) ostrich. But the "big finish" (and God's clear favorite) is the sea-monster, Leviathan, who occupies God's attention for the bulk of chapter forty-one. If Job has any doubts left about the gulf between creature and creator, God's mastery of Leviathan must surely banish them. "Can you draw out Leviathan with a fishhook?" God asks almost casually. "Will you play with it as with a bird, or will you put it on leash for your girls?" (41:1, 5). And yet, Job must also be overwhelmed by the utter glee that God takes in each one of God's creatures — of which Job is one. And perhaps, in the midst of his terror, Job also realizes that he is the only creature whom God has honored with such a vision.

God's words from the whirlwind are an overwhelming reminder of both the distance and the indelible bond between Creator and creature. Perhaps this is precisely the reminder Job needs at this point. And perhaps he needs it more than he needs an explanation for his suffering.

One wonders if some of the dissatisfaction people feel with God's re-

---

3. Ellen Davis, "Job and Jacob: The Integrity of Faith," in *The Whirlwind: Essays on Job, Hermeneutics, and Theology in Memory of Jane Morse,* ed. Stephen L. Cook, Corrine L. Patton, and James W. Watts (Sheffield: Sheffield Academic Press, 2001), p. 115.

sponse is based on the assumption that this book is "about" the problem of human suffering. If we assume that this is the book's main theme, then we, with Job, are poised for an explanation and disappointed when we don't get it. But if the book is not *primarily* about human suffering, then God's words in these chapters do not seem evasive at all. On the contrary, once we understand that the book is about the limits of human wisdom, they are "spot on." They, along with everything that's gone before in this book, work together to remind us that we live, love, lose, and learn within the limits of our "creatureliness."

Job Responds to God: Chapters 40:3-5; 42:1-6

That Job dares to respond at all is remarkable, but perhaps this is out of his control as well when God declares, "Anyone who argues with God must respond" (40:2).

Job's first response to God in 40:3-5 says very little. He essentially speaks just long enough to say that he is not going to speak anymore. This reply does not seem to pass muster with the Almighty, and God launches into another list of humbling questions.

Job's second response in 42:1-6 has significantly more substance, and is evidently much more satisfactory from God's perspective. (No new questions ensue, after all.) It has not been as satisfactory for centuries of interpreters, however, who have often seen it as either an admission of the "secret sin" of which the three friends had accused him, or an expression of shame and self-loathing. Both readings are equally wrong. A fresh look at the translation of 42:6 may help us to see why.

Many translations (KVJ, RSV, NRSV, NIV) render the second half of the verse along these lines: "Therefore I despise myself, and repent in dust and ashes." But take a look at the way this is rendered by the translators of the Jewish Publication Society:

Therefore, I recant and relent,
Being but dust and ashes.[4]

---

4. *Tanakh: The Holy Scriptures* (Philadelphia/New York: Jewish Publication Society, 1985), p. 1402.

The first thing to notice is that the phrase "despise myself" has disappeared. Instead, we find the word "recant." This is almost certainly a better choice for the Hebrew word here, *ma'as,* since in this case it occurs without an object ("myself" is not in the Hebrew). The traditional translation of the next word, *nhm* (Niphal), is "repent," which for most modern readers has a negative connotation; one "repents," after all, of sins. While the word can have this meaning in Hebrew, it can also simply mean a change of heart or mind. Another modern translator has simply rendered the word here as "reconsider."[5]

What, we may ask, has caused Job to "relent" or to "reconsider"? If we look to the context, we would guess that it is his newfound awareness of his creatureliness. And, sure enough, the last phrase of 42:6 makes reference to this very thing. "Dust and ashes" (a pun in Hebrew — *'apar wa'eper*) is a biblical metaphor for what it means to be a creature in contrast with the Creator. In Genesis 18:27, for instance, Abraham works up the courage to bargain with God for the fate of Sodom by saying, "Let me take it upon myself to speak to the Lord, I who am but dust and ashes." So, in Job 42:6, as Ellen Davis explains,

> Job does not heap literal or metaphorical ashes on his head. With humility and dignity, he attests to his new understanding of the human condition, as befits one whom God has honored with a vision. Job accepts the fact that God's unsentimental and exquisite regard for the creature is bestowed as freely and no more reasonably on Job than on Leviathan. And with that acceptance, the transformation of the saint is complete. Stripped at last of the final defense of his ego, Job claims full affinity with the world as God's creation.[6]

In short, he admits that his own wisdom is limited; he bows to a God whose wisdom is limitless.

Job's position at the end of this second speech is precisely where he needs to be — and we need to be — in order to worship God fully and rightly. He understands, at last, "about dust and ashes" — that is, about what it means to be human. This meaning has two important reference points, both of which were made clear by God's relentless questions. First,

5. Davis, "Job and Jacob: The Integrity of Faith," p. 118.
6. Davis, "Job and Jacob: The Integrity of Faith," p. 118.

human beings are, for all their glory, still distinct from their Creator. (God is God, and we are not.) Second, human beings are aligned with the rest of the created order in a much more intimate way than we often assume. (How often have you heard someone refer to "nature" as if it were something distinct from human beings?)

More will be said below about the implications of this "reality check" for worship. First, however, we need to finish our reading of Job in the light of the limits of human wisdom.

The Epilogue: Chapter 42:7-17

Once again, the critics have not always been kind to the authors and editors of Job. Job's "restoration" in the prose epilogue has taken more heat than any other part of the book. Perhaps we owe it to the faithful of every age to at least ask "Why?"

First, there is the matter of its looking — at first glance — like a vindication for the mechanistic application of the doctrine of retributive justice. A more sustained scrutiny reveals that this is not the case, however. As we have seen, Job does not "repent" of his sin so much as re-orient himself to God's reality. If that is the case, then his restoration in the epilogue does not represent "reward" so much as a "return to normal." The heavenly bet has been settled; life goes on.

The second source of dissatisfaction is not so easily dealt with, however. To give credit where credit is due, I would like to indulge in a personal story at this point. I had just finished reading the story of Job to my two children (then ages ten and eight). At the conclusion of the epilogue in the children's Bible (condensed version), my son Andrew (the elder of the two) beat his usual hasty retreat from the table. My daughter Ellen, however, remained rooted to her chair with a look of utter consternation on her face. Trying to be a sensitive parent as well as a good Bible professor, I asked, "So, Ellen, what did you think about the ending to the book of Job?" She was silent for a minute, then looked me straight in the eye and asked, "If Andy and I died and you got new kids . . . would that make it OK?"

I hastened to tell her, of course, that it would most certainly not be "OK." Then I congratulated her for seeing straight into the heart of the problem of Job's ending. (I am afraid this was cold comfort; years of therapy will probably ensue.) Her question has haunted honest readers of this book for centuries, leaving us unsatisfied about the character of Job's restoration and uncertain about the character of the God who engineered it.

Once again, help arrives in the application of the theme: the limits of human wisdom. Things are not, after all, exactly the same as they were in the prologue. Not only are the children different, but Job is different as well. He is no longer a man who assumes that the world is as neat as a mathematical equation. He no longer assumes that obedience will guarantee blessing. He no longer assumes that God owes him an explanation when things don't work out. Yet, remarkably, he is willing to live — and love — within these limits. It is part of what it means to be human. And it finally answers the question that the satan posed so succinctly in the prologue: "Will Job serve God if there is nothing in it for him?" (1:9; author's paraphrase). The answer, in contrast to what the satan expected, turns out to be "Yes."

Again, Ellen Davis says it best. She suggests that we see the value of the epilogue if we look at it from Job's perspective rather than God's. "From this angle," she says,

> . . . it is seen to be consistent with the rest of the book, a portrait of tenacious faith, stunning not so much for its reward as its cost. For what must it have cost Job, who had been stripped to the bone and borne it . . . to "reinvest" in family and community life, with its obligations, ethical ambiguities, and terrible risks?[7]

Far from being a concession to the theology of the friends, then, the epilogue to Job issues the most profound challenge we as human beings will ever face: life within the limits of human wisdom. It is a life of radical faith, a free fall into what we hope will be God's outstretched arms.

Worship as Reality Check

What does it mean to worship God in light of our reading of the book of Job? What are the implications of this reminder that we are creatures with limits to what we can understand about God and the way life "works"?

In his novel *The Glory of the Hummingbird*, Peter DeVries observes

---

7. Davis, "Job and Jacob: The Integrity of Faith," p. 119.

with appropriate irony, "Anyone informed that the universe is expanding and contracting in pulsations of eighty billion years has a right to ask, 'What's in it for me?'"[8] While it is true that one does have a *right* to ask, one might also pause to consider whether this is the most appropriate question. Frequently, however, it *is* the question that is foremost in our minds as we come to worship. The reasons for this are undoubtedly legion, but here are a few of the most obvious. All of them have at their heart the false assumption that *worship is about us.*

Worship as Entertainment

Those of us in a North American context are saturated with outpourings of the entertainment industry. While many of these are not "bad" in and of themselves, the pervasiveness of the product does have a way of shaping our expectations. Because we are so used to being entertained, we often assume that worship should function for our entertainment as well. We reflect this assumption in subtle ways. For instance, how often have you heard the congregation referred to as an "audience"? Does your congregation applaud after musical "performances"? Do you have a door to the area behind your chancel marked "backstage"? Do you ever complain of being "bored" by the sermon? What do you expect when you see a screen at the front of a sanctuary? How often have you heard (or said), "I just didn't get anything out of that service"?

This is not to say that worship services are always inspiring or that sermons are never boring. (I once observed to my teenagers that while sermons are often boring, God never is.) The point is that all of these examples spring from the assumption that worship is "about" our own entertainment. It is not. It is about God. (Kierkegaard's famous observation about God being the "audience" of our worship fits here, though it may be safer to avoid the language of audience altogether.)

Like Pavlov's proverbial dogs, worshipers respond to certain familiar stimuli in predictable ways. Because of this, worship leaders need to be especially careful about the signals we send lest we activate people's conscious or subconscious assumptions about worship as entertainment. One simple way to do this is to watch our language. Avoid calling the congrega-

8. Peter DeVries, *The Glory of the Hummingbird* (Boston: Little, Brown, 1974), p. 6.

tion an audience. Avoid the temptation to function like a master of ceremonies. And at every turn, let liturgy be what it literally is: "the work of the people." We are not "on stage" to worship for them; we arise from among them to lead. Let someone from the congregation pray the prayer for illumination, or, better yet, have the whole congregation pray it in song. Let the "pastoral prayer" become the "prayers of the people," and invite the congregation to participate, either in their preparation or in their actual presentation to God. Make sure the choir and the other musicians genuinely lead the people in song rather than drowning out or confusing their efforts.

These are just a few examples of practical ways to undermine an assumption that gets worship off on the wrong foot every time.

Worship as Therapy

Let's admit it. Sometimes worship *is* therapeutic. Yet, if we expect it to function that way every time, we are bound to be disappointed. That is as it should be, since, as we've already pointed out, worship is not primarily "about" us, but about God.

Churches that regard worship as primarily therapeutic are misguided on two fronts. Not only is their orientation falsely focused on the human rather than the divine, but the "therapy" itself is by definition doomed to failure. What worship leader can possibly function as a responsible "therapist" for the myriad of individuals who show up for worship on any given Sunday? One person is grieving the death of a parent, child, or spouse; another is celebrating a new job, a new marriage, or a new child. One person needs to be confronted with their destructive behavior; another needs to be reassured of their worth. Where does a worship leader/therapist begin?

Too often, worship that is designed under the therapeutic rubric tends to settle for a single generic task rather than try to do justice to every worshiper's needs. That task is to try to make everyone feel better. The pressure is to make the service uniformly upbeat, so that no matter where people are, they'll leave feeling inspired and uplifted.

Odd decisions get made on the basis of this assumption. Confession of sin is ruled out altogether as being "too much of a downer," or the prayer is simply made so innocuous as to take out its teeth altogether. Sermons are judged by their number of heartwarming stories instead of their faithfulness to Scripture. Music is chosen not because of its appropriateness but because of its ability to manipulate the emotions of the congregation according to an "inspiration quotient." Prayers of intercession are not included because the focus of worship is not on others but on all of the individual "me's" that have shown up on any given Sunday.

In contrast, worship that is focused on God rather than the therapeutic tends to relativize the question of "What's in it for me?" We come not to make ourselves feel better, but to worship a God who is both utterly beyond us and intimately interested in us. Ironically, the effect of this kind of genuine worship encounter is very often to make us feel better — if only because it has given us a break from our own narcissistic self-absorption! We realize at last that we are not the center of the universe, and that both God and the rest of God's creation are worthy of our attention.

Worship as a Vehicle for Self-Expression

Closely related to the "worship as therapy" fallacy is the assumption that worship should function primarily as a vehicle for self-expression. The key word here is "primarily." No one could argue that worship does not give us the opportunity to express our love for God. Even a quick survey of the book of Psalms underscores the power and importance of both baring our souls before God (as in the laments) and expressing our love for God (as in the hymns of praise).

If one looks closely at the form of such biblical hymns, however, one sees that such expressions are focused more on God than on the one worshiping God. One of the most typical traits of a biblical hymn is its insistence on giving God particular praise. That is, the praise is almost always linked to some specific reason for it. The link itself is often signaled by the use of the Hebrew word *ki,* meaning "for." This link is especially easy to see in William Kethe's 1560 paraphrase of Psalm 100 (usually sung to the tune "Old Hundredth," attributed to Louis Bourgeois). After three verses of calling "all people who on earth do dwell" to praise, the reasons for that praise are enumerated in verse four:

> For why? The Lord our God is good; His mercy is forever sure;
> His truth at all times firmly stood, and shall from age to age endure.

Praise in the Bible, then, is not typically detached from the reasons for that praise. This has the effect of keeping worship's focus on God rather than on the worshiper.

How might this biblical pattern impact the ways we worship now? Perhaps it could simply encourage us to take a hard look at the songs we sing in worship. Perhaps it could caution us against singing songs whose primary focus seems to be on self-expression that is disconnected from God's acts and attributes. Perhaps it could nudge us toward worship that is God-centered rather than self-centered.

Preachers would do well to remember that the sermon is not a vehicle for their own self-expression as well. Sermons ideally help congregations to see and hear God's self-expression (that is, Scripture) more clearly. When worship planning for a Service of the Word starts with Scripture and works outward, the whole service points in a "God" direction and not in a "me" direction. The more a preacher and a congregation buy into the notion that the preacher is a celebrity, the less likely this kind of God focus will be.

Worship as a Way of Earning Brownie Points

Most of us would never admit it, but some of us worship because we're trying to "be good." Underneath it, we are trying to impress someone. That "someone" is not necessarily our neighbors (though they often factor in as well). The "someone" we are most concerned to impress is God.

This assumption is often so deeply buried within our subconscious that it only springs out in situations of extreme fear or danger. "But I go to church every Sunday!" we blurt out in the emergency room, as if this is a telling argument for why we should not be suffering. We then feel taken advantage of when God is apparently not persuaded.

Job's friends would have appreciated our disappointment. This assumption — that we can somehow earn our way into God's good graces and thus guarantee success — is at the heart of the doctrine they defended. On one side of the equation is the proposition that "obedience yields blessing." On the flip side is the proposition that "disobedience yields suffering." While this doctrine works fairly well as a *prescription* for how to live, it has serious limitations as a *description* of how life often works out, at least within the limits of what we as human beings see and experience. The book of Job is, among other things, an extended caution-ary tale about this doctrine's rigid application. It is particularly eloquent on the dangers of trying to read the equations backwards. Suffering, after all, is not always a symptom of a specific sin; neither is success a reliable indication of religious devotion. On the contrary, if we take an honest look at the evidence, the wicked frequently prosper, and the righteous of-ten suffer.

These observations ought to make us automatically suspicious of any form of worship that advocates a theology of "success" or "the good life." God, as Job reminds us, cannot be bribed. The only question is this: Are we willing to serve God if there's nothing in it for us?

What Are We Doing Here?

Now that we have cleared the air of some false assumptions about worship, let's return to what the book of Job teaches us about the character of true worship.

One of the most important lessons that Job learns in his encounter with the God who speaks from the center of the whirlwind is that he him-self is not at the center of the universe. Because of this, the book of Job functions as a kind of reality check for us as we contemplate what it means to worship the One who made heaven and earth. This is particularly true of God's speeches in chapters 38–41. God's questions about the genesis of so many of the splendors of the natural world illustrate both God's extrav-agant freedom and Job's inherent limitations.

Annie Dillard's much-quoted comments on this topic are worth quot-ing again. "Why," she asks, "do we people in churches seem like cheerful, brainless tourists on a packaged tour of the Absolute?" She continues,

On the whole, I do not find Christians, outside of the catacombs, suffi-ciently sensible of conditions. Does anyone have the foggiest idea of what sort of power we so blithely invoke? Or, as I suspect, does no one believe a word of it? The churches are children playing on the floor with their chemistry sets, mixing up a batch of TNT to kill a Sunday morn-ing. It is madness to wear ladies' straw hats and velvet hats to church; we should all be wearing crash helmets. Ushers should issue life preservers and signal flairs; they should lash us to our pews. For the sleeping god may wake someday and take offense, or the waking god may draw us out to where we can never return.[9]

No wonder our first response in a genuine encounter with this magnificent God is to realize our own human shortcomings. This is the logic behind the liturgy that, in many traditions, places a prayer of confession after the opening hymn of praise. There is broader biblical precedent for this than just Job. In his vision of God, for instance, Isaiah pauses only long enough to let the seraphim finish their song before he cries out, "Woe is me! I am lost, for I am a man of unclean lips, and I live among a people of unclean lips; yet my eyes have seen the King, the LORD of hosts!" (Isa. 6:5). Only after one of the seraphim touches his lips with a live coal from the altar does he dare utter another word — and that word is an offer to do whatever God tells him!

Similarly, Job's encounter with a wild and uncontrollable God causes him to radically reconsider what it means to be "dust and ashes." It is a reality check we could all benefit from when we approach the throne. Indeed, if we are to be sufficiently "sensible of conditions" as worshipers, we might begin every worship service with some appropriate acknowledgment of our human limits, "touching the altar," as it were, only with fear and trembling.

John Bell's simple but eloquent song is a nice summary of where we as humans need to be as we approach God in worship. It acknowledges both our own limits and God's ability to work in spite of them:

> Take, O take me as I am;
> summon out what I shall be;
> set your seal upon my heart
> and live in me.[10]

---

9. Annie Dillard, *Teaching a Stone to Talk* (San Francisco: Harper & Row, 1982), pp. 40-41.

10. John L. Bell, "Take, O Take Me as I Am," in *Come All You People: Shorter Songs for Worship* (Chicago: GIA Publications, Inc., 1994), p. 88. Text copyright © 1995, Wild Goose Resource Group, Iona Community, Scotland. GIA Publications, Inc., exclusive North American agent, 7404 S. Mason Ave., Chicago, IL 60638 (www.giamusic.com; 800.442.1358). All rights reserved. Used by permission.

All Nature Sings

Now that we have considered the "where were you when" part of God's questions to Job in chapters 38–41, let us look at the other most prominent feature of God's speeches — namely, God's wild delight in the created world.

In what has to be the most extravagant game of "show and tell" ever recorded, God holds up the whole spectrum of creation for Job's admiration (and ours). Each object or phenomenon is honored with a divine caress as it passes in review. The "waterskins of the heavens" have their moment in the spotlight (38:37), as does the wild ostrich: "When it spreads its plumes aloft, it laughs at the horse and its rider" (39:18). Even Leviathan gets his fifteen minutes of fame (chap. 41). Yet, one gets the sense that the participants in this parade are not passive. Each has a job to do: namely, to praise and worship God. Let's take a moment to look at how this takes place, since it is so significant for both how we worship and how we regard the world.

More than a Metaphor

Creation's praise of God is most evident where the poetry seems to suggest that a particular feature has a "voice." Verse seven of chapter thirty-eight is a case in point when it makes reference to the moment "when the morning stars sang together/and all the heavenly beings shouted for joy." Here as elsewhere in these chapters, it is easy to hear an echo of the Psalms. Psalm 19, for instance, asserts,

> The heavens are telling the glory of God;
> > and the firmament proclaims his handiwork.
> Day to day pours forth speech,
> > and night to night declares knowledge.

> (vv. 1-2)

Yet, the psalm goes on to counter the obvious human objection that "there is no speech, nor are there words;/their voice is not heard" (v. 3) by asserting that nonetheless "their voice goes out through all the earth,/and their words to the end of the world" (v. 4).

Usually passages like this are written off as "mere metaphors." The first difficulty with this cavalier dismissal is its underestimation of the power and meaning of metaphor. Metaphors allow us to say what we mean — only more so. As each side of the implied comparison is held up, we automatically apply the emotions and associations of the one side to the other. Hence, when the psalmist laments in Psalm 22:6 that "I am a worm," we suddenly know that he feels like all the slimy, squirmy, vulnerable things we know worms to be. This is a group of words that paints a thousand pictures, as it were. We need to take care that we do not "domesticate" metaphors too quickly.[11]

The second reason not to dismiss such references to creation's "voice" too quickly is that it is very possible that creation's voice may manifest itself in a variety of ways. Human beings, then, have one kind of voice, and other aspects of creation have another. Perhaps "praise occurs when the creature fulfills the task for which it was created."[12] Perhaps "all nature sings" simply by virtue of its essence. After all, just because human beings are deaf to the voice of the rest of creation does not mean that God is.

Solo versus Symphony

This section of Job suggests that all God's creatures really do have a place in the choir. One wonders what Job felt and thought as he realized this. For surely, this realization is as much a reality check as the "I'm God and you're not" aspect of these chapters. If the "where were you when" questions form the vertical axis of the passage, then surely the description of nature's praise forms the horizontal one. Up until this point, Job may have fancied himself to be singing a solo; now he knows he's singing with a symphony! This is an observation I owe to Terence Fretheim, who adds that "God is enthroned not simply on the praises of Israel" but "on the praises of all [God's] creatures."[13]

God's gleeful descriptions of the nonhuman dimensions of creation

---

11. A. A. Andersen, *The Book of Psalms*, II (London, 1972), p. 950; quoted by Terence E. Fretheim in "Nature's Praise of God in the Psalms," *Ex Auditu* 3 (1987): 23.

12. Fretheim, "Nature's Praise of God in the Psalms," p. 22.

13. Fretheim, "Nature's Praise of God in the Psalms," p. 29.

are an integral part of this passage's reality check. Other parts of the Bible function this way as well. (See Genesis 1 and Psalms 104 and 148 for examples.) Fretheim makes this important point:

> One fundamental problem relating to this issue has certainly been our preoccupation with the human as the center of the universe. In Psalm 148 one is no doubt pleased to be listed among the angels in the call to praise God and perhaps not so pleased to be included among creeping, crawling things and crabapple trees. One of the major difficulties with such a psalm is that it offends our anthropocentric sensibilities to be on a list with hills, horses, and hurricanes. Certainly human praise to God means more to God than the clatter of hail on tin roofs or the clapping of the musically inclined leaves of the aspen trees. Perhaps, but not as much as we would like to think.[14]

Passages like these, then, may well make us uncomfortable, since they will certainly disillusion us about our place at the center of the universe. But as Barbara Brown Taylor observes, disillusionment is not always a bad thing. After all, "disillusionment is the loss of illusion — about ourselves, about the world, about God — and while it is almost always painful, it is not a bad thing to lose the lies we have mistaken for the truth."[15]

Once disillusioned, we may find ourselves with a very different sense of what it means to worship God. Let's look at some of the ways this revised perspective on God's creation and our place in it might have for worship.

A Room without a View

I remember visiting a Protestant church in Iowa that was billed locally as the "cutting edge" in worship. My first visit there was in the middle of the week, and a custodian graciously unlocked the doors and ushered me into

---

14. Fretheim, "Nature's Praise of God in the Psalms," p. 16.

15. Barbara Brown Taylor, *The Preaching Life* (Cambridge: Cowley Publications, 1993), p. 8.

an unusually dark sanctuary. "Just a minute, while I get the lights," he said, disappearing into the gloom.

After a short time (it felt longer), the lights were switched on to reveal a sanctuary without a single window. I remarked on this lack of natural light and scenery to my host, and he explained, "Oh, they designed it that way so that the light wouldn't interfere with the screen." He pointed toward the huge screen at the center of the "stage."

In that moment I understood a lot about that congregation's priorities, and they did not involve "hearing creation's voice." To be fair, there were some dramatic natural scenes projected on the screen at certain points during the worship service that I later attended. But they were not enough to counter the architectural message that nature was a negligible part of the praise of God.

We often assume that we shape our buildings. More and more I suspect the opposite is true: our buildings shape us. I wondered how that congregation's theology was being shaped by their windowless worship space. As you enter a worship space, look around for signs that creation has at least some sort of voice.

Singing Creation's Songs

There was a time when the "creation hymn" category in most hymnals was exhausted after "All Creatures of our God and King," "All Things Bright and Beautiful," and "Fairest Lord Jesus." Recent hymnals have reflected a happy reverse in this trend, however. It is no exaggeration to say that there has been a veritable explosion of hymns that celebrate creation.

Some of the most profound prayers and hymn texts to have come on the scene in recent years have hailed from Scotland, particularly from the Iona Community. To those who are familiar with the importance of creation in Celtic Christianity, this should come as no surprise. Celtic Christianity's strengths in this regard may make it uniquely suited to helping the rest of the Christian world with a long overdue "reality check."

One example will have to suffice. There is a hymn in the recent ecumenical collection called *Common Ground* that epitomizes the possibilities for a Christian response to Job 38–41. It is called "God's Will for Creation." Not surprisingly, the text has its origins in a collection of ancient Celtic prayers, *Carmina Gadelica.*

God's will for creation is Jesus' to do:
new branches to wither,
old trees to renew.

  Refrain: Jesus! Jesus! Jesus!
      How can we help but praise him?

Each plant in its growing,
each shape in the strand,
are filled with God's blessing,
are stirred by God's hand.

All life in the river,
all fish in the sea,
earth's numberless creatures
God summoned to be.

Each bird in the morning,
each star in the sky,
proclaim the Lord's goodness
which never can die.[16]

This hymn text is typical of a genre of new hymns that reveal a renewed sensitivity to the importance not only of hearing creation's voice but also of caring for it. Many of them contain an element of confession for our neglect and misuse of creation, as well as a commitment to ecology as a form of the worship of God. Both dimensions are, it seems to me, faithful reflections of Job's wisdom on this subject.

God's Fierce Freedom

Job was a changed man after he heard God's voice from the whirlwind. Now that we have heard it, may the same be true for us.

---

16. "God's Will for Creation," in *Common Ground: A Song Book for All the Churches,* ed. John L. Bell et al. (Christian Churches in Scotland; Edinburgh: St. Andrew Press, 1998), 44. Copyright © 1997 by the Panel on Worship, Church of Scotland.

not Measure How You Heal

ot measure how you heal
er every sufferer's prayer,
elieve your grace responds
ith and doubt unite to care.
ids, though bloodied on the cross,
o hold and heal and warn,
all through death to life
le children yet unborn.

that will not go away,
that clings from things long past,
of what the future holds,
ent as if meant to last.
ent too is love which tends
we never hoped to find,
ite agonies inside,
iories that haunt the mind.

have come who need your help
e have come to make amends,
which shaped and saved the world
ent in the touch of friends.
your Spirit meet us here
the body, mind, and soul,
angle peace from pain
e your broken people whole.

Creation Hymns

The following list is but the tip of the iceberg in the category of "creation hymns," but it does give a sense of the breadth and momentum of the genre. The hymnals sampled represent a range of Christian traditions.

"Children from Your Vast Creation" (SNC, no. 58)

"Father Eternal, Ruler of Creation" (H, no. 573; LBW, no. 413)

"Let There Be Light" (UMH, no. 440)

"Thank You, God, for Water, Soil, and Air" (HPSS, no. 266; PsH, no. 437)

"Today We All Are Called to Be Disciples" (HPSS, no. 434)

"Touch the Earth Lightly" (CH, no. 693; NCH, no. 569)

"We Are Not Our Own" (CH, no. 689)

"We Cannot Own the Sunlit Sky" (GC, no. 710; NCH, no. 563)

Abbreviations:

CH	*Chalice Hymnal* (St. Louis: Chalice Press, 1995)
GC	*Gather Comprehensive* (Chicago: GIA Publications, Inc., 1994)
H	*The Hymnal 1982* (New York: Church Hymnal Corporation, 1985)
HPSS	*The Presbyterian Hymnal: Hymns, Psalms, and Spiritual Songs* (Louisville: Westminster John Knox Press, 1990)
LBW	*Lutheran Book of Worship* (Minneapolis: Augsburg Publishing House, 1978)
NCH	*The New Century Hymnal* (Cleveland: Pilgrim Press, 1995)
PsH	*Psalter Hymnal* (Grand Rapids: CRC Publications, 1987)
SNC	*Sing! A New Creation* (New York: Reformed Church Press; Grand Rapids: Faith Alive Christian Resources, Calvin Institute of Christian Worship, 2001)
UMH	*The United Methodist Hymnal* (Nashville: United Methodist Publishing House, 1989)

One of the ways it will make us wiser is in our worship. Perhaps we will be less likely to "darken counsel without knowledge," attempting to force God into our rigid doctrinal equations. Perhaps we will be less likely to assume that we, as humans, are the center of the universe. Perhaps we will be less likely to discount and destroy creation's voice.

Perhaps we should look to Annie Dillard for the last word. In the final paragraphs of her Pulitzer prize–winning book, *Pilgrim at Tinker Creek,* she captures the essence of both life and worship when she says,

I think that the dying pray at the last not "please," but "thank you," as a guest thanks his host at the door. Falling from airplanes the people are crying thank you, thank you, all down the air, as the cold carriages draw up for them on the rocks. Divinity is not playful. The universe was not made in jest but in solemn incomprehensible earnest. By a power that is unfathomably secret, and holy, and fleet. There is nothing to be done about it, but ignore it, or see. And then you walk fearlessly, eating what you must, growing wherever you can, like the monk on the road who knows precisely how vulnerable he is, who takes no comfort among death-forgetting men, who carries his vision of vastness and might around in his tunic like a live coal which neither burns nor warms him, but with which he will not part.[17]

17. Annie Dillard, *Pilgrim at Tinker Creek* (New York: Harper/Perennial, 1998), pp. 275-76.

Creation Sings! Each Plant and Tree

Creation sings! Each plant and tree,
each bird and beast in harmony;
the brightest star, the smallest cell,
God's tender care and glory tell.
From ocean depths to mountain peaks,
in praise of God, creation speaks.

Creation speaks a message true,
reminds us we are creatures too.
To serve as stewards is our role,
despite our dreams of full control.
When we disparage what God owns,
in turmoil, all creation groans.

Creation groans to see the day
that ends all bondage, all decay.
Frustrated now, it must await
the Lord who comes to recreate,
till round the universe there rings
the song God's new creation sings!

Text: Martin E. Leckebusch (b. 1962), 1995
Text copyright © 2000 Kevin Mayhew Ltd., Buxhall, Stowmark
permission, license no. 705051/2 (www.kevinmayhew.com).

We Ca

We car
or answ
yet we
where
Your h
survive
to carr
and cr

The pa
the gu
the fea
are pre
But pr
the hu
the pri
the m

So sor
and sc
as har
are pr
Lord,
to me
to dis
and m

Text: J
Text c
licatio
(www

For Further Reading

Stephen L. Cook, Corrine L. Patton, and James W. Watts, eds. *The Whirlwind: Essays on Job, Hermeneutics, and Theology in Memory of Jane Morse* (Sheffield: Sheffield Academic Press, 2001). This collection of essays by nine contemporary scholars honors "fierce believer" and colleague Jane Morse. It includes essays by two of the authors in the present volume, Ellen F. Davis and Corrine L. Carvalho, and brings fresh perspectives to a book that has sparked lively discussion for centuries.

Marva J. Dawn. *A Royal Waste of Time: The Splendor of Worshiping God and Being Church for the World* (Grand Rapids: Eerdmans, 1999). This book is a thoughtful and approachable exploration of the theological foundations of worship. Particularly relevant in the present context is Dawn's chapter entitled "Keeping God as the Infinite Center of Our Worship."

Terence E. Fretheim. "Nature's Praise of God in the Psalms" (*Ex Auditu* 3 [1987]: 16-30). This article is a beautifully articulate interpretation of nature's voice in the Psalms. It has obvious implications for the "whirlwind" speeches of Job, but also for our sense of where we as human beings fit into the choir.

Don E. Saliers. *Worship as Theology: Foretaste of Glory Divine* (Nashville: Abingdon Press, 1994). This book may be one of the sharpest tools ever forged in the fight against narcissism in worship. The first section, "Liturgy and Theology," is especially useful in this regard.